CONNECTING IN THE ONLINE CLASSROOM

connecting in the online classroom

building rapport

between

teachers & students

REBECCA A. GLAZIER

JOHNS HOPKINS UNIVERSITY PRESS | *Baltimore*

© 2021 Johns Hopkins University Press
All rights reserved. Published 2021
Printed in the United States of America on acid-free paper
9 8 7 6 5 4 3 2 1

Johns Hopkins University Press
2715 North Charles Street
Baltimore, Maryland 21218-4363
www.press.jhu.edu

Library of Congress Cataloging-in-Publication Data

Names: Glazier, Rebecca A., 1982– author.
Title: Connecting in the online classroom : building rapport between teachers and
    students / Rebecca A. Glazier.
Description: Baltimore : Johns Hopkins University Press, 2021. | Includes
    bibliographical references and index.
Identifiers: LCCN 2021011259 | ISBN 9781421442655 (paperback) | ISBN
    9781421442662 (ebook)
Subjects: LCSH: Web-based instruction. | Education, Higher—Computer-assisted
    instruction. | Teacher-student relationships.
Classification: LCC LB1044.87 .G57 2021 | DDC 371.33/44678—dc23
LC record available at https://lccn.loc.gov/2021011259

A catalog record for this book is available from the British Library.

*Special discounts are available for bulk purchases of this book. For more informa-
tion, please contact Special Sales at specialsales@jh.edu.*

For my parents

CONTENTS

The heart of rapport is human connection. So, the acknowledgments section of a book about rapport seems an especially fitting place to express my gratitude for the incredible circle of supportive people in my life. Being connected with all of you is a blessing.

At the top of that list are my parents, whose unconditional love has been a shining beacon in my life. Neither of them was able to finish their college degree, but from my very earliest memories they have always taught me to love learning and they have always believed in me. Anyone should be so lucky as to have a mom like mine. She sends me a text message of love and support every night and, as I was in the home stretch of finishing this book, she started sending one every morning, too. My dad is one of the most brilliant people I know and he was often on my heart as I was writing. My parents have not had easy lives and I can't help but wonder, if college would have been a little more accessible 40 years ago, how things might have been different. My parents have given me everything that matters and I love them more than words can say.

I also want to acknowledge my wild and wonderful son, Wilk, who turned 8 while I was writing this book. I didn't expect to finish a book during a homeschooling spring and a pandemic summer of adventure together, but every 5:00 a.m. writing morning and afternoon creek exploration was worth it. Wilk is such a sweet, happy boy. He is the light of my life, and I love him an infinite amount. I consider myself a person of faith and spending time with Wilk, spending time outdoors, and spending time in prayer kept me centered and connected when things got challenging. I am thankful for my church home in Little Rock and for the many prayers I know were offered on my behalf.

When it comes to people who have read, edited, provided feedback on, and listened to me talk about this book, I owe my hugest debt of gratitude to my colleague, best friend, godmother to my only child, and all-around the best human I know, Amber Boydstun. From the first time I pitched the idea of writing a book on online teaching to Amber and her mom, Faye, on a drive into San Francisco in 2019 until the very final draft, Amber has been brilliant, insightful, patient, kind, and simply the best. Beyond that, she is the greatest friend a person could have. My life is orders of magnitude better for having her in it. I am forever grateful to have her as my person.

To my partner in conducting a number of the research studies discussed in the book, and my dear friend, Heidi Skurat Harris, I also owe a great deal of thanks. Heidi is a great collaborator and fantastic qualitative researcher—she has a much higher tolerance for wading through open-ended student comments about their worst online classes. I am grateful for her partnership and for the fact that she is always up for chocolate crème brûlée. Heidi is part of a wonderful group of women, the Professor Moms, who get together once a month for dinner, conversation, and emotional support and for whom I am very grateful.

I am incredibly thankful to be surrounded by such a kind and supportive community. I have a wonderful family, including three younger brothers: Mo, Calvin, and Zack. Calvin earned his undergraduate degree entirely online while working full-time; Zack had to grit his teeth through classes the Air Force moved online because of the pandemic in the summer of 2020. They were often on my mind while I was writing. Thank you to my Glazier family, especially Gary and JoDy, whose love never wavers, and who would find time on their visits to take Wilk on adventures so I could write for a few hours. I've had my book club cheering me on, thoughtful neighbors sending me encouraging text messages, and a circle of friends I could call on at a moment's notice. Liz Holman, Maria Mae Tobler, Sayra Crandall, Yvonne Wiebelhaus-Brahm, Jessica Feezell, and Jennifer Kines have come through for me so many times. I am especially grateful for Ceanne Warner, the sister of my soul, whose kindness and early morning hikes kept me spiritually grounded and always made me feel loved.

When I was finishing my dissertation and searching for a job as a professor, I interviewed at an institution where I was told that I should stop doing pedagogical research because it wouldn't count toward tenure. I am grateful I landed at a university and a department that values teaching. Because of that support, I have been able to publish both in my field of political science and in the scholarship of teaching and learning. Much of the research in this book was funded by internal grants from the University of Arkansas at Little Rock. Two of my colleagues and close friends in the School of Public Affairs, Joe Giammo and Eric Wiebelhaus-Brahm, read drafts of the book and provided very helpful comments. Eric was kind enough to read the entire thing while on sabbatical and stop me from submitting a manuscript with far too many instances of the word "literally." These are colleagues to hold on to.

Johns Hopkins University Press thankfully had six anonymous external reviewers take a look at the manuscript, and their comments greatly improved the final product. I am also grateful to my colleagues and friends who agreed to read chapters—on very short notice, during a pandemic. A huge thank-you to Shawna Brandle, Charity Butcher, I-Chant Chiang, April Chatham-Carpenter, Terry Gilmour, Eric Loepp, Michael Rogers (figure 3.1 was his idea!), and Renée Van Vechten. Thank you also to my wonderful colleagues in the American Political Science Association's Political Science Education Section, especially Kerstin Hamman and Victor Asal, who are dear friends and mentors. I am lucky to have such a thoughtful community of scholars to call home. Kerstin was kind enough to connect me with Patsy Moskal at the University of Central Florida, who was such a great resource for the case study in chapter 7. I am also grateful to Michelle Pacansky-Brock for her very helpful feedback and for connecting me with Tracy Schaelen at Southwestern College and Mike Smedshammer at Modesto Junior College, who were both such huge helps for the case studies on those institutions in chapter 7. I am also grateful to Jim Lang for his feedback and encouragement when this project was in an early stage.

I am also thankful to work with a really great team at Johns Hopkins, including my smart and thoughtful editor, Greg Britton. Thanks also to Juliana McCarthy, Adriahna Conway, Kathryn Marguy, and Hilary Jacqmin. Mike Baker is an incredible copy editor. And I have to give a huge shout out to Martha Sewall in the design department, who humored my request to hide a coded message for my son in the background math of the cover art for the book. What a great press!

Finally, thank you to my students. You inspire me every day. You are working so hard to build something better for yourselves and for the people you love. I am proud to be your professor and I hope you always know that I am on your side.

Introduction

Teaching online can be hard. I miss seeing my students' faces when I teach online. I miss walking around the room, the give-and-take of discussion, the random current events tangents we sometimes go off on, and the simulations that get students out of their chairs and interacting with each other. But teaching online can also be incredibly rewarding. Given the time to think, students make really insightful discussion posts; asynchronous online simulations push students, and me, outside our comfort zones; and some of my most meaningful teaching interactions have occurred with students in my online classes.

When online classes are working well—the students are engaged, the professor is responsive, and the technology runs smoothly—they can represent a great resource for higher education.* Online classes can expand access and improve equity. They make it possible for students to attend college when it otherwise wouldn't be an option due to

---

* A note about language here. I use the terms *college, university,* and *higher education* interchangeably, although *university* typically refers to an institution of higher education that offers graduate degrees and *college* refers to an institution that offers exclusively undergraduate or associate degrees.

the constraints of time, distance, or resources. But all too often, online classes don't work so well—students are checked out, professors are absent, and technology falls short. In the end, repeated studies show that students fail and drop out of online classes at significantly higher rates than face-to-face classes (e.g., Xu and Jaggars 2014, 2011b; Glazier 2016). Even when statistical studies account for demographic and academic variables, there remains a persistent gap in retention between online and face-to-face classes (Jaggars 2013; Willging and Johnson 2009). Things have gotten so bad, we are facing an online retention crisis.

Take the case of one student, who described their experience returning to college after being away for a few years: "I have so much respect for people that juggle work, home life, raising children, and returning to complete a degree because it is a struggle but a blessing!" You can hear this student's optimism coming through as they attempt to put a positive spin on what is obviously a trying first semester back at college. Knowing the potentially overwhelming challenges facing this student, engage in a short thought experiment with me. First, imagine that this student returned to *in-person* classes where they connected with faculty members,* found an active support system at the university, and made friends with their fellow students. How likely are they to be successful, despite all of their challenges? Now, imagine that same student returning to *online* classes where the faculty members are distant, there is no mention of university support systems, and they have little interaction with their fellow students. How likely is it that this student's challenges will overwhelm them in their first semester back? Given the stark differences between these two hypothetical

---

* Another note about language: I use the terms *faculty, professor,* and *instructor* interchangeably. *Instructor* is the most inclusive term, and includes anyone who is teaching a college course, but is the least used in common conversation. *Professor* and *faculty* both refer to those who teach at universities, but there are hierarchical structures in university systems that mean that part-time teachers or those not on the tenure-track may not officially be titled "faculty." It is not my intent to exclude adjunct faculty from any categories here, so again when I use any of these terms I mean to include anyone who teaches a college course.

college experiences—which are very much the reality for many students—it's no wonder that there is a gap between online and face-to-face retention rates.

This problem is a crisis because the students who would be succeeding in face-to-face classes are failing and withdrawing from online classes. Often, these are the very same disadvantaged students that online classes are intended to help—lower-income students, working parents, students of color, and first-generation college students. This book is about what we can do to reverse the online retention crisis. The key lies in bridging the distance inherent in online classes that make students feel like they are out in the cold. To do that, we have to build *rapport* with our students—to make real human connections with them. Doing so would improve both the teaching and the learning experience in online classes.

The case I make for building rapport in online classes is not based on my personal experience alone. It is built on extensive academic research, original experimental studies, and surveys of online students. Throughout the book, I use quotes from real students, just as I did with the case of the returning student above, often drawn from research studies I have conducted with colleagues. We have surveyed thousands of students over the years, including through the Best/Worst Study, the Minimum Rapport Experiment, and the Rapport Impact Study, projects on which I collaborated with Dr. Heidi Skurat Harris, an expert in online writing instruction, and the results of which I will discuss in later chapters. I have included students' words just as they wrote them, and they add a depth of understanding to the retention crisis revealed by the data. What the evidence shows is that building rapport helps students succeed. For individual instructors and institutions looking for data-driven solutions to improve online student success, building rapport is a low-cost option they can implement right away. Online higher education has great potential to expand access to college to help disadvantaged student populations. But to meet that promise, we have to connect with our students and close the online retention gap.

Why Connecting with Online Students Matters

Online courses are solidly in the mainstream of higher education. Even before 2020, when the COVID-19 pandemic unexpectedly shifted universities to a much greater reliance on online education, the integration of online courses was already well underway. Instead of students taking their course load either entirely online or entirely face-to-face, students often take courses from a mix of modalities (Botsch and Botsch 2012; Glazier et al. 2019a). In 2016, for example, about a third of all college students chose to take at least one online class (Seaman, Allen, and Seaman 2018). A student living on campus may take an online class to fit in practice with the volleyball team, whereas a student living off campus and taking most of their classes online may commute in for the last senior seminar they need to graduate. In fact, for most students, "distance education" through online courses isn't very distant at all; about half of all students who take online classes also take classes on campus (Seaman, Allen, and Seaman 2018).

When we talk about online classes today, that category includes asynchronous classes, where students work completely virtually and at their own pace; synchronous classes, where students often log in to attend video lectures or discussions at a particular time; hybrid classes, where students sometimes attend in person, but at other times complete coursework online; and hyflex classes, where students can choose the modality of instruction that works best for them in any given week. This variety of options and increased flexibility means more students are taking online classes and attending college than ever before.

Students taking online classes represent a key part of the college-attending population, but they are often treated as second-class students. Because they may not be physically present on campus as much, they may not know about or access campus support services. Although decades of research tells us that positive student relationships with faculty members are one of the strongest predictors of college success (e.g., Kezar and Maxey 2014a), few online classes involve anything more than limited interactions between faculty and students

(Cox 2006; Jaggars and Xu 2016). Without opportunities to connect across the digital divide, students in online classes are missing out on what could be a much more engaging and fulfilling learning experience (Felten and Lambert 2020).

For decades, colleges and universities have been increasing enrollment in their online programs while high retention gaps between online and face-to-face classes have persisted. We should not simply accept as given that many more online students will fail and drop out than face-to-face students. The online retention crisis has disastrous consequences for university graduation rates and budgets, as well as tragic consequences for students whose lives are marred by dashed dreams and burdened by student debt. But it doesn't have to be this way.

A Solution: Human Connection through Building Rapport

How can we correct the online retention gap that is so prevalent in academia and revive the promise of online higher education? One key lies in addressing the fundamental difference between online and face-to-face classes: the distance between the instructor and the students. Although low retention can be a thorny problem, the data I present in this book show that, if instructors can bridge that distance by building positive relationships, or rapport, with their students, the retention gap between online and face-to-face classes can be completely eliminated. Numerous studies examining online student retention have consistently identified this lack of connection between students and instructors as a key factor leading to student withdrawal from online courses (e.g., Bowers and Kumar 2015; Eom, Wen, and Ashill 2006; Morris 2010; Willging and Johnson 2009). The students who are more likely to stay enrolled and ultimately succeed are the students who have positive interactions with faculty members.

Study after study shows that these positive interactions improve the quality of student learning and their educational experience overall (Chickering and Gamson 1987; Kezar and Maxey 2014a; Kuh 1995; Kuh et al. 2006; Light 2004). To put it simply, "teaching is— and has always been—about making authentic connections with students" (McCabe and Gonzalez-Flores 2017, 1). This fundamental truth doesn't change if the classroom happens to move online. Teaching, and student retention, is best accomplished in online classrooms where faculty build rapport with their students and students feel genuinely cared about (Jaggars and Xu 2016). We all know this intuitively, which is why the thought experiment with the returning student had such an obvious answer: get that student some connection and they will be much more successful! As the rest of the book establishes, we don't just have to rely on intuition—research, data, and experimental studies all demonstrate that building rapport with students improves retention and success.

Faculty-student interaction is particularly important for retaining first-generation students and students of color (Kezar and Maxey 2014a). In fact, research indicates that the positive effects of faculty-student interaction are particularly strong for first-generation college students, but for students of color, they can be decisive (Allen 1992; Lundberg and Schreiner 2004): even when other variables are accounted for statistically, the strongest factor for students of color is a positive relationship with a professor (Kezar and Maxey 2014a, 31–32). Wood, Harris III, and White (2015) looked at successful teaching practices for working with men of color in community colleges and found that personal relationships based in trust and authentic care were so important that they consider them a necessary precondition for effective teaching.

Yet, the very nature of online education means that faculty have fewer opportunities to interact with students in both casual and meaningful ways (King and Alperstein 2014). There are no direct online equivalents to conversations about current events after class that may turn into talks about career goals or the best graduate school. For students who are entirely online, there are no chance encounters at a speaker series, in line for coffee, or walking across the quad. There are no opportunities to have your professor recognize you outside the context of the classroom, ask how you are doing, and invite you to apply for the research assistantship they have opening next fall. These moments of human connection may seem trivial, but both qualitative and quantitative data demonstrate that they can have a significant impact on student success and retention in college.

The lack of personal, face-to-face interaction is one of the major challenges of building rapport with students in online classes. Instead of just shrugging our shoulders and thinking that it is too bad that online students will miss out on these moments of connection, faculty can be more thoughtful and creative in engaging with our online students and in generating moments of genuine human connection with them. This is rapport building: connecting with students on a human level to support their learning, so that students feel that their success matters to their instructor. This book shows you how to do it and how significant its impact is on students.

What to Expect from the Rest of This Book

The goal of this book is to help faculty members, administrators, policy makers, and others identify a clear path, grounded in research and data, that will improve online retention rates and student success at the institutions of higher education they care about. In the coming chapters, I walk through what we know about online retention and present specific strategies that can be adapted to individual teaching styles in order to build rapport with students and help them succeed.

In part I of the book, I discuss the online retention crisis that is currently facing colleges and universities. In chapter 1, I lay out the current state of online higher education and how it provides both promise and peril for students and for universities. Students are promised expanded access but may find succeeding in an online environment difficult. Universities are promised new student populations but may find that they have a hard time retaining and graduating them. In chapter 2, I discuss the reasons why online students are more likely to drop out and the efforts that are currently underway to address the crisis of online retention. A major problem with the efforts at most institutions is that they are deeply invested in technological solutions—automatic early alert systems, data collection on student participation, training on navigating Learning Management Systems (like Canvas and Blackboard), and other EdTech fixes. While these efforts may be helpful for some students, they do not address a key component that online classes are often lacking: a connection between the instructor and the student. I highlight those interventions that are working and identify the human element at the heart of those successes.

In part II of the book, I present a solution to the online retention crisis: making real human connections between faculty and students, or what I call rapport building. In chapter 3, I discuss the importance of building rapport between faculty members and students and the impact it can have on student success. For generations, we have known the difference that a great teacher can make in face-to-face classrooms. This chapter takes that concept into the online realm, reviewing the literature on instructor presence in face-to-face and online classes, and making connections between rapport and success. In this chapter, I also present results from the Rapport Teaching Experiment, a study conducted in my own online classes, to demonstrate the efficacy of teaching with rapport. This multiyear teaching experiment involving hundreds of students resulted in a 13% increase in retention for those students taught with rapport-building techniques, completely eliminating the retention gap in my online Introduction to Political Science classes.

Chapter 4 provides specific strategies for building positive instructor-student relationships in online classes. Instructors who already believe it is important to connect with their online students, but may not know exactly how to do that, can skip right to this chapter for a wealth of specific strategies for building rapport. The rapport-building techniques are organized into three general categories: humanizing the instructor, providing personalized feedback, and reaching out to students. Each category contains multiple strategies, which are adaptable to each instructor's specific teaching style and level of commitment to rapport building. Faculty can start small and build on the ideas shared in this chapter. It may spur new ideas as instructors read and think about how they teach their own classes and ways that they can do so to better connect with students.

Chapter 5 looks closely at students on the margins. These are students for whom success is precarious—exactly the kinds of students that expanding access to higher education is supposed to help. Students of color, first-generation students, and lower-income students may be more likely to take online classes and are more likely to struggle in them. What can we do for these students? Using original survey data and student demographic data from the Rapport Impact Study, I demonstrate that rapport building is particularly helpful in retaining these students on the margins. I also talk about how central empathy is to my teaching approach and how feeling cared about can make a huge difference for our students.

Building rapport is a commitment. Part III of the book looks at what it will take to change the way we teach online to more authentically connect with students. Chapter 6 looks at the tradeoffs from a faculty perspective, including addressing the difficult balance between supporting students—especially those who are first-generation, underserved, or who have many other demands on their time, as students in online classes often do—and helping students develop responsibility. Striking this balance is personal and will vary from one instructor to another. This chapter helps instructors think through how to reach that balance in their own teaching and provides evidence from the Minimum Rapport Experiment to demonstrate just how little rapport building it takes to have an effect on student retention.

Whereas most of the rapport-building strategies in this book focus on the role of instructors in improving student success, chapter 7 brings in concrete strategies for administrators, parents, mentors, and students, to support the success of online students through a holistic approach. The online instructor is on the front lines of the retention battle, but the problem of online student retention is a large and persistent one. It is not one that can be solved by faculty alone. Case studies of institutions that are successfully closing the retention gap by building rapport provide potential models to follow in this final chapter.

Conclusion

Higher education is facing an online retention crisis. It is already harming our students and our universities, with the potential to get much worse. But it is a crisis we know how to address. The data and research presented in this book clearly demonstrate that building rapport with students in online classes can significantly improve retention and success. It will take administrators investing more in online classes and faculty. It will take faculty dedicating more time to our online students. But the payoff is significant. There are specific things that instructors can do in our classes starting today to connect with online students and lead to measurably better retention rates. This is a problem we can solve. When we build rapport with our students and connect with them on a human level, it improves both the teaching and the learning experience. Online higher education has great potential to help expand access and improve equity. But to meet that potential, we have to address the online retention crisis. Our students are counting on us, and the long-term financial stability of higher education might depend on it.

PART I   THE PROBLEM

Higher education is facing an online retention crisis

My reason for taking online classes was because of my job and the hours I needed to work . . . The instructor was not interested in working with my situation . . . That class was my only option and so I was set up for failure.

Online student at the University of Arkansas at Little Rock

ONE

The Promise and the Peril
of Online Higher Education

I teach at an urban-serving university in Little Rock, the capital city of Arkansas, a state in the southern United States. Arkansas is in the bottom quartile for educational attainment for the 25- to 44-year-old age cohort. For this critical category of early to mid-career adults who represent the heart of a state's workforce, only 25.7% of them hold a bachelor's degree in Arkansas, compared to 36.4% in the United States as a whole, and 52.4% in Massachusetts, the state with the highest average educational attainment (National Science Board 2020). Lower levels of education attainment are bad for the people of Arkansas, and for the state as a whole, because they slow economic growth, make companies less likely to build here, and make stable employment more difficult to find (Sweeney 2015). How can communities who find themselves in this situation improve educational attainment? Enter online higher education.

For colleges and universities in Arkansas and around the world, online classes can be a valuable resource for expanding access to students who otherwise wouldn't be able to attend. In the first half of this chapter, I present data in support of that promise for both students and institutions. Online classes can help increase access for students, increase enrollment for universities, and increase educational attainment for communities. This golden promise is one reason that so many have embraced online higher education.

In the second half of the chapter, however, I demonstrate the peril that is lurking in the current online higher education environment: low retention rates. Tragically, the golden promise of online higher education is a false one. Even as enrollment in online classes continues to climb, many more students are failing and dropping out of online classes, compared to face-to-face classes (e.g., Glazier 2016; Xu and Jaggars 2014, 2011b). Instead of the expanding availability of online classes leading to more students from disadvantaged populations earning college degrees, research indicates taking more online classes actually leads to lower persistence in a given field and a lower likelihood of graduating (Huntington-Klein, Cowan, and Goldhaber 2017). This reality has created an online retention crisis that higher education must address if we have any hope of recapturing the promise of online education to improve the situations of our students, our universities, and our communities.

The Promise of Online Higher Education

The online modality has introduced a level of flexibility and affordability to higher education that has greatly expanded student access. Lower-income students, nontraditional students, and students of color are all accessing college in greater numbers, in part due to the increased availability of online classes (Jaggars and Bailey 2010; Parsad, Lewis, and Tice 2008). This is the great promise of online higher education—to expand access to underserved populations.

Affordability for Lower-Income Students

Financial considerations are a major reason students are drawn to online classes. Much of the growth in higher education over the past 20 years has come from lower-income students who were previously unable to access a college education (Fry and Cilluffo 2019). In recent years, lower-income students have begun to enroll in college at numbers approaching those of middle-income students. Whereas in 1990, 44% of lower-income students and 56% of middle-income students enrolled in college; by 2015, the numbers were statistically indistinguishable at about 64% each (Fry and Cilluffo 2019).*

As lower-income students enter the world of higher education, they often find that online classes are a more affordable and accessible alternative to the traditional college classroom, even if they would prefer to take classes in person. Lower-income students often select institutions where they can take less expensive online classes, like community colleges or for-profit colleges, where the percentage of students in poverty has doubled over the past 20 years (Fry and Cilluffo 2019), even though the financial model of for-profit colleges often leaves students worse off than when they started (Cottom 2017; US Department of Education 2017).

The increase in lower-income students attending college is encouraging, but these numbers don't tell the stories of the students struggling financially to make it through. These are the stories we heard when Skurat Harris and I surveyed students about online classes, like the student who felt online classes were their only option because of the price of gas: "If I had gas to get back and forth I'd take it in classroom, but I wish I could live on campus cuz it would be easier to get involved."

Attending college at all may be financially intimidating to students from lower-income backgrounds because, to put it very simply, college costs a lot. In 2019, the cost of in-state tuition, fees, and room and board at a public university averaged $21,950 a year. If you are attending an out-of-state college, you can up that price to $38,330 a year. And if you want to attend a private, four-year institution, it is going to cost nearly $50,000 a year (specifically, $49,870) (College Board 2019). As a reality check, the most recent available data

---

* Over time, high-income students remain consistently about 20 percentage points above middle-income students in terms of college enrollment, but the gains for lower-income students are promising.

in the United States from 2018, puts the median household income at $61,937 (Guzman 2019).

To put into perspective just how much the cost of college has increased over the past generation, in 2000, the average cost of a year of college, including room and board, at a public four-year institution was $8,653 (Snyder, de Brey, and Dillow 2019) and the median income was $42,148 (DeNavas-Walt, Cleveland, and Roemer 2001). So, it cost about 20% of median income to attend a state college in 2000, but it will cost between 35% and 61% of the median income today. The rising costs of college have far outpaced inflation, which averaged about 2% a year since 2000, whereas in-state tuition and fees increased 221% from 2000 to 2020 (Boyington and Kerr 2019).

And if you felt overwhelmed reading through those statistics on the cost of college, imagine being a first-generation college student going over them with your working-class parent or parents. It's no wonder that, when potential students consider the high cost of tuition and fees, plus the expense of living on campus, many are deciding that they would prefer to live at home or to take courses entirely online in order to reduce college expenses and be able to work more hours (King and Alperstein 2014, 10). Attending college in the current fiscal environment almost always means that students will need to both work and take out loans (Goldrick-Rab 2016).

Lower-income students are the most sensitive to the costs of attending face-to-face classes (Osei 2019). At my own university, the University of Arkansas at Little Rock, completely online students pay lower fees, resulting in an annual cost savings of $4,166, or about 34% (What It Costs 2020).* Using data from the Integrated Postsecondary Education Data System (IPEDS), Deming et al. (2015) find that those institutions that have more online students tend to charge lower tuition, providing some evidence that online higher education

---

* Lower tuition costs are not necessarily the norm in online higher education; in fact, 74% of institutions report charging the same for online and face-to-face classes (Craig 2019). A study from the North Carolina General Assembly found that the cost of developing an online class is actually slightly (6%) higher than a face-to-face class but that the cost of delivery is the same (North Carolina General Assembly 2010).

can "bend the cost curve" for students. When lower-income students are considering the costs of college, they are thinking of far more than just tuition. There are other costs associated with attending classes on campus (Hurt 2008). Students at California State University Channel Islands, for instance, specifically mention how taking online classes can help with hidden costs, like gas and parking (Hannans, Leafstedt, and Pacansky-Brock 2017). As one online student with young kids at home said about his reasons for choosing online classes, "For my wife and me, it was the fact that we wouldn't have to put the kids into day care" (Schaarsmith 2012). One of the great promises of online education is expanding access for these students. Online classes make college affordable when it otherwise would not be.

Flexibility for Nontraditional Students

The flexibility that online courses provide is another part of their allure—they hold out the possibility of making a college education accessible to populations that otherwise wouldn't be able to reach it. A working father can take one or two online classes at a time and finish his degree over the course of six to eight years. Without set meeting times, a first-generation college student taking online classes and working to help her family make ends meet can be available for the sometimes unpredictable hours that retail or food service industries require, while still being able to complete her classwork. Online enrollments have grown remarkably over time, increasing 17.2% just from 2012 to 2016 (Seaman, Allen, and Seaman 2018, 12), with much of this growth coming from students who are considered nontraditional—students who may attend part-time, work full-time jobs, or care for dependents (Layne, Boston, and Ice 2013). Without online classes, these students might not be able to finish their degrees as quickly, or they may not enroll in college at all (Xu and Xu 2019).

When Skurat Harris and I surveyed students at the University of Arkansas at Little Rock, many of them mentioned the flexibility of online classes. For instance, one student said, "I generally have the freedom to schedule classwork around my life instead of missing out on life to attend a brick and mortar class." Another student specifically noted that they appreciated that the professor in their online class was "in tune with today's non-traditional adult student working on master's level classes while raising a family and having an active career." Students today have a lot going on and nontraditional students often turn to online classes for the flexibility they need to complete their degrees (National Adult Learner Coalition 2017; Tung 2012).

Recent research looking at the Georgia Institute of Technology's Master of Science in Computer Science program demonstrates that providing an online option for this degree significantly increased overall enrollment, mostly among midcareer professionals (Goodman, Melkers, and Pallais 2019). The average age of a student applying for the face-to-face program was 24, but the average age of a student applying for the online program was 34. Although it is focused on a single, advanced degree program, this research indicates that online programs are not just substituting for face-to-face ones, but are, in fact, expanding access to students who otherwise wouldn't attend.

These nontraditional students represent an important higher education population. They are more likely to take online classes and enroll part-time, but they are also more likely to be engaged academically (Rabourn, BrckaLorenz, and Shoup 2018). They tend to spend more hours studying and more hours working, compared to traditional students (Woods and Frogge 2017). These are often students who are paying for school themselves, who have families to support, and who are taking their education very seriously. They need online courses in order to fit college into their busy lives.

Accessibility for Underserved Ethnic and Racial Groups

Recent decades have also seen an increase in the ethnic and racial diversity of the students attending college (Lumina Foundation 2019; Snyder, de Brey, and Dillow 2019), in part due to increasing accessibility as a result of online courses. The percentage of students of color taking online classes has also increased over time (Ortagus 2017). Institutions that offer more online classes are also more likely to enroll students of color. Between 1996 and 2016, the percentage of the community college student population comprising students of color increased from 31% to 50% (Fry and Cilluffo 2019). Students of color also make up 58% of the student population of private for-profit universities (Fry and Cilluffo 2019), the majority of which specialize in online programs (Deming, Goldin, and Katz 2012), compared to about 42% of college students overall (Lumina Foundation 2019). Some studies also show that students of color are more likely to take online classes, compared to white students (Chen, Lambert, and Guidry 2010; Classes & Careers 2011).

Despite this, US Census data reveal that, at 57%, Black high school graduates enroll in college at rates about 15% lower than the national average of 72% (Snyder, de Brey, and Dillow 2019). One promise of online higher education is the ability to close these racial gaps (Killion, Gallagher-Lepak, and Reilly 2015; Kronk 2017). Students from disadvantaged backgrounds have not had the same educational opportunities as other students (Engle and Tinto 2008). More students of color are enrolling in online classes in part due to cost considerations, as they are also more likely to be lower-income and more likely to attend affordable community colleges, where online classes are common (Fry and Cilluffo 2019). Research on Latinx students shows that online classes can help them graduate, because many Latinx students work full- or part-time jobs and they benefit from the flexibility of online classes (Contreras and Contreras 2015; Elliott and Parks 2018).

Online classes may also hold additional, less obvious, benefits for disadvantaged groups. Looking at African American students attending Predominantly White Institutions (PWIs), Stanley (2014) finds they have greater learning outcomes in online, compared to face-to-face, courses, arguing that the online environment provides a more neutral space where African American students are able to expend less energy on the intercultural efforts of engaging at PWIs and can instead focus on learning (Dowd, Sawatzky, and Korn 2011; Tanaka 2002). Along these same lines, some scholars argue that online courses may feel safer for students from marginalized groups because they provide some distance from peers and faculty, along with some degree of anonymity (Erichsen and Bolliger 2011; Humiston et al. 2020; Sullivan 2002).

Despite decades of effort, higher education remains stratified by race (Bowen, Chingos, and McPherson 2009; Carnevale and Strohl 2013; Long and Bateman 2020; Sublett 2020). Online courses can help close racial gaps in higher education attainment by putting a college education within reach for students of color, although there remain important "digital divide" issues regarding access to technology and internet infrastructure (Ortagus 2017).

Other Benefits of Online Learning

Beyond these specific benefits—affordability for lower-income students, flexibility for nontraditional students, and accessibility for students of color—there are many additional benefits of online learning. When students aren't required to be in a physical classroom at the same time, access expands to potentially include students from all over the world (Rovai and Downey 2010). When students can watch or read lectures multiple times, it can be more accommodating for different learning abilities (Hollins and Foley 2013; Mikołajewska and Mikołajewski 2011; Policar, Crawford, and Alligood 2017). A Universal Design for Learning approach in an online classroom, which prioritizes creating a flexible environment to accommodate different learners, disabilities, limitations, and needs, can be welcoming for all students (King-Sears 2009). When class discussions take place asynchronously, students who are less outgoing or less confident in their language skills have more of an opportunity to participate (Bassett 2011; Campbell 2007; Erichsen and Bolliger 2011). Even absent a pandemic, online learning is a good option for students who might be immunocompromised.

Online classes are often thought of as the second choice for higher education, but there are benefits to online courses that should be appreciated in their own right (Bayne et al. 2020). For instance, online classes can provide improved access to primary sources, the ability to take virtual field trips, collaboration across more diverse student populations, and opportunities to use technology to engage students in innovative ways (Journell 2007).

Online learning helps make higher education accessible for all kinds of previously hard-to-reach student groups, including students from rural areas, older students, and those who are primary caregivers (Thomas, Herbert, and Teras 2014). Those who live in what Rosenboom and Blagg (2018) call "geographical higher education deserts" are too far from a college campus to attend in person and so online courses provide higher education access they otherwise wouldn't have. There are many populations who benefit from taking online classes—that is one reason online enrollment has been growing so quickly! Almost a million more students were taking online courses in 2016, compared to 2012 (Seaman, Allen, and Seaman 2018, 15). The promise of online classes is that they serve a crucial function in higher education: expanding access to college. Among this greatly expanding pool of college-attending adults are increasing numbers of lower-income students and students of color, signaling positive forward progress for society and for universities. More students are depending on online higher education than ever before, which makes a focus on equity in online courses even more imperative (Sublett 2020).

What a Degree Can Mean for Students

The promise of online higher education is not just about access to college but also about what a college degree can mean for graduates. Receiving a college degree can make a significant difference in terms of earning potential and quality of life, especially for the categories of students discussed above, who are relatively new in the higher education market (Ma, Pender, and Welch 2016), and especially if they are coming from lower-income backgrounds or are the first in their families to earn a college diploma.

Higher education can mean the key to upward social and economic mobility (Johnson, Brett, and Deary 2010) and can raise entire communities. The unemployment rate is consistently lower for those with a bachelor's degree or higher, with the gap between college graduates and those with less educational attainment only growing during times of economic uncertainty (Snyder, de Brey, and Dillow 2019). During the Great Recession (2008–2013), the unemployment gap between a 25- to 34-year-old with a high school diploma and one with a bachelor's degree was about 12 percentage points (Snyder, de Brey, and Dillow 2019, 657). Early data from the pandemic recession of 2020 indicated that those with a college degree had an advantage of 8 to 14 percentage points over those without one when it came to finding themselves unemployed (Whistle 2020). We also have to consider the devastating reality that the types of jobs that require college degrees are the ones more likely to be able to be done from home. Tragically, low-wage workers bore the brunt of both financial and health losses in the early months of the COVID-19 pandemic in 2020, illustrating how people without college degrees are at greater risk not only for economic hardship but also, in the case of the pandemic, for infection (Kinder and Ross 2020). College degrees, in other words, give people more than just an education (which is a laudable thing on its own); they give people greater economic (and sometimes health) security.

As high school counselors regularly advise, the economic payoffs in terms of salary gained make a college degree well worth the investment. US Census data reveal that the median annual earnings of year-round, full-time workers age 25 and older are $61,830 for college graduates but $36,715 for those with only a high school diploma (Snyder, de Brey, and Dillow 2019, 658). What that means in very real terms for students is that, if they can graduate, they can boost their earning potential by an average of $25,000 a year. That gain in earnings can make a world of difference for them and their families, particularly for those students who come from lower income brackets. We see this promise of upward mobility in a very real way when we look at the data from Minority Serving Institutions (MSIs) of higher education, where the extended mobility rate—students moving from the bottom two income quintiles to the top two—is more than double that of non-MSIs (20%, compared to 9%) (Espinosa, Kelchen, and Taylor 2018). College is a major engine of upward mobility, especially for students of color. This is how students and their families get out of poverty and into the middle class.

Beyond the cold calculations of financial well-being, these students also get to engage in the process of learning. They get to come into our classrooms and leave transformed. A first-generation college student enthusiastically told my colleagues and me in a survey about an online class she took, "I learned so much about things that I can actually apply in my life! This class was very enlightening." Another was just starting graduate school and said, "I'm very excited to finally be in grad school and to be learning!" Without online classes, many of our students wouldn't have these opportunities and, as I discuss below, colleges and universities would lose out on these amazing students from diverse backgrounds. This is the promise of online higher education.

The Importance of Online Education for Universities

The promise of online education is not just in the benefits it holds for students. As access has increased, universities have been happy to welcome new students. As we have seen, the students in higher education today are drawn from a broader and more diverse population than ever before, thanks in part to advances in technology that provide students with the flexibility to access content anywhere, at any time (Herbert 2006; Layne, Boston, and Ice 2013), making for a richer learning experience for all students. Seeing the potential to bring in new students, many universities have prioritized online education as a strategic approach to increase enrollment (Clinefelter and Aslanian 2016), especially in the face of declining traditional enrollments (Gering et al. 2018). University administrators explicitly see online education as a way to expand access and broaden the pool of potential students. Fifty-seven percent of university leaders say that online learning can help them "attract students from outside the traditional service area," and 71% say it can "increase student access" (Smith, Samors, and Mayadas 2008, 98).

In fact, as students have increasingly taken more online classes, universities have increasingly become financially dependent on online enrollment. Although certainly an outlier, Arizona State University grew from around 400 students enrolled in online programs to more than 30,000 in just six years (ASU Online 2020). At a time when many colleges and universities are facing enrollment challenges, online courses are an enrollment bright spot. For instance, in the state of Oregon, enrollment in community colleges declined by 28% from 2009 to 2019, but enrollment in online classes increased by 1% (Wallis 2020). Similarly, from 2002 to 2012, the California Community College system increased online enrollments by almost 850,000, while at the same time enrollment in face-to-face classes declined by about 285,000 (Johnson and Mejia 2014; Xu and Xu 2019). Greater numbers of students—even students who live on campus—are opting to take online classes. In 2018, more than 30% of all college students in the United States were enrolled in at least one online class (Seaman, Allen, and Seaman 2018, 3).

It is critically important to note that at the same time that online enrollment has been increasing, traditional enrollment has been declining. From 2012 to 2017, 44 of the 50 states saw a decline in enrollment at their colleges and universities, with 28 states declining 5% or more. Nationally, annual enrollment numbers for 2017–2018 are about 10% lower than for 2010–2011 (Snyder, de Brey, and Dillow 2019). And these numbers are pre-pandemic. Note that while these *overall* enrollment declines have plagued institutions, the number of students taking *online* courses has steadily climbed. Looking to the future, many institutions of higher education are concerned about the coming "enrollment cliff" due to demographic changes and a reverse baby boom as a result of the Great Recession (Grawe 2018). With fewer children born from 2008 to 2013, universities with enrollment-based funding models, especially non-elite universities, are likely to find themselves in a tight spot, with predicted enrollment drops of up to 15% over just five years (Grawe 2018).

Many university administrators see these current and future enrollment declines, together with the real and potential growth in online education, and they view online classes as critical to the strategic future of their institutions (Allen and Seaman 2016; McCarthy 2009). Before the COVID-19 pandemic hit in 2020 and moved virtually all of higher education online, about 90% of higher education institutions offered some form of online education (Bowers and Kumar 2015; Capra 2011). Online education is attractive to institutions from a business perspective because it does not come with the physical costs of buildings and infrastructure and because it broadens the pool of prospective students (King and Alperstein 2014, 11). Online education is thus seen as a revenue-positive endeavor (Bacow et al. 2012). Online classes are also often taught by contingent faculty, who are paid less than tenured or tenure-track faculty and have fewer benefits (Chapman 2011; Franklin 2015; Kezar, DePaola, and Scott 2019; Mandernach, Register, and O'Donnell 2015). The COVID-19 pandemic only heightened the focus on online education beginning in 2020, as universities around the world shifted to emergency remote teaching on very short notice (Hodges et al. 2020). The need for physical distance raises the prominence of online education in the short-term strategic calculations of colleges and universities around the world, and some may find value in keeping a portion of their courses there.

At a time when students are well aware of the rising costs of tuition, universities would much rather choose an entrepreneurial path of market expansion through online education than have to issue another tuition hike (Dykman and Davis 2008). Online courses are a quick and easy way to gain access to a larger market. When asked about whether the growth of online education excited or frightened them, 80% of university administrators were more excited than afraid, compared to just 42% of faculty (Allen and Seaman 2012). While there is certainly not a universal embrace of online education, many who are thinking long-term about the strategic future of institutions of higher education are turning to online courses.

The promise of online education is the golden win-win situation it provides. Online college courses provide underserved populations with access to higher education, all while ensuring enrollment growth and fiscal stability for universities. What more could you ask for?

The Peril of Online Higher Education: Low Retention Rates

Although online courses have the potential to provide an ideal symbiotic arrangement in which a greater number of students are able to access higher education and universities are able to access a greater number of students (King and Alperstein 2014, 26), they are hiding a difficult truth, one university enrollment officers are often loath to confront and faculty may prefer to stay in the dark about. Many more students are failing and dropping out of online classes, compared to face-to-face classes (Boston, Ice, and Burgess 2012). We have seen from the data that many different kinds of students are taking online classes today and, although some students do better than others, students are generally more likely to drop and fail online classes, compared to face-to-face classes. Repeated studies across different types of universities, different kinds of programs, and different student populations all indicate persistent and significantly lower retention rates for online courses. Students are simply more likely to fail and withdraw from online classes. This is the reality that has created an online retention crisis.

What do I mean when I say that higher education is facing an online retention crisis? *Retention* is sometimes used like a higher education buzzword that is casually dropped in administration meetings, along with *flexible classrooms* and *student-centered,* but without any real intent behind it. Different institutions and researchers use the term *retention* in different ways, so that it sometimes means keeping a student enrolled in a single class and other times means ensuring they graduate from the institution. In all cases, retention looks at the issue from the institution's perspective—and improving retention comes down to keeping students enrolled and getting them graduated in a timely manner. From another perspective, we could talk about student persistence, or the student's decision to stay enrolled in a particular class or in college (Mortenson 2012). Although institutions want to retain and graduate as many of their students as they can, when we take the student's point of view, being retained at a particular institution may not be the best choice for them. A student may see transferring to another institution or even leaving higher education as the best option (de los Santos and Sutton 2012; Hagedorn 2012).

No matter which way we look at it, a crisis arises when we notice the *gap* between online and face-to-face classes. All else being equal, retention rates are significantly lower for students in online classes, compared to face-to-face classes (Xu and Xu 2019). There are many reasons why students may leave college, but for any given class, any given semester, students who need (or have) to take a class online should not be significantly more likely to fail or drop out just because the class is online. Currently, lower retention rates for online classes are the reality for the vast majority of students. Given the increasing numbers of students taking online classes, and the higher education need online classes fill for underserved student populations, the online retention gap is a crisis for higher education. There is no excuse for letting this gap persist and letting so many of our students fail.

The gap between online and face-to-face retention is not a small one. Although there is no systematic, national study of online retention rates (Angelino, Williams, and Natvig 2007; Frankola 2001), single-campus studies usually place the online retention rate between 5% and 35% lower than the in-person retention rate (Dutton, Dutton, and Perry 2001; Patterson and McFadden 2009; Stover 2005; Terry 2001), and some reviews roughly estimate that "students enrolled in distance education are twice as likely to drop out than on-campus students" (Willging and Johnson 2009, 115–16). Patterson and McFadden's (2009) study of students seeking master's degrees found online retention six to seven times lower than face-to-face retention rates. The retention gap persists across disciplines and universities (Carr-Chellman and Duchastel 2000; Levy 2007; McLaren 2004; Tello 2007). Looking specifically at community colleges, Aragon and Johnson (2008) find that online retention rates lagged behind traditional face-to-face classes by at least 20%. Simply put, more students are failing and dropping out of online classes. Imagine being a student, excited to finally go to college, and then having an experience with a professor in an online class like the one this student reported in one of our research surveys: "He needs to be more involved and less contemptuous with students . . . I know several students that have dropped this class because of the lack of communication." This is just one qualitative example of what might be behind the retention gap.

The online retention gap is even worse for underserved student populations. Studies show that lower-income students, first-generation students, and students of color are attracted to the flexibility of online classes, and are more likely to enroll at institutions that cater to online students, like community colleges and for-profit colleges (Deming, Goldin, and Katz 2012; Fry and Cilluffo 2019; Snyder, de Brey, and Dillow 2019). But work by Xu and Jaggars (2014) finds, consistent with other research (Glazier et al. 2019a; Hamann et al. 2020), that the more online courses students take, the less likely they are to complete their degrees. This finding holds across demographics but is even stronger for some groups, including Black students, male students, younger students, and students with lower grade-point averages. In fact, both performance and retention gaps are significantly greater for those students who have less academic preparation, are from underrepresented racial or ethnic groups, or are younger (Figlio, Rush, and Yin 2013; Jaggars and Bailey 2010; Johnson and Mejia 2014; Krieg and Henson 2016; Peterson and Bond 2004; Xu and Jaggars 2014).

Further research affirms that some students of color are struggling to succeed in their online classes (Jaggars and Xu 2014). In California Community Colleges, dropout rates for Latinx students in online classes are twice as high as those in face-to-face classes (Kaupp 2012). Multiple statistical studies across different student populations demonstrate that the racial achievement gaps that are already a problem in face-to-face college classes are exacerbated even further in online college classes (Bennett, McCarty, and Carter 2019; Figlio, Rush, and Yin 2013; McCarty, Bennett, and Carter 2013). And, although one might think that online courses would reduce biases, a field experiment by Baker et al. (2018) finds that professors still show implicit bias in online classes, responding to comments by students with stereotypically white male names more often than to comments by students with stereotypically Black, South Asian, or female names. Although more students of color are accessing college through online courses, online classes can be hard on them. Low retention rates are harming the very student populations we thought were being helped by expanded access to college through online courses (Jaggars and Bailey 2010).

The peril of online education thus boils down to a problem of retention. What this means in practice is that institutions of higher education are inviting students to pursue college degrees through online courses yet making it difficult for them to successfully complete those courses and earn those degrees because of the medium through which the courses are delivered. Even if a student is only taking a few online classes, if they are failing and dropping out of those classes, it can harm their degree progression, preventing them from passing important prerequisites, reducing their chances of graduating, and harming their sense of self (Bailey, Jeong, and Cho 2010; Tinto 2006; Urwin et al. 2010). It is not just fully online students who are harmed by the online retention crisis. It is the millions of students each year who enroll in online classes. When retention rates in online classes are significantly and persistently lower than in face-to-face classes, and we continue to ignore that fact, we are setting our students up to fail.

This is a dire situation for both universities and students. Federal financial aid covers a smaller proportion of the cost of college than in years past, and the vast majority of students are taking out loans to attend (Goldrick-Rab 2016). Students who drop out of college are financially devastated—not only do they fail to realize the higher earning potential they could have achieved with a degree, but they are also often saddled with student loan debt. This double whammy can leave them worse off financially than before they enrolled: buried under a mountain of debt that can be quite literally inescapable (Hilton-smith 2017). Dropping out can also be emotionally devastating, damaging a student's sense of self and belief in what they can accomplish (Hoeschler and Backes-Gellner 2019; Ramsdal, Bergvik, and Wynn 2018; Urwin et al. 2010). As one student wrote on an anonymous survey, "When a student drops, it's hard as hell to get the student loans or the scholarships . . . we are already losing our home and cars."

While the reality of low online retention rates can be disastrous for students, it is also harmful for universities, who find themselves spending valuable limited resources to recruit students only to lose them when they drop or fail. Low retention rates can lead to millions in lost revenue, at an increasingly financially difficult time for universities (Nelson and Creagh 2013). This situation is even more perilous due to the growing use of performance-based funding models that use retention and graduation data as key metrics (Atchley, Wingenbach, and Akers 2013; Polatajko and Monaghan 2017). The growth trajectory of online enrollments over the past 20 years has made it possible for many colleges to overlook their online retention problems. With so much online growth, what is the loss of 10%, or even 20%, of those students? The very real long-term enrollment problems many universities are facing, together with the detrimental impact low retention rates have on our students, mean that this time of naiveté, perhaps even willful blindness, is quickly ending. The bottom line is that the cost of losing our students—whether counted in terms of time, money, or effort—is simply too high to bear, for students, faculty, universities, or society as a whole (Willging and Johnson 2009, 118). We can no longer afford to ignore this problem.

Finding a Solution

In order to know how to reverse the online retention crisis, we have to better understand what is causing it. In the next chapter, I look closely at the research on student retention and ask why so many students are dropping out of and failing online classes. Although this problem is complex, at the heart of it is a lack of human connection. Online classes inherently create distance between instructors and students. Chapter 2 also looks at successful retention efforts and identifies those that close this distance and build rapport with students as the most effective at improving student outcomes. There is hope for restoring the promise of online higher education for our students, our universities, and our communities. But in order to do so, we have to make real human connections in our online classes by building rapport with our students.

TWO

The Digital Divide

Online higher education is facing a retention crisis. And I have to warn you, looking at the data on online retention rates can be downright demoralizing. In this chapter, I present data from diverse courses, institutions, and student populations to demonstrate just how staggering the online retention crisis is. I then take a close look at the research on student retention and three key explanations for why students don't succeed in online classes. In doing so, I introduce the concept of *rapport* in the online classroom and the academic research in support of its importance to student success. Next, because many universities are trying to address the online retention crisis right now, I take a look at some of those solutions, specifically ones targeted at improving student skills and setting early alerts for when students are struggling. Ultimately, I argue that increased human connections are at the heart of most successful online retention efforts. Building rapport with our students is a key way to close the retention gap and reverse the online retention crisis.

The Online Retention Crisis

Heartbreaking retention gaps between online and face-to-face classes as high as 40% (e.g., Jaggars 2013) bear witness to the wasted potential of students who might have succeeded if the circumstances had been different. A sample of just some of the published research studies on university online versus face-to-face course retention rates is provided in table 2.1. These data provide, as closely as possible, an apples-to-apples comparison of the same courses, taught at the same university, often by the same professors, via different modalities (online vs. face-to-face). These data starkly demonstrate the seriousness of the problem. We are losing our online students.

Because community colleges have been leaders in providing online higher education, a great deal of excellent scholarly research has focused on online community college students. For big-picture comparisons aggregated across entire community college systems, see the data in table 2.2. In both tables, retention rates are significantly lower in online classes.

Although there may be slight differences in how each study in tables 2.1 and 2.2 defines retention, retained students are usually defined as students who successfully pass a class by earning at least a C. Students who earn a D, an F, or withdraw from the course completely are not

Table 2.1. Online and Face-to-Face Retention Rates in Specific Courses (in percentages)

Course	Face-to-Face Retention Rate	Online Retention Rate	Gap in Retention Rates	Citation
Beginning Algebra	85	50	35	Blackner (2000)
Intermediate Algebra	73	51	22	Summerlin (2004)
Basic Algebra	80	61	19	Zavarella and Ignash (2009)
Introductory Computer Science	94	53	41	Kleinman and Entin (2002)
Political Methodology	90	71	19	Roberts (2015)
Introductory Political Science	70	57	13	Glazier (2016)

Table 2.2. Online and Face-to-Face Retention Rates,
across Community College Systems (in percentages)

Institution	Face-to-Face Retention Rate	Online Retention Rate	Gap in Retention Rates	Citation
Aggregate of six Ohio community colleges	90	77	13	Chambers (2002)
Aggregate of Virginia community colleges	81	68	13	Jaggars and Xu (2010)
Aggregate of Washington community colleges	90	82	8	Xu and Jaggars (2011b)
Aggregate of California community colleges	70	60	10	Johnson and Mejia (2014)

considered retained (Mortenson 2012). Lower online retention rates present many challenges to universities, damage already flagging university finances, and harm university reputations (Crosling, Heagney, and Thomas 2009). Universities want to keep these students enrolled. As we will see, those universities that have begun to confront the online retention crisis often sink vast amounts of time and resources into complex technological fixes (Beer and Lawson 2017, 774).

Not only are low online retention rates bad for universities, but withdrawing from a course can be financially devastating for students (Jaggars 2013). When students drop out of a class in the middle of a semester, or even when they complete the class but earn an F or a D and do not get credit for it (as is the policy at many universities), they are less likely to take the next required class, less likely to enroll in the university in the subsequent semester, and less likely to graduate (Bailey, Jeong, and Cho 2010; Jaggars and Xu 2010; Xu and Jaggars 2011b). Failing or dropping a course interrupts students' education, while also negatively affecting both their career advancement and their self-esteem (Tinto 2006; Urwin et al. 2010). Dropping out of college can lead to a spiral of failure and debt that can mar a student's life and finances for years to come (Alexander 2014; Hilton-smith 2017; Scott-Clayton and Li 2016).

Although some amount of failure or withdrawal is inevitable (Urwin et al. 2010)—a college degree is not the right fit for every person who enrolls—the gap between online and face-to-face retention tells us that something is seriously wrong with our online classes. The more cynical among us might venture that low online retention rates are a design feature of the current academic system. Higher education does not care so much if students drop out halfway through the semester, so long as they pay their tuition up front. I will admit that over a decade of teaching at a public university has left me a bit more jaded than when I started. Nevertheless, it is financially shortsighted for institutions to let students fail in the short term when they could be returning for subsequent semesters and eventually graduating in the long term. There are too many ways that low retention hurts institutions and students. Even from a cold, pragmatic, financially driven perspective, this retention crisis is bad news for colleges and universities.

Some have suggested that the key to reducing the retention gap is to allow only students who meet a particular GPA or experience threshold to take online classes (e.g., Cochran et al. 2014). Although this may seem like a tempting solution, it would undermine a fundamental promise of online education: expanding access to broader student populations. For some students, the ability to take classes online is key to their success (Shea and Bidjerano 2014). Indeed, our most vulnerable student populations are often the ones who most need online classes to graduate. They won't be able to finish otherwise.

Data from my own school, the University of Arkansas at Little Rock, show that retention numbers increase slightly when students take some of their course load online (see figure 2.1). UA Little Rock is an urban, state university serving a nontraditional student population; many of our students need the flexibility that online classes provide. Research based on data from over half a million community college students similarly indicates that students taking a mix of online and face-to-face classes are more likely to succeed (James, Swan, and Daston 2016).

The data in figure 2.1 show a slight uptick in retention for students taking some online classes but also illustrate how those retention numbers decline when we look at students who are taking more

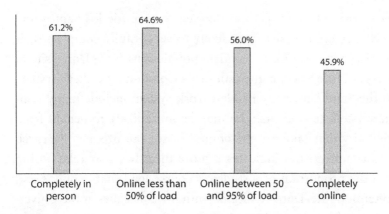

61.2%   64.6%   56.0%   45.9%

Completely in   Online less than   Online between 50   Completely
person   50% of load   and 95% of load   online

Figure 2.1. University of Arkansas at Little Rock Retention Rate by Course Load, 2017–2018

than 50% of their course load online. The lowest retention rate is in the category of students who are taking all of their classes online—they are 20% less likely to be retained than the students who are taking some, but less than 50%, of their course load online.

Similarly, in their study of California Community College students, Johnson and Mejia (2014) find that students who take at least some of their courses online are more likely than those who take only traditional courses to earn an associate's degree or to transfer to a four-year institution. Shea and Bidjerano (2018) looked at data from more than 45,000 community college students in the State University of New York system and found that there was a "tipping point" in terms of course load. Taking some online classes helped students complete their degrees, but when students took more than 40% of their courses online, they were less likely to graduate.

Importantly, the effect of online classes on retention rates is likely to vary by student population. It can be difficult to track students who take a mix of online and face-to-face classes; sometimes students even take classes across different universities as they start and restart college (Cuba 2016; Katsinas et al. 2019). Students who engage in this institutional "swirling" behavior, often nontraditional students who are searching out the needed classes at any institution or underserved students who are taking as many classes as possible at a community college before transferring to a four-year school (de los Santos and Sutton 2012), are actually more likely to successfully complete their degrees (Kolodner 2016). The student populations at the University of Arkansas at Little Rock, in the California Community College system, and in the State University of New York system include many nontraditional college students who may be more likely to benefit from the flexibility that taking some online classes can provide. Research from other universities indicates a more directly linear relationship between the proportion of a student's course load that is online and their retention rate. Data I collected with my colleagues at the University of Central Florida indicate that, for their student population, *any* additional online classes lead to lower retention rates (Glazier et al. 2019b; Hamann et al. 2020).

While advising students to avoid a fully online load if at all possible is probably a good idea (Shea and Bidjerano 2018), preventing students from taking online classes is not going to help them succeed or expand access to higher education. We need to do a better job of reaching students through the online classes we are offering.

Why Do Students Drop and Fail Online Classes?

In order to reach our online students, we need to start with understanding *why* they fail and drop out at consistently higher rates than students in face-to-face classes. What is driving the online retention crisis? This question has lurked in the background of higher education since courses first moved online. Often, it has been overshadowed by the remarkable growth of online enrollment—when students keep signing up for online classes, lower retention rates tend to fall down the priority list. But for years, scholars of online teaching and learning have been seeking to better understand why online students are significantly less likely to succeed (e.g., Moore and Fetzner 2009; Muljana and Luo 2019; Willging and Johnson 2009). There are many reasons why students drop and fail online classes. Here, I look at three categories of explanations: online student characteristics, online student skills, and the online course environment. In these sections, I use quotes, both from others' research and my own, to illustrate the student experience beyond the academic research.

Explanation #1: Online Students Are Inherently Different

I value my education and am appreciative that I am able to obtain an education with as little time away from my family as possible. Because education is important to me and I want to show my sons . . . there is just no way that I could do it in any kind of time, without that online.

Online student at Utah State University

(quoted in Maxfield 2008, 65)

One intuitively popular explanation is that students who take online classes are just different from students who take face-to-face classes. Students in online courses tend to be older (Cochran et al. 2014; Horn 1998; Murtaugh, Burns, and Schuster 1999; Patterson and McFadden 2009; Xenos, Pierrakeas, and Pintelas 2002), are more likely to be women (Kearsley 2002; Willging and Johnson 2009), and are more likely to have the kind of work and family responsibilities that might disrupt coursework (Aslanian and Clinefelter 2012; Cochran et al. 2014; Daymont, Blau, and Campbell 2011; Frydenberg 2007; Hannay and Newvine 2006; Hirschheim 2005; Jaggars 2014; Kramarae 2001; McEwen 2001; Tello 2007; Woodyard and Larson 2018;). When researchers ask students about their online experiences, concerns about family, childcare, and finances are regularly the reasons students give for dropping online classes (Fetzner 2013; Martinez 2003). For instance, Beer and Lawson (2017) surveyed 2,643 non-reenrolling online students at an Australian university and found that personal reasons were most likely to be cited for not returning to the university. In their survey of 305 students in a rural community college, Aragon and Johnson (2008) found that a lack of time due to work and family commitments was a significant predictor of students dropping online classes. Using survey data collected at the University of Illinois at Urbana-Champaign, Willging and Johnson (2009) find that most online students who leave do so for a variety of personal, financial, and family reasons that can be hard to predict (see also Thompson 1997). Looking at students in Malaysia, Tung (2012) similarly finds that many students drop online classes because of family matters and job commitments.

According to the "online students are inherently different" explanation, the students who are self-selecting into online classes just have more complicated lives and are more likely to drop out of college anyway. Online students who tell us about using the flexibility of asynchronous online classes to balance work and caretaking responsibilities, as well as college classes, reinforce this point. Take, for instance, the student who responded to a survey Skurat Harris and I conducted with this comment, "As an online student I need to be able to work ahead when I have available days. I work full time and have a family so I need plenty of time to plan my schedule of studying." Not all face-to-face students may be carrying such a full load. The conclusion that many faculty members and administrators draw from such data is simple and absolving: there is nothing we can do about it.

However, Jaggers's (2013) rigorous research in repeated studies involving tens of thousands of community college students and dozens of control variables over multiple states clearly illustrates that lower completion rates in online classes are not due to the effects of students self-selecting into online classes. Yes, online student populations are often different, but those differences are not driving them to drop out at higher rates. This research suggests that the same students would be *more successful* if they took the same class in person. Selection effects are not the answer (Willging and Johnson 2009; Xu and Jaggars 2011a). The modality—and the way we as faculty are teaching via that modality—is having the effect. We also see the causal relationship between online modality and student success through experimental studies, like the one by Alpert, Couch, and Harmon (2016), which looked at students randomly assigned to three different sections of a microeconomics course: one online, one hybrid, and one face-to-face. The final exam grades for the students in the online section were significantly lower than for those students in either the hybrid or the face-to-face section.

In short, it is clear that personal, work, and family challenges lead students to drop online classes, but not necessarily any more often than students drop face-to-face classes. Willging and Johnson (2009) conclude that "the reasons given by the online students for dropping out of the program were not very different from those typically given by dropouts from traditional face-to-face programs" (p. 125). In fact, Johnson and Mejia (2014) argue that *more* motivated students enroll in online classes, at least at the community college level. When it comes to the personal characteristics of students, online students are actually better off, compared to students in face-to-face classes. Thus, looking just at the raw retention numbers, like in table 2.1, without accounting for personal factors, actually undercounts the negative effect of the online medium on retention. In their research, Johnson and Mejia (2014) find that the gap "between online and traditional courses becomes larger once we control for student characteristics that cannot be observed" (p. 9). That is a sobering thought. The actual gaps in retention rates between in-person and online courses could be even larger than they appear in table 2.1.

Thus, although it feels like an easy out to blame busy, older, working students for low online retention, the data don't support that explanation. We have to dig a little deeper to figure out what's really going on.

Explanation #2: Online Classes Require Specific Skills That Online Students Lack

It was very student-paced and I think that kind of put the student in the professor's position. You taught yourself.

Online student at the University of Alaska Fairbanks

(quoted in Gering et al. 2018, 71)

Success in online classes may be more likely with a particular set of skills. It is no surprise that students with lower GPAs are less likely to persist in online courses. One study found that students who successfully completed online courses had an average GPA of 2.47, compared to 1.66 for noncompleters (Aragon and Johnson 2008).

But beyond GPA or academic ability, there are particular skills that contribute to online success. Computer literacy, time management, and even the ability to interact well online, all contribute to online course success (Rovai 2003). Online courses are sometimes considered "learner-autonomous" interfaces, which require students to have high levels of self-direction, motivation, and self-discipline in order to be successful (Bambara et al. 2009; Ehrman 1990; Eisenberg and Dowsett 1990; Guglielmino and Guglielmino 2003; Jaasma and Koper 1999; Roll and Winne 2015; Xu and Xu 2019). In fact, repeated studies indicate that self-motivated, self-regulated, and independent learners tend to do better in online classes (Bell and Akroyd 2006; Blocher et al. 2002; Diaz 2002; Diaz and Cartnal 1999; Gaytan 2015; Lee, Choi, and Kim 2013). In addition to motivation (Waschull 2005), study skills, time commitment, and goal setting also matter for online student success (Leeds et al. 2013; Schrum and Hong 2002; Tung 2012). As one online student surveyed at the University of Arkansas at Little Rock put it, "My attention span and discipline is not focused enough to do online courses."

Research by Lee, Choi, and Kim (2013) focuses on students' Academic Locus of Control—basically, whether students believe their academic success is in their own hands or whether they believe it is at least partly subject to luck or circumstance. The more students externalize control, together with other metacognitive self-regulation skills, the less likely they are to persist and be successful in online classes. In her book, *Minds Online,* Michelle Miller (2014) writes about the connection between motivation and belief. Students who think they can do well are more likely to succeed. It can be difficult for students— or anyone—to recognize their own weaknesses, but if students are struggling in online classes and see it as within their power to change things, they are more likely to succeed.

A related concept is grit, or perseverance for long-term goals such as a college degree, even in the face of challenges (Duckworth et al. 2007). Research shows that grit can help online learners; not if they have it coming into a class, but if their instructor utilizes deliberate strategies to encourage the development of grit and a growth mindset—

like allowing for failure and multiple attempts at assignments, providing positive encouragement, and being open to taking risks (Buzzetto-Hollywood et al. 2019; McClendon, Neugebauer, and King 2017). This research is particularly interesting because it switches the focus from the student to the instructor.

One student survey response from the University of Arkansas at Little Rock captured how a student's ability to recognize their own challenges and persist through them can bolster academic success: "Because of the difficulties I was having with online classes and self-discipline, I moved to doing strictly face-to-face on campus classes to improve my GPA and my relationships with my professors." Of course, not all students will realize that they have difficulties succeeding in an online environment and not all students will have the luxury of moving to face-to-face classes.

When Skurat Harris and I surveyed students about their preferences in taking online versus face-to-face classes, one student said, "I enjoy online but if I could I would choose face-to-face. I feel like I pay more attention to what's going on around me." Students who struggle with time management or self-regulation may do better in face-to-face classes, where the regular schedule of in-person class meetings keeps them engaged with the course material, but the same students would not do as well with online classes, at least those held asynchronously, where they would have to impose that structure themselves.

At the same time, the online format really works for some students. Another student surveyed wrote, "I actually have a better time with focusing on classes that I take online rather than classes that I take face-to-face." To a certain extent, the ability to succeed online may be less about skills and more about learning preferences and constraints. The format of online classes, especially asynchronous online classes that are more self-paced, tend to play to particular strengths among learners. Not all students do well in these circumstances. In fact, Palacios and Wood (2016) argue that building positive personal relationships with faculty is so important to the success of men of color attending community colleges—and happens so rarely in online classes—that community colleges should consider carefully before recommending online classes to men of color. Improving student time management, organization, and self-regulation may improve retention, but greater improvement will likely come by focusing on connection and belonging, the explanation covered in the next section.

Explanation #3: Online Classes Lack Connection and Belonging

It was a very hands-off approach to teaching. All the assignments were loaded onto Blackboard on the first day of the semester, including weekly discussions that the instructor very obviously paid no attention to . . . About a month into the class, I stopped trying to learn.

Online student at the University of Arkansas at Little Rock

One of the key themes in the research on student retention at colleges and universities is the need for students to integrate—both socially and academically—if they are going to graduate (Stavredes and Herder 2013). Integration means being part of a community and feeling connected. Building a sense of belonging and community among students makes them more likely to stay enrolled (Karp 2011). Making the kinds of connections that will take a student—particularly a first-generation or nontraditional student—from feeling like an outsider to feeling like they belong, can be challenging in an online class. Connecting is often simply easier in person. But a sense of connection can be that much more important for online students, who don't necessarily have the same opportunities for personal, face-to-face interactions that naturally foster a sense of community.

This connection is sometimes talked about in terms of "presence" (Lowenthal 2010) as with the Community of Inquiry framework (Garrison, Anderson, and Archer 1999; Garrison and Cleveland-Innes 2004), which has been used in hundreds of teaching studies over the last 40 years. In a course with a high degree of social presence, the professor and the students perceive each other as real people (Garrison, Anderson, and Archer 1999). A class with positive presence from the instructor means a low-risk learning environment where self-disclosure and humor are possible and students can communicate on an emotional and not just an intellectual level. Although it may sound like I'm describing a class that differs from other classes by just being more "fun," research shows that it's more than that; instructor presence significantly improves student retention and learning (Daigle and Stuvland 2020; Liu, Gomez, and Yen 2009; Wei and Chen 2012). For instance, Boston et al. (2009) analyzed data from over 28,000 students and found that a large amount of the variance in retention rates between online and face-to-face students is explained by accounting for presence.

A growing body of work emphasizes the importance of a positive connection between faculty and students. Michelle Pacansky-Brock (2020) talks about humanizing the online classroom and the interactions therein. Sean Michael Morris and Jesse Stommel (2018) focus on critical digital pedagogy to bring the heart and soul of compassionate teaching back. Researchers in an older school of thought more stringently seek to measure perceptions of instructor immediacy, or how much instructors respond to and interact with students, and its impact (Arbaugh 2001; Hutchins 2003; Richardson and Swan 2003; Woods and Baker 2004). More recently, movements toward creating welcoming online classrooms have been termed "pedagogical warmth" (Bond 2019), "pedagogy of empathy" (Eyler 2018), or, arising in the wake of the 2020 COVID-19 pandemic, "pedagogies of care" (Mondelli and Tobin 2020).

I draw from and build on this work for my concept of connecting with students through building *rapport*. Building rapport with students means letting students know that we are on their side in this whole learning endeavor. It means good communication, supportive messages, informative feedback, and authentic caring. In short, building rapport with students is connecting with them on a human level to support their learning so that students know their success matters.

Unfortunately, human connection is something that online classes are often lacking. Students report feeling isolated and unsupported in online classes (Aversa and MacCall 2013; Hammond and Shoemaker 2014; Pinchbeck and Heaney 2017), feelings that can be especially prevalent for students of color at predominantly white institutions (Crosson 1991; Rovai and Gallien Jr. 2005; Rovai and Wighting 2005). As a student responded in one of my research surveys, "I just feel alone in this course." Students aren't the only ones who miss the human connection in online classes. Faculty say they hesitate to teach online because they miss the interaction with students (Lin 2002; Nelson 2003; Shattuck 2013; Shea, Pickett, and Li 2005). To faculty, online classes can seem like cold and distant places that just don't support their pedagogical values. As I argue throughout the rest of this book, most of our problems with retention come down to this—a lack of human connection.

What Have Universities Tried Already?

The fact that online classes have lower retention rates than face-to-face classes is not news to most universities. Many universities with large online programs have been working to address this problem for years. Arizona State University, which housed the largest public online higher education program in the United States in 2019, with over 36,000 students (Moody 2019), also runs a multi-million-dollar EdPlus Action Lab to improve online teaching and learning. The University of Central Florida's Center for Distributed Learning has a staff of 90 working to support online students and faculty (Bailey et al. 2018). The California Community College system has a massive online professional development program for faculty called @ONE, Online Network of Educators, which serves over 60,000 instructors and won the 2019 Online Learning Consortium Award for Excellence in Faculty Development for Online Teaching. These universities and others are addressing online education on a scale that is far beyond individual faculty members and their classes, and far exceeds the reach of most institutions. In chapter 7, I look more closely at different institutional models by presenting three case studies of universities that are successfully improving online retention. In this chapter, I take a big-picture look at academic research and data.

I draw from a variety of sources throughout the book—including reports, raw data, original studies, and peer-reviewed research—but I consistently rely on rigorous, academic scholarship in making my claims. The evidence is compelling. By the end of the book, I hope you will agree that the online retention gap represents a crisis for higher education and that building rapport is an excellent approach to addressing it.

As both a social scientist and an academic, I am upfront about my bias toward evaluating online retention efforts through published, peer-reviewed studies. Every university has an incentive to make itself look better to potential students, to donors, and to administrators, so internal reports and website statistics, not to mention pitches from for-profit companies hoping to sell universities the latest technology to improve retention, should all be taken with a grain of salt. Published peer-reviewed studies, on the other hand, are held to rigorous scientific standards and can provide data-driven insights into successful retention efforts. The downside is that not many unsuccessful retention efforts reach publication, because academia tends to favor publishing research on things that do work over things that don't (Ferguson and Heene 2012; Therrien and Cook 2018).

The published, academic literature on online retention generally points to two, non-mutually exclusive, categories of interventions to reverse the retention gap between online and face-to-face classes: improving the skills of online learners and using early alert systems to identify struggling students. Both of these categories of interventions are targeted at the characteristics and skills of students (explanations 1 and 2 from earlier in the chapter) and not the characteristics of and pedagogy of online classes (explanation 3). I will look closely at both categories of interventions in the next sections. In the end, I argue that the efficacy of either strategy is improved by building rapport between students and faculty. The success of most retention efforts is bolstered by the extent to which university faculty and staff are able to make real human connections with online students. The more we move beyond blaming students for the retention crisis and begin to address the ways we can improve online classes, the more easily we will be able to turn this ship around.

Improving the Skills of Online Learners

One of the obstacles to higher online retention rates is students' overestimation of their capabilities in online classes (Bawa 2016). Although students may go into a class thinking that they will do fine, they often don't have the time, the time management skills, and/or the technological skills to succeed (Boston et al. 2014; Lee and Choi 2013). As mentioned earlier, the lack of preparation for online classes has led some scholars to suggest that one approach to improving retention would be to restrict enrollment and exclude risky students—perhaps students with low GPAs or little college experience—from online courses (e.g., Cochran et al. 2014). This approach is unlikely to yield the desired outcome. Looking just at community college classes, a major hub for online higher education, enrollment would have to be limited to those students with a GPA of 3.0 or better in order to see significant gains in retention, which would impose severe accessibility restrictions, and likely run counter to many colleges' missions (Hachey, Wladis, and Conway 2013).

Instead, most institutions have sought to intervene and improve students' skills before they begin online classes. Highly successful online programs—those with retention rates above 85% and equal to or better than on-campus retention rates—provide 24/7 help desks, prepare students through orientations, support them with tutors, and help them gauge their own readiness with online skill assessments (Moore and Fetzner 2009). Requiring students to attend orientation is one way to ensure that they have some baseline level of information before classes begin and also that they personally connect with faculty, staff, and other students. Requiring the orientation may be necessary, because otherwise students will view it as optional and may not complete it (Bawa 2016; Bozarth, Chapman, and LaMonica 2004), but a required orientation places another hurdle in front of potentially overwhelmed first-time students and may actually end up reducing retention on the front end.

While the specifics may require some thought, given the student population, online student orientations have led to impressive retention gains for some universities. Boise State University requires first-year online students to attend an online boot camp, where they learn about course navigation, email etiquette, and get a chance to interact with classmates before courses start (Carnevale 2000). On the cutting edge when it first began in the early 2000s, Boise State's online boot camp improved online retention from around 60% to over 80% in just the first year. A nursing program at the University of Southern Mississippi held a one-day intensive, face-to-face orientation for its online students and improved retention from 80% to 99% (Gilmore and Lyons 2012).

At Kennesaw State University, professors organized a multifaceted intervention for students in a single online undergraduate business information systems course (Ali and Leeds 2009). Students were contacted by email, received course documents ahead of time, were contacted by phone, and were invited to a pre-course face-to-face orientation. In the end, there was a massive difference between the retention rates for students attending the orientation at 91% (n = 35), and the retention rates for students who didn't attend the orientation at 18% (n = 29). These orientations represent resource-intensive interventions for institutions, faculty, and students, but the outcomes suggest significant improvements in retention.

However, other attempts at relatively nonintrusive skills interventions have had minimal success. For instance, Baker et al. (2019) did an intervention to help students with their time management skills, where some students in an advanced undergraduate STEM class were required to schedule watching a lecture video. The intervention helped a little in the short term—the ones who scheduled did slightly better on the first quiz—but the intervention had no lasting impact on their time management, their later quiz grades, or their overall grade in the class. Bernacki, Vosicka, and Utz (2020) find that a short (two-hour) online training in study skills did lead students to better utilize digital resources in a course and earn higher grades, but we don't know if these results last beyond a single class. More intensive orientation and skill building may be required for the long-term benefits universities are interested in.

In terms of skill building, orientations seem to have the biggest pay-off, as students learn basic skills in navigation, start dates, where to find resources, and so on. These skills may seem rudimentary, but we can compare students without them, as Darby and Lang (2019) do, to students showing up to campus on the first day of class and not knowing where the building is, or finding the classroom locked, or realizing that the professor is gone and there is just a stack of syllabi waiting on the desk. We would do all we could to prevent that situation from happening on campus—distributing maps ahead of time, having directional signs on campus, posting numbers to call for help, or having volunteers available to answer questions. We should similarly prepare and support our online students.

One reason orientations are helpful in improving retention is because they are excellent rapport-building opportunities. Sure, students may get a campus map at orientation, but they also make personal connections with faculty, staff, and classmates. Those connections can be key to their success. At a minimum, the effort put into an orientation, either at the university level or at the level of a single course, likely signals to students that their success matters to the university or instructor. That signal alone marks an important step toward building rapport.

Early Alert Systems

Another popular intervention is the use of so-called early alert systems. These systems take advantage of big data to determine which students are most at risk of dropping out (Arnold and Pistilli 2012; Romero and Ventura 2010). Online programs with better than average retention records tend to use a Learning Management System, or LMS (like Blackboard, Canvas, Moodle, or any other number of platforms) to observe and track how students are doing and intervene with those who are not doing so well (Moore and Fetzner 2009). A systematic review of 40 empirical articles on online retention in higher education published between 2010 and 2018, determined that early interventions are one of the most effective ways that universities can improve their online retention rates (Muljana and Luo 2019).

One example of an early alert system comes from a group of scholars in Brazil, de Castro e Lima Baesse, Grisolia, and de Oliveira (2016), who developed and patented Monsys, a pedagogical monitoring tool to enable data mining in Moodle, one type of Learning Management System. Developed through a partnership with the government of Brazil, Monsys helps faculty and institutions make sense of all of the data that the LMS collects and uses it to identify students at risk of dropping out. Monsys aggregates and organizes the data into a user-friendly format that pedagogical teams can then use when deciding which students to reach out to via email, phone call, or Whatsapp message. One class of Family Health graduate students was taught without it in 2010 and one with it in 2011. Students were then matched on demographics for comparison (n = 444), and the students in the class with the early alert data used by the pedagogical teams were 13% more likely to be retained.

Another example is the Course Signals system at Purdue, which is integrated with the Blackboard LMS, provides user analytics, and allows faculty to send personalized emails to students informing them of problems (Arnold and Pistilli 2012). Researchers found that taking a course with Course Signals led to higher retention, a statistic that was improved if the student took more than one class using Course Signals.

Effectively using early alert systems can be resource intensive, though. An example comes from the University System of Georgia (USG), which created eCore, a collaborative program to help students easily take and transfer online core classes. This online education portal includes 60 people on staff and over a dozen people working on a student success team. It's this student success team that does the challenging work of personal engagement with those students who are at risk of dropping out—making hundreds of personal phone calls every day (Zatynsk 2013). In six years, they were able to reduce the dropout rate by 11%. Importantly, some of the students they were able to keep in classes were still not able to *pass* those classes—that is, they stayed enrolled just to earn an F—but the efforts of the student success team to make personal contact and help students through challenges did pay off in measurable ways (Clay, Rowland, and Packard 2008). The important fact remains that the extent to which early alert systems help "students succeed in online learning environments largely depends on the quality of follow-up supports that instructors and advisers provide" (Xu and Xu 2019, 28).

Some data scientists caution that the data inputs used by most early alert systems are not detailed enough to capture the unique circumstances of students of color and nontraditional students—populations that tend to take online classes but tend not to follow linear degree progression paths (Berzenski 2019; Cano and Leonard 2019). Thus, they may fail at accurately predicting online student success and may lead to poor recommendations—like increasing course loads in order to shorten the time to degree—that will not lead to more success for these students. We can't data mine and algorithm our way to knowing our students (Veletsianos 2020). Overrelying on technological solutions, instead of personally knowing the students in our classes, may even lead to worse outcomes. These early alert systems are most successful when coupled with a human touch—someone who sees the warning signs and reaches out to students in need.

A Common Denominator in Retention Success: Human Connection

Retention is not just a problem for online courses. There is a vast body of literature on how to retain college students more broadly. Vincent Tinto, who has been studying the topic since the 1970s, argues that, among other things, students need to feel valued through frequent and quality contact, especially with faculty members (Tinto 2007). Felten and Lambert (2020) similarly argue that a "relationship-rich" educational experience in college is much more likely to lead to successful learning and graduation, and that this experience should be available to all students, not just those in the Ivy League or in honors programs at their universities. Although much of this work focuses on traditional students taking face-to-face classes, the importance of quality contact persists for any student population taking classes in any medium. In fact, it becomes even more important when classes move partially or fully online (Davidson and Wilson 2013).

When we look closely at the successful efforts to improve online retention just reviewed, we see a simple and consistent theme: personal connections with students lead to success. An orientation is about more than learning how to log into a Learning Management System. It is about meeting the person who is on the other side of the screen, connecting with the other students in the class, and finding out about the support services the campus offers. Similarly, early alert systems get a lot of the credit for online retention, but monitoring by itself will make no difference. You need real humans who will act on the data to reach out to students and help them do better. Early alert systems improve retention because they tell real people—whether it be faculty or retention teams—where to focus their attention (Villano et al. 2018). As researchers from the University of Central Florida's very successful, and data-driven, online program put it, "Data do not make decisions, people do" (Dziuban et al. 2012, 27).

The success of the early alert system at the University of Georgia didn't come because of a new piece of technology. It came because of a dedicated investment in human connection, *facilitated* by the eCore technology. Its success required a massive staff, a reporting portal that faculty had to be trained on, and literally thousands of outreach efforts made within the first few days of each semester, many to help with technical problems like forgotten passwords (Zatynsk 2013). All the early alerts in the world will not retain a student if a real human being doesn't take the information and then reach out to the student with an offer of help and support (Hachey, Wladis, and Conway 2013). The staff at the University of Georgia talk about serving "more as counselors than technical support" (Zatynsk 2013, 3). They check in with students, encourage them, and remind them of assignment deadlines. They are constantly making individual, personal contact with students.

Whether it is meeting faculty at orientation or receiving check-in phone calls from support staff, these examples represent universities that are fostering a culture of connection. These connections make a difference on the university level, but they matter even more when it comes to individual classes. A sense of belonging and good communication with the instructor are strongly associated with online course persistence (Hart 2012). High-quality, collegial interactions with faculty get students to stay in the class (Ivankova and Stick 2005).

One study of institutions that performed above expectations to defy the usual retention gap between online and face-to-face classes found that successful colleges and universities included a personal touch with students at every possible step of the way: "via marketers, advisors, troubleshooters, peers and coaches throughout the student's academic career, even dedicating individual administrative or programmatic advisors" to work with individual students (Moore and Fetzner 2009, 6). Universities with successful retention efforts have first-year experiences, online and face-to-face student orientations, and online student community websites. They use every possible opportunity to make personal connections with students.

When the *New York Times* did an investigation into "The College Dropout Crisis" in 2019, it identified a number of universities that outperformed their expected graduation rates, as well as those that underperformed (Leonhardt and Chino 2019). One institution that was high on its list of successful universities was Alfred State College, in the State University of New York system. Given the student demographics at Alfred State, its expected six-year graduation rate was 50%, but its actual graduation rate was 74%. Alfred State's online learning website is full of encouraging messages to students, telling them, "Our faculty love what they do and truly want you to succeed" (Alfred State 2020), while also providing links to an online readiness assessment, a place to check technology requirements, and a list of tips for online success. Alfred State provost Dr. Kristin Poppo says, "When a student chooses a degree that we offer 100 percent online, we still promise to provide personal attention and experiential learning. These are traits for which our college is well known" (Alfred State News

2017). Show me a college that is successfully improving its online retention rates and I will show you a college that is building rapport with its online students.

Human connection is what matters—and what is often missing from online classes. The good news is that building rapport through human connection can be purposefully introduced into online courses. The common denominator among successful retention efforts is real human connections with students. When we make those connections, students are more likely to stay enrolled in our classes.

Bridging the Digital Divide

Eliminating the large and devastating online retention gap will not be an easy task. When we look at the many factors that contribute to students dropping out of college, we find that, as Australian professors Beer and Lawson (2017) put it, students are "socially complex, diverse and fluid, which means they resist mechanical, time-limited solutions" (p. 775). To translate that from professor-speak: it's complicated.

Rapport is not the only solution to the online retention crisis, and faculty are not the only problem solvers. With the complex layers of personal, circumstantial, and course problems that may lead students to withdraw (Gering et al. 2018), universities will need to take a multifaceted approach, working across bureaucratic layers toward a common goal, to address it. Colleges and universities may find that they need a variety of interventions—some inside the classroom, some through support services, and some targeted at training students. Each institution should consider its own needs carefully.

Research and data indicate that there are other strategies, and other people, who can move the needle on the retention problem (Kirp 2019; Leonhardt and Chino 2019). More funding for students is probably the most critical and immediate need. Many students drop out because they can't afford to keep attending (Boston, Ice, and Gibson 2010; Parkes et al. 2015). Others get caught at choke points, like continually repeating remedial courses (Bahr 2010; Hoyt 1999). Student support services, like counseling and tutoring, could also help with retention (Aversa and MacCall 2013; Nichols 2010). But when it comes to solutions that can be implemented immediately, without any academic red tape, or even any budget allocations, rapport rises to the top. It works best when there is a university culture of rapport, administrative support, and budget allocations as well, but even without those things individual faculty can make a difference for individual students by connecting and building rapport with them.

It is critically important to recognize that the people on the front lines at universities, the ones coming into the most frequent contact with students, and the ones that the research shows have the greatest impact on their retention, are professors. The classroom is the most important place for building and fostering relationships (Felten and Lambert 2020, 11). That doesn't mean that solving the retention crisis should rest on the shoulders of college faculty alone. Building rapport is resource-intensive. Chapter 6 talks about faculty strategies for balancing that workload, and chapter 7 speaks to the other players who should be supporting faculty in their front-line role. But faculty, as human beings, have the agility to deal with complex human problems; we can consider context and adjust on the fly. Just look at the incredible ability professors around the world demonstrated in adjusting their classes, their teaching format, their grading schemes, and their interactions with students in the face of the COVID-19 pandemic in 2020.

While this singular moment meant nearly everyone moving online, there has been a consistent trend over time toward colleges and universities relying on online courses to boost their overall enrollment numbers. Those who are paying attention are aware that retention in their online courses is significantly lower than retention in their face-to-face courses. Most of the interventions to address this problem are resource-intensive, requiring large investments in time and capital across multiple organizational levels—from student support services, to administration, to instructors. They also may require online students to act like face-to-face students, for instance, by attending in-person orientation events. These large investments sometimes pay off in terms of increased retention, but the costs to both the institution and to the students are high.

A common denominator across all successful efforts is that they address the driving reason behind the online retention crisis—the lack of human connection in online education. Successful retention efforts bridge the digital divide by helping students build relationships with each other, get support when they need it, and connect with engaged faculty members. The truth is that the retention problem is complex and multifaceted. But whatever angle we take on it, at the heart we will find a lack of human connection exacerbating the problem. Building rapport can help fix it.

PART II THE SOLUTION

We can improve retention by building rapport with our students

The teacher's instructions were straight forward and she cared about student success. She even emailed me when I missed an assignment. The teacher engaged with students and really cared about the students.

Online student at the University of Arkansas at Little Rock

THREE

Relationships Matter

Anyone who has ever taught a class, or who has even been a student in a class, knows that there is a real difference in learning and motivation when the students connect with the instructor. Think all the way back to elementary school. Didn't it make attending fourth grade that much better if you knew that your teacher liked you and was cheering for you to succeed? And didn't you come home from a challenging day of long division even more discouraged if you felt like "the teacher just hates me" or "the teacher doesn't even care about this stuff"? The same basic principles carry forward to college. When professors connect with their students, the students are more likely to come to class, stay enrolled, put forward greater effort, and earn higher grades. Whether we are talking about online classes or face-to-face classes, decades of research consistently demonstrate that involved and caring professors are one of the most important factors in student success.

In fact, as discussed in the previous chapter, a common thread underlying almost all successful retention efforts is human connection. One root cause of poor online course retention—a key difference between online and face-to-face classes that makes students more likely to drop and fail them—is the lack of a personal connection between the instructor and the students. Professors are thus perfectly placed to play a critical role in retaining students. Research clearly shows that involved and engaged faculty can make a significant difference when it comes to student success and retention. In this chapter, I take a close look at data and research demonstrating that when faculty build rapport with their students by making real human connections they can eliminate the retention gap between online and face-to-face classes completely. First, I demonstrate how critical faculty are in face-to-face classes. Using original data from the Best/Worst Study, I then demonstrate how, without those same personal connections that face-to-face students make with faculty, our online students are being treated as second-class. Next, I draw on a wide range of published research studies to show how faculty are just as critical for the success of the students in their online classes. I further make this case with evidence from my own multiyear Rapport Teaching Experiment. Using data from my classes, I show how employing rapport-building techniques in online teaching—even in completely asynchronous online classes—can lead to real human connections with students and eliminate the online retention gap.

The Impact of Faculty in Face-to-Face Classes

One of the most consistent and effective predictors of student success in college is the extent and quality of their interactions with faculty. As George D. Kuh, the founding director of the National Institute for Learning Outcomes Assessment, and his coauthors put it, "In general, for most students most of the time, the more interaction with faculty the better" (Kuh et al. 2006, 55). Kezar and Maxey (2014a) reviewed dozens of studies over more than forty years (e.g., Braxton, Bray, and Berger 2000; Johnson 1997; Lundquist, Spalding, and Landrum 2002) and concluded that both the amount of time students interact with faculty and the quality of their relationships with them "effectively decreases student dropout rates and increases their persistence toward degrees" (p. 31). National data from over 1,500 first-year college students show significant and positive relationships between interaction with faculty and perceived growth in knowledge, academic adjustment, and satisfaction with courses (Delaney 2008). Statistical regression analysis using these same data reveals that, even after controlling for demographic and academic variables, interaction with faculty significantly predicts academic performance.

Indeed, personal relationships can play a surprisingly decisive role in student success at college. Chambliss and Takacs (2014) followed over 100 students at a liberal arts college in New York for eight years and found that their professors were far more important than any technology, program, or curricular innovation. Relationships with peers, even a few good friendships, also predict successful graduation (McCabe 2016). Felten and Lambert (2020) conducted 385 interviews with students, faculty, administrators, and staff at 30 different institutions, and they make a compelling case that all students should experience welcome and care in order to get the most out of college. The beneficial impact of positive relationships with professors is a finding that comes up again and again in the literature.

Not only are positive interactions with professors associated with positive student outcomes across the board, they can be especially impactful for at-risk student populations. For instance, first-generation students who have positive interactions with faculty are more likely to be successful than those who do not (Amelink 2005; Ishiyama 2002), and students with lower GPAs and lower SAT scores are the ones who benefit the most from engagement with faculty members (Carini, Kuh, and Klein 2006). Research has found that positive informal interactions with faculty significantly improve the academic achievement of Hispanic students (Anaya and Cole 2001) and that a positive relationship with a faculty member can improve retention for African American students (Lee 1999). In fact, data show that the race of the faculty member is not as important as the quality of the mentor relationship, which is good news, because our faculty are not nearly as diverse as our students (Espinosa et al. 2019).

Why do interactions with faculty have such a strong effect on success and retention? When we get down to the methodological operationalization, we find that the heavy lifting of the instructor interaction effect is often done by rapport. A high-rapport relationship between an instructor and a student means the instructor is present, cares, and communicates well (Creasey, Jarvis, and Gadke 2009; Shevlin et al. 2000; Wilson, Ryan, and Pugh 2010). When students believe their instructors care about them, they are more engaged in their courses and motivated to do well (Kezar and Maxey 2014a). Engaged and motivated students earn better grades and are more likely to persist in their studies (Braxton, Bray, and Berger 2000; Chickering and Gamson 1987; Cokley 2000; Wang and Grimes 2000), so it is no wonder that studies of rapport have repeatedly shown strongly positive outcomes in student learning in face-to-face classes (e.g., Benson, Cohen, and Buskist 2005; Frisby and Martin 2010; Frisby and Myers 2008; Granitz, Koernig, and Harich 2009; Wilson 2006).

Importantly, in statistical analysis aiming to explain variance in student success, rapport has added explanatory power above measures of friendliness, as well as nonverbal behaviors like eye contact (Wilson, Ryan, and Pugh 2010). This means that rapport is not just a superficial measure of niceness or good public speaking. Professors who have high-rapport relationships with their students are approachable, supportive of what the students need, and respond when contacted (Lundquist, Spalding, and Landrum 2002). When students reach out in a time of crisis, like if they are considering dropping a class or dropping out of college altogether, they will find a listening ear in a high-rapport professor. With someone they trust to talk to, students may be more likely to find a solution to their problem that doesn't involve withdrawing from classes.

Students feel respected and valued when faculty make time for them, respond quickly to their emails, and give them personal attention (Hurtado et al. 2011; Lundquist, Spalding, and Landrum 2002). These interactions build rapport one by one, over time. On the other hand, students are less successful when they feel isolated or alienated from faculty (Cole 2007; Komarraju, Musulkin, and Bhattacharya 2010), with especially negative consequences for women and students of color (Bush and Bush 2010; Hurtado et al. 2011; Sax, Bryant, and Harper 2005; Wood 2014b).

Although many faculty-student interactions that build rapport take place in the traditional classroom environment, some of the most impactful interactions take place outside of the classroom. Kuh et al. (2010) looked at 20 institutions doing better than expected on student success and retention and concluded that faculty-student interactions outside of class were critical to that success. Pascarella and Terenzini (2005) reviewed 30 years of empirical research and concluded that student-faculty contact outside of the classroom, even after controlling for other factors, positively affects student persistence and degree completion.

When we think of faculty-student contact that builds rapport outside the classroom, we may think only of intensive mentoring or one-on-one undergraduate research supervision. These types of interactions do lead to improved student outcomes (Ishiyama 2002; Kuh and Hu 2001; Thiry et al. 2012), but more casual interactions are also associated with increased retention and graduation rates and with positive student development outcomes (Komarraju, Musulkin, and Bhattacharya 2010). Think about the many informal ways faculty interact with students on campus: talking after class about academic or personal issues, a simple greeting on the quad, giving advice about a major or a job in office hours, or chatting about a speaker after an event. These interactions are huge rapport-builders—making professors more approachable, easy to communicate with, and even more human. These casual interactions signal a willingness to engage with students. And students pick up on those signals and internalize them.

In other words, students can tell when faculty want to be in contact with them and when they are annoyed by having to interact with them as a requirement of their jobs. Hurtado et al. (2011) found that students even read into the times that office hours are scheduled and the ways that they are posted as cues of whether or not faculty really want to meet with them. So, putting your office hours for only two hours a week at 8:00 am on Mondays and posting that in a tiny corner of your bulletin board sends a message—I am only doing this because I have to; meeting with you is not my top priority. In his book, *Radical Hope: A Teaching Manifesto*, Kevin Gannon (2020) challenges faculty to think critically about the things we tell our students. What are we saying to them in the way we communicate our office hours? In the way we structure our syllabus? Students pick up on those messages. Choosing to be unavailable has real consequences. If faculty instead choose to build rapport with students, even with relatively minimal effort, we can have a meaningful positive impact on our students' success in college.

Second-Class Students

Since contact with faculty is incredibly important to student success, and a great deal of that contact happens outside of the traditional classroom, what does this mean for our online students? As mentioned earlier, I often use student quotes drawn from research studies I have done with colleagues to bring in students' perspectives and deepen our understanding of the student experience. In this chapter in particular, I use a number of quotes from a 2018 study my colleague Heidi Skurat Harris and I conducted at the University of Arkansas at Little Rock, which we call the Best/Worst Study. For this study, every student enrolled at the university received two email invitations: one to participate in a survey about the best class they had ever taken at the University of Arkansas at Little Rock and one to participate in a survey about the worst class they had ever taken there. A breakdown of the responses is given in table 3.1, illustrating that about half of the students told us about their worst class (n = 1,070, 53.31% of the total sample) and about half told us about their best class (n = 937, 46.69% of the total sample).[*] Table 3.1. also breaks down the student response by course medium—whether the class was taught face-to-face or online. More than twice as many student respondents told us about face-to-face classes (n = 1,376) than online classes (n = 631).

Whereas students telling us about face-to-face classes were slightly

---

[*] Students could fill out both surveys, but due to confidentiality, we are unable to determine how many did so.

Table 3.1. Student Respondents by Course Designation (Best/Worst) and Medium (Face-to-Face/Online)

	Best	Worst	Total
Face-to-Face	714	662	1,376
Online	223	408	631
Total	937	1,070	2,007

more likely to tell us about the best class they had ever taken (n = 714, 51.89%), compared to the worst class they had ever taken (n = 662, 48.11%), students telling us about online classes were much more likely to tell us about their worst class (n = 408, 64.65%) than their best (n = 223, 35.34%), by almost a two-to-one margin.

The skew in our Best/Worst survey data fits what we know from the academic research. Although online students want and expect an equivalent experience to their on-campus peers, despite geographical and time constraints, they clearly aren't getting it (Eliasquevici, Seruffo, and Resque 2017; Muljana and Luo 2019). Our online students frequently tell us some version of what this student expressed in the survey about the worst class experience: "I feel like I don't have the same relationships and opportunities for dialogue with my professors as those individuals who live locally. It is a real disadvantage to the online only community." Another student told us, "There is more personal contact and a greater ability to network in live classes." Online students might seek out the convenience of learning off-campus for at least some of their courses, but they still want to be a part of a campus community (Magda, Capranos, and Aslanian 2020). Instead of equal opportunity, in the world of higher education, online students are often treated like second-class students. Online students are not present on campus, have access to and use fewer campus resources, and are often taught by part-time adjunct and non-tenure-track faculty (Bettinger and Long 2010; Fagan-Wilen et al. 2006). These contingent faculty lack the job security, resources, and institutional incentives that tenure-track faculty may have (Kezar, DePaola, and Scott

2019), and research indicates that the result can be a negative impact on student learning (Ehrenberg and Zhang 2005; Jaeger and Eagan 2009, 2011; Ran and Xu 2019).

Instead of high-quality faculty-student interactions that build rapport and improve retention, students who take online classes often acutely feel the absence of an engaged instructor. Not only do students lack high-rapport relationships with their online professors, students often express feelings of going it alone in their online classes, which feel unsatisfying and impersonal (Lee et al. 2011; Paechter, Maier, and Macher 2010; Song et al. 2004; Vonderwell 2003). As one student put it, "Obviously we are the student, but I think when it comes to the online course, we're also the professor because we have to teach ourselves" (quoted in Gering et al. 2018, 71). Another student said that the downside of online classes is "the lack of interpersonal communication . . . not knowing who your professor might be . . . what they may be like in real life" (quoted in Nate' Evans 2009, 69). Open-ended responses from surveys I have conducted, like the Best/Worst Study, have returned similarly heartbreaking responses, like this student who said, "The online book homework/test is a joke. I have never been more frustrated than having to struggle with automated assignments that are buggy and completely unpersonal."

Student learning and retention suffers when students feel isolated and unimportant in online classes. And, to our shame, many of them do. A study of Virginia Community Colleges found that 43% of students complained of not getting enough feedback and interaction from professors (Virginia Community College System 2001). Data from my own research demonstrate that lack of instructor engagement is far and away the number one complaint of students in what they have categorized for us as poor-quality online classes (Glazier and Skurat Harris 2020).

Huss and Eastep (2013) found, in their survey of online students, that many felt "that their professor was 'missing' from the educational conversation. The ability, or willingness, of instructors to communicate online was perceived to be a crucial component of online learning" (p. 13). In our Best/Worst Study, we saw extreme examples of this lack of communication. One student said about the worst class experience:

> Absolute absence of professor-student interaction. Tests are not difficult and automatically graded, which is convenient for student to get an easy A, but not actually learn much. The rest of the grade is based on weekly discussion boards with no grade known until the end of the semester when it is too late to respond or improve. Professor does not respond to emails or phone calls. Does not read discussion boards or participate. Does not make comments . . . I question whether the professor actually exists.

If your students are questioning whether or not you exist, something has gone seriously off the rails. Most classes aren't nearly this bad, but many students express frustration with poor communication in online classes. When we asked students to tell us about the worst online class they had ever taken, 17% of students named poor instructor communication as a reason for their selection in open-ended comments. This statistic gives poor communication the dubious honor of being second only to a lack of instructor engagement as the top reason why students said a class was the worst one they had ever taken (Glazier and Skurat Harris 2020).

Nowhere is the second-class status of online students clearer than in the online retention gap. Even in the exemplary programs Bailey et al. (2018) profile as case studies of online education excellence, like the Kentucky Community and Technical College System, retention rates are 9% lower for online classes (pp. 44–45). This is an online program in the spotlight for excellence! Any gap between the retention rates of online and face-to-face students should be unacceptable. To do otherwise is to treat our online students as second-class.

The Impact of Faculty in Online Classes

The academic research on rapport in face-to-face classes shows, both in the classroom and out, that availability, engagement, good communication, and positive interactions with students all lead to better outcomes in terms of grades, student satisfaction, and retention. Is rapport just as important in *online* classes?

While faculty members still engage with students online, the kinds of informal exchanges that take place in the hallway, before class starts, at events, and at socials are not available in the same ways. Thus, one of the downsides of online education is the lack of both formal and informal physical gathering places for instructors and students (King and Alperstein 2014, 49). Without these opportunities to interact, professors have to work harder to build relationships with students. Building rapport in the online classroom is more challenging than doing so in person.

Instructors are pivotal in online education (Eom, Wen, and Ashill 2006; Morris 2010) but, without the obvious spoken and visual cues of communication we are used to in face-to-face classes (Alman, Frey, and Tomer 2012), online students can often feel isolated and unsupported (Aversa and MacCall 2013; Hammond and Shoemaker 2014; Pinchbeck and Heaney 2017). Teaching college students can be challenging enough, but trying to keep students motivated and engaged online adds an additional layer of complexity to the pedagogical mix (Bennett and Lockyer 2004; Thomas, Herbert, and Teras 2014). Instructors have to set the curriculum, design the course, use the time effectively, model participation in discussion boards, and facilitate discourse (Garrison, Anderson, and Archer 1999)—all while providing "direct instruction," or communicating content knowledge, which is what most of us think of when we think of teaching. Add to that the difficulties online instructors have to face when they are expected to put out technology fires for students and deal with non-intuitive electronic interfaces themselves and online teaching can become quite a challenge.

Even after doing all this well, even exceptionally, instructors may lose a large number of their online students if they don't also take the time to connect with them and humanize the sometimes sterile electronic environment (Gustafson and Gibbs 2000). The students need to see the professor as a real person, and the professor needs to see the students the same way (Gunawardena and Zittle 1997). Although adding rapport building on top of everything else professors do may seem overwhelming (a subject tackled head-on in chapter 6), paying attention to human connection often pays dividends: when students are engaged, they are more likely to stay enrolled and be successful (Crosling, Heagney, and Thomas 2009; Dhilla 2017; Meyer 2014).

In fact, when it comes to effective online learning, the instructor is more important than any other aspect of a course and plays a vital role in driving course completion (Muljana and Luo 2019; Nistor and Neubauer 2010). Jaggars and Xu (2016) examined four design features in 23 online classes at two community colleges but found that only the quality of interpersonal interaction within a course was positively and significantly related with student retention and achievement. Gering et al. (2018) similarly found that only teaching presence was a statistically significant factor for student grades in online classes. Muilenburg and Berge (2005) conducted a large-scale factor analysis of survey data from over 1,000 students and found that, from eight potential barriers to online learning, the most significant impediment was a perceived lack of social interaction. Somewhat ironically, the least important barriers were technical issues, a lack of technical skill, and a lack of academic skill, the things at which we so often target our top-down retention solutions. Instead, it is a lack of social interaction in online classes that is the biggest barrier to student success.

This is not to say that technical issues don't matter—they absolutely do. Chapter 7 details some key steps students, administrators, and supporters can take to ensure that basic technological needs are met. But once you meet a pretty low baseline of technical skill and accessibility (e.g., a computer, a stable internet connection, and course navigation skills), the rest is just technological icing. The real difference is made by human connections.

Instructors may not realize just how powerful an effect they can have on retention in their courses. A student's relationship with their instructor is often a significant predictor of whether or not they will drop out of an online class. For instance, students who are dissatisfied with instructor communication are more likely to drop out (Astleitner

2000; Thompson 1997). Instructor presence, availability, and communication are among the most important things to students when it comes to evaluating their courses (Huss and Eastep 2013). In the research I have done with colleagues, we often hear comments from students like this one we received on a survey about online classes: "I think that the most important thing for any kind of class is that the instructor promptly responds to emails and other communication from students." Poor communication can have a devastating effect on student learning and motivation, like the student who responded to the Best/Worst Study by telling us, "This was by far the worst online class that I have taken. The teacher would either not respond to emails, would be rude to where I felt like I was bothering her, or didn't provide the information that I was asking for. It was not helpful."

We know the online retention gap is even worse for students of color (Figlio, Rush, and Yin 2013; Johnson and Mejia 2014; Sublett 2020; Xu and Jaggars 2014). This may be in part because many online classes have such isolating designs, intended to be "self-directed" courses, whereas some students of color may thrive in more collaborative or communal environments (Ashong and Commander 2012; Boyette 2008; Rovai and Ponton 2005). Kaupp (2012) looks specifically at the retention gap for Latinx students in California community colleges and finds that "the absence of a strong student-instructor relationship was identified as the key difference between their face-to-face and online educational experience" (p. 8). Merrills (2010) studied African American students in online world literature classes and found that they had stronger preferences for offline communication with their professors and oral communication among students. Wood, Harris III, and White (2015) similarly find that building trusting relationships between men of color and faculty is critically important to their success. When online environments make these relationships more challenging to forge, the success of men of color is thwarted (Palacios and Wood 2016).

When instructors build rapport with their students, it has a positive impact on student learning and motivation in online classes (Baker 2010; Liu, Gomez, and Yen 2009; Russo and Benson 2005; Tu 2002).

Just as with face-to-face classes, when professors in online classes demonstrate that they care about the students, students put more effort into their work for the class and end up doing better academically (Jaggars and Xu 2016, 280). When that happens, you get comments like these from students, who seem pleasantly surprised to encounter such a professor: "the instructor actually taught and interacted with the students, providing feedback and helping them to understand the concepts . . . he provided comments that motivated the student to continue." And, "she was tough in a way, but she was right there with you all the way. She senses when students under her watch are struggling and will NOT let them go down without fighting for them and with them. She is so wonderfully rare."

Another great example of how good communication can build rapport and improve retention comes from this student comment: "The professor was so involved and he made the subject fun. I have taken a lot of online classes at [the University of Arkansas at Little Rock] and the professors are rarely involved. They assign and grade work. No lectures, no interaction. I learned so much more from this class than almost any other. Because he cared, I cared."

Did you catch that last part? "Because he cared, I cared." When we show our students that we really care about a class and their success in it, they are motivated to work harder and do well.

Both research and student feedback make clear just how critical relationships are in online classes. Their value becomes even more apparent when students are in crisis. We know from published research (and many of us from personal experience) that a high-rapport relationship with a faculty member can save a student in crisis in a face-to-face class (Lundquist, Spalding, and Landrum 2002). That same effect may be amplified in an online environment. Students often drop online classes because they get behind or their life circumstances make success in the class difficult (Fetzner 2013). Some faculty may feel like, when "life circumstances" lead students to drop a class, there is nothing they could have done. But, in many cases, a positive relationship with the instructor may make it possible for the student to pass the class, even given challenging life circumstances in that semester. A key difference is that, in a face-to-face class, more students will feel comfortable asking the professor for help. In an online class—without eye contact, opportunities to talk after class, the ability to drop by office hours, and other casual interactions—students may be less comfortable admitting they are in trouble. So, a high-rapport relationship with a professor becomes even more crucial.

Take, for instance, a nontraditional student of mine* who was already feeling overwhelmed by the workload in his first semester returning to college after a very long hiatus, when the grandchild for whom he was a primary caretaker fell ill. With his grandchild in the hospital, he didn't think he would be able to take the third exam by the deadline, and he figured he should just drop the class. Because we had emailed and had positive interactions previously, this student reached out to let me know of his situation. I responded that the last thing he should be thinking about when he had a sick grandchild was an exam. I would be happy to work with him to reschedule it. Instead of dropping the class, he took the exam a week later, and finished the class with a B. His grandchild fully recovered and he went on to earn a college degree. This student's success required two things: him reaching out to ask for help when he needed it and me trusting him enough to give him the grace he was asking for. Because we had built rapport through real human connection, both of those things were present when we needed them and he was able to successfully complete the class. We can begin building these relationships before the semester even starts, by preemptively reaching out to students via email to welcome them to our class. Chapter 4 details this and many other ideas for building rapport.

Our students experience all kinds of difficult life circumstances that we can't do anything about. But, if we have spent the semester building rapport with our students, when those difficulties arise, they will let us know that they are struggling, instead of just dropping our classes. That gives us the chance to do our part as professors to work with

---

* In this case and elsewhere in the book where I give specific examples using my own students, all names, details, and identifying information have been changed.

them, if possible, and to help them stay enrolled and succeed. Chapter 5 talks more about how building rapport is particularly helpful for students who are in crisis or who may be on the margins of academia.

It may also be helpful to consider what rapport *doesn't* look like for our online students. Rapport isn't built through automated systems or formulas. Remember the success story of the eCore teams at the University of Georgia from chapter 2? They were able to make a major dent in the online retention gap (Zatynsk 2013). But the classes they had the hardest time with were math classes. No matter how many resources they threw at them, the retention rates in introductory math classes stayed stubbornly high. What was different about math? Well, for one thing, math is challenging to learn online (Smith, Heindel, and Torres-Ayala 2008). In a classroom, you can see the professor working out the problem on the board in real time and ask questions as they come up. Not so in an asynchronous online class. But more than that, the eCore math tutoring system was automated.

Although eCore provided some amazing resources, the main thing students are looking for when they reach out for help in an online math class is a real human to talk them through something they are struggling with. Imagine instead meeting an automated tutoring interface. No wonder students wanted to quit! The same thing happened when California Community Colleges implemented self-directed learning support services for math in 2015: the intervention had no significant impact on retention in math classes (Chatteinier 2016). Sometimes, there is no electronic substitute for a little human contact.

Students have remarkably well-attuned authenticity detectors and they want professors who actually care. Putulowski and Crosby (2019) ran an experiment where they varied the frequency of instructor-initiated communication with students in an online class. They found that students who received weekly contact initially rated their courses more highly, but that effect dropped off after about four weeks, as the students began to feel that the contact was rote and insincere. The authors conclude that consistent instructor-student communication is important, but that approaching it in a formulaic way is unlikely to be successful. There is not going to be a shiny new "rapport-building" technology that will do it for us. Building relationships requires real human connection—that is a feature, not a bug.

The Impact of Meaningful Faculty Connections with Students

When faculty connect with students—whether in class or outside of class, in-person or using technology, in intensive mentor relationships or through casual contact, in response to student requests for help or when faculty reach out proactively—they have significant impacts (see figure 3.1). We see these positive impacts in the short term, when it comes to the specific classes students are taking; in the long term, when it comes to overall improvement for the university; and in the long term, when it comes to positive outcomes in students' lives and careers.

First, in terms of enrollment, students who have positive relationships with their professors are more likely to be retained (Astleitner 2000; Jaggars and Xu 2016; Kezar and Maxey 2014a; Thompson 1997) and are more likely to graduate (Chambliss and Takacs 2014; Kezar and Maxey 2014a). There is also a direct equity impact here, as faculty connections with students have a particularly strong positive effect for first-generation students, low-achieving students, and students of color (Amelink 2005; Anaya and Cole 2001; Carini, Kuh, and Klein 2006; Ishiyama 2002; Kaupp 2012; Lee 1999; Strayhorn and Terrell 2007; Wood and Williams 2013). Second, in terms of academics, those students also gain greater knowledge in their classes (Baker 2010; Liu, Gomez, and Yen 2009; Russo and Benson 2005; Tu 2002; Wilson, Ryan, and Pugh 2010) and earn higher grades (Gering et al. 2018; Jaggars and Xu 2016; Wilson, Ryan, and Pugh 2010). Third, these effects are further amplified because faculty relationships with students have a direct impact on student behavior—resulting in greater engagement and motivation on the part of the students (Jaggars and Xu 2016; Kezar and Maxey 2014a)—which then lead to both enrollment (Crosling, Heagney, and Thomas 2009; Daigle and Stuvland 2020; Meyer 2014) and academic gains (Chickering and Gamson 1987; Cokley 2000; Wang and Grimes 2000). As faculty con-

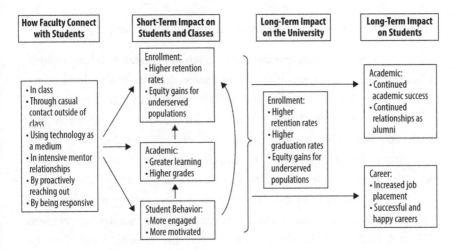

Figure 3.1. The Impact of Meaningful Faculty Connections with Students

nections with students positively impact enrollment, academic outcomes, and student behavior in individual classes, these effects aggregate up to result in higher retention rates, higher graduation rates, and great equity gains for the university as a whole.

Perhaps not surprisingly, the effects of high-rapport relationships last beyond graduation, benefiting students for the long term, as well. Positive interactions with faculty lead to success in academia with better letters of recommendation and success in upper division courses and in graduate school (Calarco 2020; Eby et al. 2008; Johnson 2015), as well as success in the workforce with higher rates of job placement, and more successful and happier careers (Gallup-Purdue Index Report 2014; Johnson 2015; Roche 1979). Simply put, these relationships are meaningful to students. For instance, one survey of 111 alumni from an online graduate program found that, even years after graduation, the alumni valued the engagement they had with the faculty in the program more than even the content they learned or the relationships they built with fellow students (Tanis 2020; see also Gallup-Purdue Index Report 2014). Even in retrospect, rapport is still the most important thing to students.

Results from an Online Rapport-Building Experiment

Like many first-time online instructors, when I started teaching online, I had no idea what I was doing. I had good student evaluations in my face-to-face classes and the best of intentions, but I had never even taken an online course, and knew very little about how to teach one. I did my best with common sense and enthusiasm, but after a few semesters of teaching online, I realized that I had a significant problem, the same problem faced by online instructors across higher education. The students in my online classes were failing and dropping out at much higher rates than the students in my face-to-face classes. When I looked at the data, I found that the retention rate for my online classes—the number of students succeeding by earning Cs or better—was about 13% lower than for my face-to-face classes.

This fact bothered me, both as a professor who cared about the success of my students and as a social scientist. I was the same professor, using the same textbook and requiring the same assignments, so why were my online students doing so poorly? After consulting the literature and discussing the problem with my colleagues and with my students, I concluded that the most important of the many factors that might be depressing the retention rate in my online classes was the lack of personal connection with my students.

Nowhere was this hard truth more evident than in the way I personally viewed online teaching. I loved teaching my face-to-face classes. I loved connecting with students, seeing them grasp new concepts, and pushing them to think deeply in class discussion. In my online classes, on the other hand, few students participated in the online discussion boards, and I found myself rarely checking them or posting in them. Whereas I would regularly come across current events and think about how I would incorporate them into my next face-to-face lecture, I could go days without thinking about my online class. No wonder my students were failing and dropping! They had an instructor who was barely engaged in the class—so how could I expect them to be?

In 2012, I began a teaching experiment to see if I could affect the retention rate in my online classes by changing the way I interacted with my students. I tried to make real human connections with my students by implementing rapport-building measures. Chapter 4 has details on the specific rapport-building strategies I used, as well as tips and advice from research and experience on how to build rapport with your students. Here, I present the results of the experiment (Glazier 2016).

I implemented rapport building measures in six introductory online classes I taught over the course of three years (n = 143). I compared data from these courses to data from three introductory online courses I taught without the rapport-building measures during the same time period, as well as data from online introductory courses I taught before the rapport experiment began (n = 322), and data from students who took my introductory political science class face-to-face (n = 125). In all of these courses, students covered the same content, used the same textbook and readings, and completed the same assignments. The online classes were fully asynchronous, and my lectures were available to the students via notes and PowerPoint slides. The online classes that received the rapport treatment were determined by random assignment. How did retention compare across these three groups?

The percentage of students in each category who passed the class with a C or better is displayed in figure 3.2. Those who earned a D, F, or withdrew from the class are not considered successfully retained.

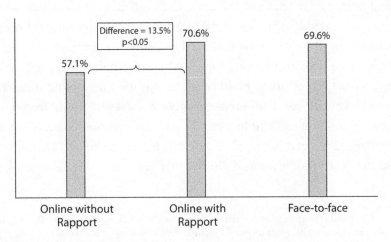

Figure 3.2. Retention Rate by Course Type

In line with data from around the country, the students in the online classes taught without rapport are retained about 13% less than students in face-to-face classes. In this introductory course at a university with a large percentage of first-generation and underserved students, that retention rate falls depressingly below 60%. When we compare the second two columns, however, we see that the retention rate for online courses taught with rapport and the retention rate for face-to-face courses are indistinguishable. These data indicate that building relationships with students in online classes can eliminate the retention gap between online and face-to-face courses. Note that in figure 3.2, when we compare the online classes taught with and without rapport, the retention gap is a statistically significant 13.5%—strong support that the rapport experiment worked.

Additionally, statistical models* that take into account the age, gender, ethnicity, year in college, transfer status, and GPA of the students also consistently return results that indicate that being in the rapport condition significantly improves retention, even when accounting for the effects of these control variables. In fact, rapport has a greater influence on student retention than any other variable besides GPA.

I had considered extending this experiment to collect more data (social scientists always want more data), but after I ran these initial numbers, I knew I couldn't go back. I felt like I had been conducting a randomized drug trial and the patients in the rapport treatment were responding remarkably well. Ethically, I couldn't keep giving the other patients the placebo. I now had hard evidence that rapport worked. I couldn't go back to teaching the way I used to before I started making a concerted effort to build relationships with my online students. I could already see a difference in my course evaluations from students in the rapport-building condition. I was getting comments like "online classes can have a disconnected feel to them, and Dr. Glazier did the best job I've seen of closing that gap" and "Dr. Glazier's lec-

---

* Logit and OLS regression models are not shown here but are available in the peer-reviewed academic journal that originally published these findings, the *Journal of Political Science Education* (Glazier 2016).

tures gave me a virtual in class experience. Matched with her availability, I was confident that I would succeed in her course." I knew I was making a difference and that I would never go back to teaching without rapport.

If instructors want to improve the retention rates in their online classes, they can start right away by connecting with their students and building relationships. In chapter 4, I outline a number of specific recommendations and detail the steps that I took, but building rapport is about your personality and how you connect with students, so it works best when you make it your own. Remember that authenticity is key. Students know when the effort to connect is sincere.

Closing the Gap

There is a gap between online and face-to-face classes that goes beyond retention rates. Moore (1991) refers to the sense of space between teacher and learner as "transactional distance" and cautions that when transactional distance becomes too great, it can increase misunderstanding and be a barrier to learning (McCabe and Gonzalez-Flores 2017). George Veletsianos similarly describes online classes as having a "distinctive quality, one that risks creating and widening the distance between us and our students. That quality is the physical distance that separates us from students and requires us to take active steps to build and foster our relationship with them" (2020, 3). Thankfully, the nature of this transactional distance is not fixed. Classes aren't categorized in a binary way as either distant or not. If we teach online we are not inherently stuck in isolating nonrelationships with our students. Instead, transactional distance runs along a continuum, with high-distance, low-rapport courses at one end and low-distance, high-rapport courses at the other.

Along this imagined continuum we could array all kinds of course delivery options—from hybrid courses that combine elements of both online and face-to-face formats, to hyflex courses that provide students with the maximum flexibility to choose the format that works for them on any particular day. We could imagine both synchronous and asynchronous online classes fitting along this continuum, as well as traditional face-to-face classes. But no matter how the course content is delivered, the level of rapport in the course could be high and the transactional distance low, or the level of rapport in the class could be low and the transactional distance high. Just because a class takes place in person doesn't mean that there is going to be a high level of rapport in that class.

For instance, in the move to online education in response to the COVID-19 pandemic in 2020, some faculty thought that they could maintain or create a sense of community in their suddenly online classes by simply holding synchronous Zoom lectures (Flaherty 2020b), as opposed to, for instance, posting asynchronous text-based lectures and hosting discussion boards. Building rapport takes a lot more than synchronous video. Think back to table 3.1. and the students who told us about their best and worst classes. There were hundreds of students who said that a face-to-face class was the worst one they had ever taken. Take the student who said, "The professor was the worst. She had no sympathy or empathy for anything or anyone. Her class was also very boring. There was very little enthusiasm in her teaching. An hour long lecture felt like 5." Similarly, there were hundreds of students who named an online class as the best class they had ever taken. The student who said, "The teacher engaged with students and really care[d] about the students. You could always count on getting a response back from them," is a great example.

Although it may be easier to build rapport in person, the course medium is not determinative. Even a little bit of human contact tends to help. The research shows that hybrid courses have retention and learning outcomes that are often similar to face-to-face courses (Alpert, Couch, and Harmon 2016; Bowen et al. 2014; Chingos et al. 2017). Palacios and Wood (2016) looked at data from nearly four million students across 112 campuses in the California Community College system and found that Black men did significantly worse in asynchronous online classes, compared to face-to-face classes, but that their performance improved when the online classes included a multimedia component.

Making a course hybrid or adding synchronous video won't automatically improve relationships between faculty and students. You need sincere effort and caring to go along with those course elements. This really gets at the heart of how present we are in our classes and how much we connect with our students (Lowenthal 2010). Even when we are not face-to-face nor synchronous, both students and instructors can project themselves and their personalities into the education environment with text by telling stories, using emoticons, and employing humor (Lindt and Miller 2018; Swan 2003; Swan and Shih 2005). It's not just about technology—for instance, whether or not you have a video camera—it is at least as much about how you use it. Many professors have successfully built rapport with engaging synchronous course discussions or office hours, but we are deluding ourselves if we think we are building connections with students who log on to a synchronous class just to be lectured at with their cameras off and their microphones muted.

How can we reduce the transactional distance in our courses and move them closer to the high-rapport end of the spectrum? How can we make online education work better for our students so that more of them stay enrolled and graduate? Closing the gap may feel like a daunting endeavor, but we can think creatively about how to bring the human connection that makes student success more likely in face-to-face classes into the online realm. An online discussion forum is never going to be the same as sitting around a synchronous discussion group in the classroom. But the elements that make the discussion great can transcend the teaching medium. Online learning provides new opportunities for creative engagement and innovating teaching, as well (Bayne et al. 2020). If faculty can replicate the human connections that make in-person classes so rewarding for both the instructor and the student, teaching and learning online might not be such a struggle. If we can't reduce the distance physically, we have to do it socially and emotionally. The next chapter describes specific, data-tested rapport-building strategies that faculty can implement in their online classes to begin to reduce that distance immediately.

FOUR

Strategies for Building Rapport

L ike most professors, I send a lot of emails. One of the most memorable responses I ever received came after I sent a "check-in" email halfway through the semester. As I detail below, I send personal check-in emails to all of the students in my online classes, to ask them how they are doing, give them their grades on assignments completed so far, and share some words of encouragement. This particular response stayed with me because of how perfectly it encapsulated the sometimes heartbreaking experience of being a struggling online student. I opened my email and found this vulnerable message: "I can honestly admit that an online course can be tricky. I know that I can perform a lot better than what I have been. Yes, if we can have a video call that would be more than helpful. Thank you for your concern as well because there aren't that many professors that care if students succeed or not. I thank you for that and I am going to give it my best."

Imagine being a student taking online classes and going through your college career believing that not many of your professors care whether you succeed or not. The data in chapter 3 present a compelling case that when professors develop positive, rapport-filled relationships with their students, the students do better in the class and are more likely to stay enrolled. The email I received from the student who was struggling epitomizes how students are motivated to "give it their best" when they believe that their professors care about their success. Not coincidentally, this is the same conclusion that scholars who study online teaching and learning have reached: "Frequent and effective student-instructor interaction creates an online environment that encourages students to commit themselves to the course and perform at a stronger academic level" (Jaggars and Xu 2016, 271).

So, how do we demonstrate to students that we care about their success? How do we build rapport with our online students? In chapter 3, I presented the results of a multiyear experiment where I changed my teaching style to prioritize building rapport with my students. The result was that the retention rates in my online classes significantly improved, by 13%, making them statistically indistinguishable from the retention rates in my face-to-face classes. To set up this experiment, I randomly selected one online class each semester to be the "experimental" condition and one to be the "control" condition. If I taught only one online section that semester, I would alternate whether I taught the course with the experimental treatment or not.

The specific techniques I used in the experimental, or "rapport-building," treatment are summarized in table 4.1, along with additional rapport-building methods I have learned and developed over the years. These strategies can be grouped into three general categories: humanizing the instructor, providing personalized feedback, and reaching out to students. Underlying each of these three categories is a core message: *the instructor cares about the success of each student.* In table 4.1. these strategies are also organized according to intensity level (meaning how much effort the strategy will likely take on the instructor's part). Building rapport with students can begin with something as simple as adding a profile picture to your Learning Management System (e.g., Blackboard, Canvas, etc.). Or, it can be as involved as holding extended one-on-one video conferences with students to update them on their individual progress in the course and develop a plan for mentoring them going forward. If you are just getting started with rapport building, you may want to stick to the low-intensity strategies in the table at first and build from there.

Table 4.1. Rapport-Building Techniques

Intensity Level	Humanizing the Instructor	Providing Personalized Feedback	Reaching out to Students
Low	Add a profile picture to your Learning Management System, email, etc.	Use students' names in replying to comments on discussion boards	Respond to emails as quickly as possible
	Apologize when you make mistakes	Leave positive comments on assignments (along with any critiques)	List expected email response times in your syllabus, and perhaps below your email signature line
	Host an introductions discussion thread with a humanizing question (e.g., the story of your name, your travel bucket list, your class walk-up song, past or current pictures of pets, your favorite foods, etc.)	When appropriate, consider using plural pronouns (e.g., "We want to make sure you get the best possible grade on the next exam)	Send emails to the whole class (as opposed to personal emails, which is the next intensity level)
			Disable Learning Management System communication so student messages don't get lost in the LMS
Medium	Add personal style to your lecture notes, including jokes (yes, even bad ones), references to current events, and to the extent that you feel comfortable, details about your life, preferences, hobbies, pets, TV shows you're watching, etc.	Respond frequently to comments on discussion boards, refer back to comments made by other students, and push the discussion forward	Send personal emails welcoming students to the class before the semester starts; consider including a short survey to learn more about your students
	Make your syllabus more accessible through friendly writing and using headings	Create a document with detailed, but often-used, feedback in your own voice that can be used to provide similar feedback to multiple students through a "copy-paste-personalize" method	Send personal reminder emails before assignment deadlines
			Send personal emails to check on students who haven't participated in online discussions recently
			Hold office hours on a video conference platform
High	Record videos (or a podcast-style audio recording) to give updates on course material, touch base on due dates, comment on current events, talk through especially thorny topics, etc.	Leave audio comments in a PDF document to provide specific feedback	Send personal check-in emails informing students of their grades on major assignments and telling them how to improve for the remainder of the class
	Hide an "Easter Egg" assignment in the syllabus requiring students to contact you and complete some task	Use the comment feature in Adobe PDF to electronically mark up a PDF document with colored pen and provide feedback	Use mail merge to send personal emails with detailed assignment feedback
		Return assignments as quickly as possible	If you have their phone number, call or text students you haven't heard from in a while

The remainder of this chapter provides detailed information on the rapport-building strategies I have honed over more than a decade of teaching online. These strategies may not work for every professor and should be adapted to suit each instructor's personality and teaching style. Hopefully, among these techniques are a few suggestions that you can see yourself using in your own online classes. This chapter, and table 4.1 in particular, might be worth discussing with some of your colleagues who teach online to kick off a rapport brainstorming session. Table 4.1 is far from exhaustive. It is more like a starting point for building rapport. As you read through these ideas, think about your own courses, and talk with colleagues; you may see how your teaching strategies fit into the chart. I would guess that nearly every online college professor will have some of their own rapport-building techniques to share and that more may come up in the course of conversation.

Humanizing the Instructor

In order to build rapport with students in online classes, it is important for the students to see their professor as a real person who cares about their success. Students have a lot on their plates, and online classes especially can easily slip their minds. Humanizing demonstrates to students that the professor is a real person and not an automatic grade-generating robot (or, perhaps even worse, a cold, unfeeling instructor who lacks both personality and emotions). When students know that there is a real person with them in the course, they feel more of a responsibility to the course and to the professor. Relationships are central to teaching and learning (Holmberg 2003). If the students know their professor, and know that their professor cares about them, the course becomes a higher priority and they are more likely to succeed. "Learning is a very human activity. The more people feel they are being treated as human beings—that their human needs are being taken into account—the more they are likely to learn and learn to learn" (Knowles 1990, 129). When we see human connection as central to learning, it makes both teaching and learning more fruitful and rewarding.

Building authentic human relationships with our students through an online interface takes time and effort. I use a number of strategies to help the students in my classes see me as a real human being who cares about their success. I include a profile picture on my Blackboard account so that with every message I send and every post I make, the students see my smiling face. I know some instructors who don't feel comfortable including their own photograph, and instead they include a picture of their pet or their favorite vista. Even this approach helps to humanize the instructor. I always provide written lecture notes to students, but instead of just bland facts, I try to include some personality in my lectures, letting my natural sarcasm come through and adding tidbits about pop culture and current events. Just to give you a taste of what this looks like for my students, here is an actual excerpt from a lecture in my US foreign policy class about how the international relations theory of constructivism would explain the end of the Cold War: "It would probably give a lot of the credit to changing ideas and pressure from within. The people of the USSR ended it, not anyone else. Ideas got in, people demanded more from their government, and they decided to fight for freedom. The Pope in Poland calling for more freedom and religious liberty; the popularity of Levi's jeans; Baywatch. This is how empires rise and fall."

One way I try to connect with students and help them see me as a human being is through making my course syllabus a little more interesting to read. The syllabus is likely the most important document in a course because it sets the tone and the expectations for the course. But some students, especially if they are first-generation or early in their college careers, may not know how important the syllabus is or read it very carefully (Cataldi, Bennett, and Chen 2018; Collier and Morgan 2008). I try to make my syllabus more accessible by having informative headings (e.g., "Email Policy" and "Inclement Weather Policy") so they can easily find what they need. I also try to make it more interesting by letting my personality shine through in snarky comments (e.g., "The best way to get ahold of me is through email.

The Blackboard email system is terrible, so I have disabled it." And "Sometimes bad weather makes it difficult to have class. I know that would be deeply disappointing to you, so the university administration requires me to put the inclement weather policy in our syllabus"). Because many students access course materials through their smartphones, Pacansky-Brock, Smedshammer, and Vincent-Layton (2020) recommend putting your syllabus on a website, not as a document, but in a "liquid" format, with active links that are formatted to be easily read by a smartphone. Universities may even have web hosting space and tech support to help with this.

One additional thing I have started doing in recent years is hiding an "Easter egg" in my syllabus. The idea here is that students who read the syllabus carefully will find an opportunity for bonus points. For my introductory classes, both face-to-face and online, I add a section at the end of the syllabus under the heading "Just Checking" that says, "Are you really reading this syllabus? It is actually shockingly important to your success in the class. It is like an agreement between you and me. It is like a map to getting an A. It is really important! Once you finish reading the whole syllabus—including the schedule and reading assignments below; those are super important—email me a picture of a panda (raglazier@ualr.edu) and I will give you an extra credit point towards your participation grade."

The panda picture Easter egg (and please feel free to pick the animal that best suits your personality or the class; sometimes I rotate in a tiger cub) accomplishes at least three things. First, submitting the panda pictures gives students an opportunity to initiate email contact with me. This can be a high hurdle for some students. Especially if a student has no one in their personal circle with a college degree, sending a professional email to someone with a PhD can be really intimidating (Jack 2016). Once they overcome this hurdle with the panda picture, it is easier for them to email at other times in the semester, when they may need help. (Plus, I now have an outstanding collection of panda pics.)

Second, and related, the email from the student allows me to return a friendly reply thanking them for the panda, welcoming them to the class, and inviting them to reach out if they ever need anything at all. This one-on-one interaction can set the tone for a successful semester and calm their fears. I like to imagine my students having fun selecting their panda pictures. They send me emails saying, "Hope you enjoy the panda!" and once a student sent a memorable picture of a raccoon with the subject line "trash panda." The lighthearted exchange is definitely humanizing on both sides.

Third, the paragraph under the "Just Checking" heading emphasizes as strongly as I know how just how important the syllabus is. Plus, the students only get the extra credit point associated with the panda picture by reading (at least that far in) the syllabus. These two things send a strong signal to the student to pay close attention to the syllabus, which will set them up for success in the class.

I know other faculty members who ask students to take selfies outside the faculty member's office and send them via email, which similarly requires the students to make contact, but also requires them to find your office, making it more likely that the students will come to office hours should they ever need to. This task might be challenging for some online students who don't get to campus very often, but a selfie task could help build rapport as students send pictures of themselves. (I would recommend including an alternative for students who don't feel socially or religiously comfortable sending pictures of themselves.) Other professors use interactive maps to build community among their online students as class members share where they are geographically and interact spatially with one another (Cavanaugh and Cavanaugh 2008). Although they don't see each other in class, they might see that they like the same taco truck or get their nails done at the same salon. You could also consider a pre-class survey to ask students about things like preferred pronouns and anything that might interfere with their success in the class (Pacansky-Brock, Smedshammer, and Vincent-Layton 2020). I like to include a few fun questions, like the show they most recently binge-watched or the place in the world they would most like to visit. A copy of the survey questions I use are available in the appendix; please feel free to use as many or as few as you would like for your own pre-semester surveys. When the students respond, keep the information in a spreadsheet and refer back to it if something comes up with a student. Nothing could be more humanizing than a professor remembering that your mom was going to be going through chemo in February and following up to ask how she's doing.

Faculty can be creative in thinking of ways to connect with online students at the beginning of the semester and broach that first hurdle of making contact outside the course Learning Management System. Students have a tendency to start, stop, and restart college, so the beginning of each course is a new opportunity to engage students and get off on the right foot (Felten and Lambert 2020). As the class first gets going, a simple introductions thread in the discussion board could also help students get to know you and each other. Consider including a question that could be fun or interesting to answer, like a travel bucket list or a request to share pet pictures or a class walk-up song.

To build rapport through human connection, I also record weekly videos. To keep students' attention and work with both mental and actual bandwidth issues, these videos are just a few minutes long (Darby and Lang 2019), but they tell students what might be particularly important in the material for the coming week, remind them of upcoming assignments, and mention current events. Through videos, instructors can act as a "living resource" for the students to help guide them through the course (McCabe and Gonzalez-Flores 2017, 127). This small effort makes a big difference to students. As one student wrote in an anonymous course evaluation,

> I genuinely appreciate you taking the time on Mondays to make and publish your videos, the outline really makes a huge difference for me, it seems to be very easy to get clouded up with online classes due to the lack of interaction one normally sees with attending an actual class. I unfortunately cannot say the same for my other classes, a little more engagement from my other professors would make a huge impact.

And if you are someone who prerecords your online lecture material and the idea of a weekly video seems overwhelming, consider even a weekly audio message. I have one colleague who realized that even the low-stakes recording of a weekly video was overwhelming enough to mean that she just wasn't recording them, and so instead she decided to record a weekly podcast about how each week's readings and pre-recorded lecture materials related to current events. She records these audio messages each week while walking her dog, and thus calls them not "podcasts" but "dogcasts." At the end of each dogcast, she gives a count of the number of squirrels her dog saw during the recording. The production quality is low, but these recordings communicate to students that their professor is (a) very human and (b) thinking about her students and the course material in real time even while walking her dog.

These weekly video (or audio) communications send students a signal that their professor is available and accessible. I even include a low-stakes opportunity for extra credit in the first video I post for the course, telling students in that video that if they make an introductory post sharing a description of the best part of their break, I will give them an extra point for the discussion board that week. This small opportunity for extra credit accomplishes a number of things. First, it encourages the students to watch the videos I post, in the hopes of earning more extra credit points (and I make sure to sprinkle these extra credit opportunities throughout). Second, it gives the students the chance to post something about themselves, making it possible to get to know each other better and build rapport. And third, it may signal to students who haven't watched the video that there is something to see there, from the posts on the discussion board, leading them to pay closer attention to assignments and posts.

Students tend to respond positively to this kind of multimedia interaction (Costa 2020). Data from surveys my colleague Skurat Harris and I have done show that students like videos both for learning and for personal connection. One student wrote, "Videos from the instructor made you feel like you got to know them." In one survey of 1,500 online students, videos and PowerPoints were named by students as the most helpful class activity—58% of students said that they were very helpful to their learning and success (Clinefelter and Aslanian

2016). Importantly, students differentiate videos made by the professor, which build rapport and they view as very helpful, from videos made by third-party content providers, which are rated by the students as the *least* helpful of all of the class activities listed. Thus, it is not the video medium itself that matters; it is the fact that the professor is using the video to connect with the class on a real human level.

We see similar evidence of this connection in research from Huss and Eastep (2013), who asked students if seeing a video message or hearing an audio message from the instructor helped them feel more connected to an online professor. Sixty-two percent of the students said that it did, 23% said that it didn't, and 15% had never had such messages (pp. 8–9). I record videos even when I am traveling with students on study abroad trips, when I am attending academic conferences, and, when my son was young, I would keep recording when a toddler would wander into the shot. I purposefully leave these markers of everyday life in the videos as a way to show my own humanity and connect with students. A great resource for creating videos that build rapport with students is Karen Costa's book *99 Tips for Creating Simple and Sustainable Educational Videos,* where she writes about bringing her dog, Rocky, into the videos she records for her online classes, as a humanizing element (Costa 2020).

Michelle Pacansky-Brock and colleagues have done a great deal of work on the importance of humanizing for student learning (e.g., Pacansky-Brock 2020; Pacansky-Brock, Smedshammer, and Vincent-Layton 2020). When students see their professor as a human being they can connect with, instead of a distant and unreachable electronic force that hands down grades, it makes opportunities for connection more likely and gives instructors the chance to help students when they need it. We don't need to worry about professionally edited videos. It's okay if your cat jumps up on your lap or your toddler asks for a cookie in the middle of a lecture. Your students may have cats and toddlers, too, and even if they don't, letting these day-to-day elements be a part of the video can help make a human connection (Pacansky-Brock, Smedshammer, and Vincent-Layton 2020).

Video and audio recordings are also helpful because students tend to equate teaching with verbal communication. When course content is only written and students have to read it, they feel like they are doing the work and teaching themselves. If you want to have a real teacher-learner relationship with them, you need to communicate with them beyond the written word (Gering et al. 2018, 76). This is especially important for students early in their college careers, before they have developed the study skills that make learning on their own easier. Because students value verbal communication so much, incorporating some synchronous features, like real-time conversations, or at least videos and images of yourself (Bawa 2016), can improve student success in your classes (Daigle and Stuvland 2020). Some research indicates that these synchronous, personal connections may be even more important for supporting the success of students of color in online classes (Ashong and Commander 2012; Merrills 2010; Palacios and Wood 2016). However, it is important to be sensitive to student schedules and not *require* synchronous attendance in an online class, unless the class is listed as synchronous in the catalog. Many students take online classes specifically because of the flexibility for their unpredictable schedules.

Unfortunately, most instructors who teach online receive some technical training but no pedagogical training, and so end up simply transferring their face-to-face courses online with minimal changes and few opportunities for synchronous interaction (Cox 2006; Jaggars and Xu 2016; Xu and Xu 2019). If you do teach an online class with a synchronous component, think carefully about how to use that synchronous time (Roberts 2020). Qualitative responses to a survey about course delivery preferences at the University of Arkansas at Little Rock in May 2020 revealed that only 5% of students (n = 15) want synchronous time to be used for lectures; instead, students want this time to be used for interacting with faculty and students (14%, n = 41) and answering questions (15%, n = 45) (Slagle et al. 2020). Lecture content can usually be delivered better asynchronously. When content is recorded as video or audio, or presented in written format, students can access it once the kids are in bed, review it again just before the test, and download it when they have a strong Wi-Fi connection. When you are synchronously present together, use that time to build rapport through interaction and to make real human connections as a class. This approach takes advantage of the strengths of both synchronous and asynchronous learning (Daigle and Stuvland 2020; Kemp and Grieve 2014).

Two examples illustrate the impact of building rapport through humanizing. The first is a simple story about human connection. When faculty teach online classes, we may not get to meet many of our students in person. One day, while talking with a colleague at a local café, I was approached from behind by someone who asked, "Dr. Glazier? Is that you? I recognized your voice from our online videos!" She was a student who had taken my online class the previous semester and was excited to meet in person. Without the videos I had recorded, she never would have become so familiar with my voice and never would have felt a close enough connection to approach me to talk about the class, her upcoming graduation, and her career plans. She knew I would be happy to see her because we had connected on a human level through our online class.

A second example comes from a student who was having a challenging semester. Early in the semester, Jennifer (not her real name) fell behind on a couple of assignments, but was quick to respond positively when I sent her an email reminding her about them and checking in. I gave her the chance to make up some low-stakes reading quizzes and gave her some advice about studying for the next exam. In our email exchanges, Jennifer confessed, "I bit off more than I could chew . . . I signed up for 19 hours this semester and being a full time working mama and that haven't meshed well." Sometimes it can be easy to write off students who fail to turn in assignments or don't check in to our online classes for days or weeks at a time, but often we simply don't know what is going on behind the scenes.

With a little bit of grace, Jennifer was able to get back on track in our class. With a few weeks to go, she wrote, "I just want to say I really am thankful for the patience and feedback you have given me this semester. I got in over my head and you have been there for me every time I've needed it." Jennifer worked incredibly hard to study for the final exam and make up the ground she lost early in the semester. I was so happy when the final exams were graded and I got an email from her with the subject line "I did it!" She wrote, "Dr. Glazier I just checked my final exam grade. I studied so hard. I can't believe I got that A! Thank you so much for your patience this semester." A student I could have easily written off after the first few weeks of class ended up with an A on the final exam and a B in the class. Not only was she successfully retained in my class, but she graduated and went on to earn a master's degree. Think back to figure 3.1 in chapter 3 and the long-term effects of building rapport. Jennifer is a great example of how real human connection in this class helped her succeed. Now, Jennifer is a smart and capable student and rapport certainly doesn't deserve the credit for her accomplishments, but in retrospect, we can see how, in this challenging semester, things could have ended up on a different trajectory.

Showing my students that I am human also means recognizing when I make mistakes. Working with online Learning Management Systems like Blackboard provides plenty of opportunities to make mistakes! I apologize to my students whenever I mess up a release date for an assignment or learning module; I told my students when my grandmother died and their exams were graded more slowly than they were used to. For some professors, this may feel too personal, but I think it gives students permission to be human with me as well. I try to be kind and understanding when it comes to family crises, missed deadlines, and assignment questions. As I will cover in more depth in chapter 5, this can make the difference for students on the margins. As one student put it in an anonymous evaluation comment, "Professor Glazier is a very understanding teacher. I have had a rough year but she assisted me when I needed it."

Students know when their professors really care about them. We communicate that message directly and indirectly in a thousand different ways (Gannon 2020). When students feel like their success matters to their professors, it has an impact on how they approach the class. My students sometimes send me preemptive emails warning me that they may not do well on an exam, but not to worry. Like the student who wrote, "I would like to apologize upfront for my exam, it was not my best work. My mind is not in a good place right now due to personal issues. I know you truly care about your students, so I just wanted to warn you up front, so you would not be concerned. I will give you much better next time." When our students know we care, they want to do their best.

Providing Personalized Feedback

Nothing can make a student feel more important and seen than receiving feedback that is clearly tailored just for them in order to help them improve and succeed. Most students are eager to receive feedback on their assignments (Gallien and Oomen-Early 2008). Less than 7% of students say that receiving just the grade on an assignment is sufficient (Huss and Eastep 2013). Students want to learn and want to know how to improve going forward. Without feedback, they may feel like they are in the dark and don't know how to do better.

When we asked students about the worst class they had ever taken at the University of Arkansas at Little Rock in our Best/Worst Study, they often told us about classes where they didn't receive feedback and never knew where they stood. This is an incredibly frustrating situation for students. You can feel the exasperation coming through in student comments like this one: "The professor gives no clear instructions as to what he expects from us in our weekly reading journals. I'm taking this class now. We are two weeks away from the end of the semester, and have yet to receive any grades or feedback whatsoever as to whether or not we're doing the assignments correctly." Another student said, "The teacher has only graded ONE assignment throughout the entire semester and there has been no active communication whatsoever. Most people like to know where they stand in a class so that they know how to improve, but that hasn't been possible with this class."

While providing good feedback is an important element of any teaching and learning relationship, it is especially important in the online classroom because students lack face-to-face interaction (Bonnel, Ludwig, and Smith 2008; Leibold and Schwarz 2015). Good feedback can help bridge the disconnect that is inherent in online courses. Researchers who study feedback suggest some helpful best practices: instructors call students by name when providing feedback, get feedback to students as quickly as possible (within 72 hours for discussions and one week for assignments), and use a positive tone, among other recommendations (Leibold and Schwarz 2015, 37).

These recommendations can help build rapport with online students, and the literature clearly points to improvements in student outcomes when students receive prompt feedback on assignments from their instructors. In fact, prompt feedback is so important to student success that Rio Salado College uses a proprietary software to alert the department chair if an instructor takes longer than 72 hours to grade an assignment (Bailey et al. 2018). I wouldn't go so far as to recommend a faculty surveillance approach to encourage timely feedback, as it is unlikely to engender the kind of positive faculty-student relationships that have really meaningful effects over time, but students do appreciate timely feedback.

In fact, it is clear that students would prefer a speed and level of detail in assignment feedback that would seem to come with heavy costs for instructors. Providing individualized and substantive feedback to students can be time consuming and challenging, especially in large classes (Ackerman and Gross 2010). Although students love to receive feedback, nothing sparks dread in the heart of a college professor more than providing rapid, personalized feedback for a large number of students.

How can we find the right balance here? First, at an administrative level, it is important that online class sizes be kept manageable so that personalized feedback is possible. Some universities may view online education as a financially wise path because it is possible to raise class sizes beyond what a typical classroom might hold. That model has proven profitable for some universities (Bailey et al. 2018), but it is difficult to build rapport in very large online classes. The best practice recommendation is that online classes be no more than 25 students for undergraduate classes (Arbaugh and Benbunan-Fich 2005) and 13 to

15 for graduate classes (Qiu, Hewitt, and Brett 2012). One survey of online instructors reports that they would prefer class sizes to be even smaller, at 15.9 students on average, to achieve the highest level of interaction (Orellana 2009). Research that further takes into account the additional effort required by faculty to engage students in online classes recommends class sizes of around 12 (North Carolina General Assembly 2010; Tomei 2006).

These numbers are miles away from recent trends toward Massive Open Online Classes, or MOOCs, which soared in popularity and then quickly faded as attrition rates as high as 90% became widely known (Chamberlin and Parish 2011; Daniel 2012; Gütl et al. 2014). Establishing relationships between faculty and thousands of individual students in a MOOC is impossible, leading many of the students in those classes to feel disconnected, uninvested, and to ultimately drop out. That said, some students in MOOCs do make connections with one another, illustrating both how important community building is to online students and the possibility of achieving it under even the most trying circumstances (Bali et al. 2015).

Yet, even when classes are kept at a reasonable size for building rapport with individual students, faculty and administrators have to come to grips with a difficult truth—one that is at the heart of this book and is critical to building rapport and improving retention. Retaining online students requires better relationships between instructors and students, and building those relationships takes resources. Most importantly, it takes instructor time. The data and evidence presented here will hopefully convince both faculty and administrators that the resources necessary to improve online retention are worth it, but we can't pretend that retention will improve without effort. The time and effort required of faculty to build rapport with students is the first and most effective means of improving online retention. Chapter 7 provides more detail about the roles that students, administrators, and others play in the process, but this chapter focuses on faculty. Simply put, online instructors can improve retention by building rapport with their students through taking the time to connect with them, including through providing more personalized feedback.

For all those online instructors gnashing their teeth in despair, there are ways to provide personalized feedback that are more efficient than writing individual comments for each student. I have learned a number of strategies from the literature and have developed a few of my own in my years of teaching online.

The great thing about leaving feedback in online classes is that students turn in assignments electronically and so expect feedback electronically. This makes it easy to use a "copy-paste-personalize" method of providing feedback that may be similar across students but doesn't require typing extensive comments that are specifically tailored to each individual student. Instructors using this strategy for providing personalized feedback would create a document with comments they often leave on a particular assignment, written in their own voice, and then slightly adjust them for each student. One simple adjustment is to use each student's name in the feedback you give them. It matters a lot to students that their professors know their names; it makes them feel valued and they feel more invested in the course (Cooper et al. 2017).

I use the "copy-paste-personalize" method to provide feedback to students on their annotated bibliography assignment in my introductory international politics course. For instance, sometimes the students might select sources that may be outdated and I want to push them to justify why a source from 40 years ago is the best one to consult to understand the question of, for example, whether economic development is a necessary prerequisite for democracy. I may leave a comment like, "This seems like a really interesting source, [student name], but I see that it was published in [year]. That is quite a while ago! If you are going to use a source that is that old, I would like to see some justification in your annotation telling me why it is still relevant today. Is this one of the foundational works in the field? Is this where you found some key definitions?"

Instead of typing out this comment each time a student uses an outdated source, with the "copy-paste-personalize" method I can copy and paste the comment, just adding in the student name and the publication date. The feedback is just as relevant as if I had not added those two specific details, but with them, I signal to the student that I am paying attention to their particular assignment and care about helping them do better in the future. That signal is just as important—maybe even more so—than the substance of the feedback.

I know of some instructors who compile a list of common mistakes on an assignment into a single document and number them, say 1 to 15, and then provide each student with the numbers of the things they did wrong. Thus, the student would get their assignment back with the numbers 3, 5, 9, 10, and 11 across the top. The student would then consult the document and see that they: didn't cite their sources properly (number 3), lacked a clear thesis statement (number 5), and so on. This method may get students some substantive feedback regarding their academic shortcomings, but it is incredibly impersonal and can literally make the students feel like a number. It doesn't take much more time to copy and paste the actual comments into the appropriate place in the student's assignment and it likely makes the student feel like you actually read the work they spent so much time producing. There are even computer-assisted grading rubrics that can help instructors get meaningful and substantive feedback to students more quickly (Czaplewski 2009).

When Skurat Harris and I asked students about the best class they had ever taken at our university in our Best/Worst Study, the theme of good feedback came up repeatedly (Glazier and Skurat Harris 2020). One student said, "What made this class the BEST class was the feedback from and interaction with my professor. She challenged me, but also let me know the things I was doing well." Student respondents also often noted that this was not the norm for online classes. Another said, "Though it was online, the professor was attentive and always made sure to give feedback on time and graded work back on time." Another illustrative example is the student who said their professor is an "example of an instructor who actually knows that teaching is possible with online classes . . . the instructor actually taught and interacted with the students, providing feedback and helping them to understand the concepts." Good feedback can be difficult to give in an online class, but our students are clearly hungry for it.

The "copy-paste-personalize" method is one very simple way to get more substantive yet personal feedback to students, but there are many other solutions. The tools provided by Adobe make it possible to provide personalized feedback in additional, creative ways that can reach students and make them feel seen. For instance, you can leave audio comments in a pdf document. This can be easier for some, compared to typing, and hearing a professor's voice can really help make a connection and communicate encouragement more clearly. A study of nursing students found a strong preference among students for audio feedback, as opposed to written feedback (Wood, Moskovitz, and Valiga 2011).

Imagine being a student and getting a worse grade than you would have liked on an assignment. Then imagine hearing your professor's voice saying, "I realize this may not be the grade you were hoping for, John, but I think you are a smart student and believe you can do better on the next assignment. You have some good ideas, and understand many of the major concepts. You just need to spend a little more time on organization to make sure you communicate those ideas clearly and on research to make sure you have the citations to back your work up. You can do it! I am happy to help you with the next paper if you need it. Please feel free to send me an email and we can talk through your ideas or questions." If you were John, you might come away from that assignment feeling like you had hope for success in the class, instead of perhaps feeling like you wanted to quit the class or even drop out of college. Of course, that feedback to our hypothetical student John is provided in my own voice and presumes a relationship with John and knowledge of his work in the course. You may not be able to imagine yourself leaving feedback like this for your students, and that is just fine! Connecting with students authentically is what matters and that has to happen on your own terms.

In Adobe pdf documents you can also use the feedback tools to mark up a document with a colorful pen. And, no matter what format a student used to turn in an assignment, you can convert it to a pdf to leave comments, even writing some of them out in virtual ink if you want. While some students may dread receiving a heavily marked up paper back, it is another way to send a signal that you really read their assignment. Importantly, electronic marks, and all kinds of comments, don't have to be negative. They should sometimes be positive. In fact, experts recommend a balance of two positive comments for every critical one (Leibold and Schwarz 2015). I like to underline or circle important ideas, leave exclamation marks by surprising points, and write "yes!" when a thesis is stated clearly.

Two other ideas for types of feedback include video feedback and peer feedback. Video feedback can be more engaging and accessible than written feedback, and it offers another way to connect with students on a human level. Research indicates that both faculty and students believe video feedback improves their feedback experience (Crook et al. 2012). And incorporating some peer feedback may be one way to relieve the feedback burden on the professor, while also helping improve students' writing. Getting feedback *both* from the instructor and from peers can lead to greater gains in learning for the students (Tai, Lin, and Yang 2015), but peer feedback is not a substitute for instructor feedback. Students need to know that their instructors are present and paying attention to the work they are producing.

Research shows that it is not so much the amount of the feedback that matters to students, but the nature of that feedback. An overwhelming amount of critical feedback is sure to be discouraging. More is not always better. Constructive comments, along with some encouragement and even the opportunity to revise, can instead lead students to be optimistic about their chances for success in a class and contribute to a positive feedback loop with greater commitment and effort by the students on future assignments (Ackerman, Dommeyer, and Gross 2017; Ackerman and Gross 2010). Feedback doesn't have to be long and detailed. Keep it personal, positive, and specific, and students will not only learn, they will build rapport.

No matter the medium through which it is provided, giving students personalized feedback does require more time from instructors. But it is time that directly builds relationships with students. Timely feedback on assignments is one of the critical things students want and appreciate in online classes. It is one of the key ways that instructors can signal to students that they are engaged in the class and care about the students' learning. There are "teaching hacks" that instructors can use to make providing personalized feedback less time consuming, but the increased effort is worth the payoff, as students feel seen and valued in online classes. Timely, personalized feedback is a key way to improve online retention.

Reaching Out to Students

Although rapport is almost by definition dyadic and mutual (Altman 1990; Tickle-Degnen and Rosenthal 1990), when it comes to the online classroom, a lot of the responsibility for creating a high-rapport environment rests on the instructor (Murphy and Rodríguez-Manzanares 2012). One of the most important ways that professors can build rapport with their students is by fostering good communication, including through responsive and helpful email exchanges and by proactively reaching out to contact students outside of class.

Email is one of the most important means of communicating with online students, and students have very high expectations about faculty response times. In one study by Zhang, Hurst, and McLean (2016), 91% of student respondents believed that faculty should return emails within 24 hours. Although the online student demand for high responsiveness from professors can be frustrating for some faculty (Hiltz, Kim, and Shea 2007; Leidman, Piwinsky, and McKeague 2010), a quick response to an email makes a student feel respected and valued (Hurtado et al. 2011; Lundquist, Spalding, and Landrum 2002). If you are able to prioritize your email replies to online students to provide that kind of responsiveness, students will feel cared for, and will be more likely to stay in the class.

However, not all online instructors want to be, or are able to be, that responsive to email. I recommend two initial steps in email communication with students to facilitate responsiveness and set expectations. First, disable any email platform embedded in your Learning Management System. My university has a contract with Blackboard, which has an internal messaging system where students can individually send me messages. I delete this widget from the menu in all of my online courses. In providing another way for students to contact me, Blackboard has provided another system in which I have to check my messages, which takes time and mental space to remember, both of which are in short supply. I have tried telling students that the best way to reach me is via my university email address, but one hard truth of online classes is that students do not read everything that instructors post online. Each semester, a student would inevitably contact me through the Blackboard system, where their message would languish for days before I happened to check it, and the student would feel ignored and unimportant. I disable the internal messaging system altogether so the students have no choice but to email me through my university email address. I put this information in the syllabus and even make a joke of it, using it as another opportunity to let my human side come through in the course materials.

My second email recommendation is to set the expectations for email responsiveness early and often. The syllabus should list your response time for emails. Mine says, "I am also readily available by email and promise to respond within 24 hours during the work week (usually sooner) and within 48 hours on the weekend. If you ever need anything at all, I hope you will email me." This statement is also on the instructor contact page in Blackboard near my email address. With this information available to students, they know what to expect from me and won't be left thinking that I am ignoring them if I take a day (or two) off on the weekend.

A harder ask in terms of responsiveness would be to do more to align our schedules as professors with those of our students. One study of nursing students found that the students' online course usage is very consistent Monday through Saturday, but they spend twice as much time in their online courses on Sundays (Huun and Kummerow 2018). Data from the University of Georgia similarly indicates that, looking just at one spring semester, the majority of online students were logged into their classes between 8 and 10 pm on Sunday night (Zatynsk 2013). Those are definitely not my working hours, but with Sundays being such a high usage day for students, and many assignment deadlines corresponding with the Monday-Sunday week, if we want to meet our students where they are, we may want to consider checking in before bed on Sunday night to see if there are any fires that need our attention. In his book *Learning Online: The Student Experience*, George Veletsianos (2020) looks at online learning from the perspective of students and argues that we need to understand our students as people. Building rapport is all about making these human connections. When we put ourselves in our students' shoes and connect with them as fellow humans, they learn better and the experience of teaching is better as well. Thinking about adjusting our work schedule to be available during the times when students might need us the most is a challenging recommendation, but both students and faculty could benefit in the end.

Responding to student emails is part timeliness, but tone and content are also critical. When it comes to the latter, many busy instructors may default to a rushed response or may even tell students to "check the syllabus" instead of providing the answer. This is certainly understandable, but it also sends students a signal that they are a bother, they are missing important things, and perhaps even that they are not cut out for college.

Even when I may be annoyed by a question that is answered in the syllabus, I always try to do four things when I respond to any student email:

1. *Address the student by their first name.* This models good email etiquette for students, who are often lacking in this department, and lets them know that you know who they are. I have a spreadsheet for each class where I keep track of students who go by middle names or nicknames and I work hard to remember those when I email students. I have found that universities are particularly slow at changing emails for students who are transgender, so having your own list can be really important for getting a student's name right. Also, beware of some email programs (like Gmail) that auto-suggest a recipient's name; often the suggestions are accurate, but sometimes the suggested

name is pulled from the student's name as listed in their official email contact and not the name they prefer to go by.

2. *Validate the question.* Building rapport with students means encouraging questions and engagement in the class. No matter what I think of the substance of the question, I always thank the student for asking the question or tell them I am glad they asked. Thus, even if a student emails to ask what citation format they should use for the research paper and the information is right in the assignment handout, I would respond by saying something like, "Thanks so much for the question; I am so glad you asked."

3. *Answer the question.* Even if you are frustrated by the question and think the student should be able to find this information on their own, answer the question. Imagine how frustrating it would be for the student to get an email response with no actual answer to their question! I like to tell students that the information is also available, for instance, in the syllabus or in the assignment description, and then attach that document to the email. That way, the student knows where to check first before emailing next time. In the example of the citation format, I would tell them to please cite using the *Chicago Manual of Style,* link them to the online quick citation guide, and attach the assignment handout.

4. *Invite them to follow up if they have additional questions.* Especially if this is the student's first time initiating an email with me, I want them to know that they can continue to email me and ask questions. I always invite them to let me know if they need anything and tell them that I am happy to help. In the case of the citation question, I would close by telling them that the research paper is a really important assignment, so they should feel free to email me again if any other questions come up.

Imagine how a first-generation college student, uncertain in their ability to succeed in college and mustering all their courage to email a professor for the first time, might feel receiving the two different emails displayed below. In email 1, in table 4.2, the professor is curt to the point of rudeness and clearly annoyed to be asked a question that is answered in the syllabus.

In email 2, in table 4.3, the professor still tells the student that the answer is in the syllabus but also validates the question and invites further communication. Also note the more accessible signature line in the second email, which provides additional means of contact. Email signatures are personal choices, but in signing with "Dr. Glazier" instead of "RG" the professor in the second email is both signaling the importance of the email (I didn't just dash off this reply; I took the time to sign my name to it) and modeling professional email etiquette. Students may be looking for cues of how to address the professor, and an email signed "RG" can be confusing for them.

Responding to student emails is an important part of building rapport with students in an online class. While good communication is always an important component of good teaching, it is critical in the online classroom (Capra 2011). When online instructors respond quickly and positively to emails from students, the students feel encouraged and seen. Students who participated in our Best/Worst Study report that instructors in the best online classes are "very interactive, instructor was very attentive to assignments posted and responding within hours to all communication" or "the instructor

Table 4.2. Email 1: Saves Time but Alienates Students

To: jxjones@ualr.edu From: raglazier@ualr.edu Subject: re: Final Exam Date
Please check the syllabus for the answer. RG Dr. Rebecca A. Glazier | Associate Professor University of Arkansas at Little Rock | School of Public Affairs On Wed., Nov 20, 2019 at 4:21 PM Jason Jones <jxjones@ualr.edu> wrote: Hey professor! I am just wondering when the final exam is. I may be traveling at the end of the semester and I don't want to miss it!

Table 4.3. Email 2: Takes a Little More Time but Builds Rapport with Students

---

To: jxjones@ualr.edu
From: raglazier@ualr.edu
Subject: re: Final Exam Date

Hi Jason,

Thanks for the email. I am so glad you asked about the final exam. As you know, it is worth 20% of your total grade for the class, so it is definitely important that you do well on it! I am glad that you are thinking about it now.

The date for the final exam is Thursday, December 12 from 9:00am to 11:00am. This information is also in the syllabus, which I have attached for you here.

If you have any other questions, please don't hesitate to ask. Hope you have some exciting travels to look forward to at the end of the semester!

Take care,
Dr. Glazier

Dr. Rebecca A. Glazier | Associate Professor
University of Arkansas at Little Rock | School of Public Affairs
501.813.xxxx (cell) | raglazier@ualr.edu | twitter.com/rebeccaglazier
research.ualr.edu/lrcs | rebeccaglazier.net

On Wed., Nov 20, 2019 at 4:21 PM Jason Jones <jxjones@ualr.edu> wrote:

Hey professor! I am just wondering when the final exam is. I may be traveling at the end of the semester and I don't want to miss it!

---

keeps open communication and responds to emails within the same day." One student even said about an online instructor, "You do not feel like its much of an online class because he is so awesome about communication." That is the power of rapport to eliminate the distance created by the online interface.

But many students in online classes—particularly those from a lower-income, first-generation, or otherwise disadvantaged background—will never initiate an email with a professor (Jack 2016). In order to truly build rapport and improve retention in online classes, instructors need to connect with *all* of their students. One critical way to do this is through professor-initiated emails. I send the students in my online classes at least five personal emails throughout the course of the semester. I have included the full text of these emails in the appendix, and my colleagues should feel free to borrow as much as they would like. The Hope Center at Temple University also has some email templates online for reaching out to students to show them that their professors care (Goldrick-Rab 2020).

1. A welcome email at the start of the semester, welcoming them to the class, telling them how to register for the online textbook, asking them to complete a brief survey about themselves, and including a link to the syllabus.

2. A check-in email after 3 weeks of a 15-week semester, asking how the online textbook is working for them, telling them what their grade is for the online textbook readings and quizzes so far, and inviting them to let me know if they need an extension on any deadlines as we get used to a new class and online textbook together.

3. An assignment reminder email about their satire assignment (in my online introduction to international politics classes, every week 1–2 students are assigned to share a piece of political satire with the class and turn in a one-page critical analysis). I send students a personal reminder a few days before their satire assignment is due, with assignment details, the assignment itself attached, and encouragement about how I am looking forward to seeing the satire that they find.

4. An assignment reminder email about their discussion leadership assignment (in my online classes, students are assigned to be online discussion leaders once during the semester). This involves coming up with discussion questions ahead of time, submitting an outline to me, and leading the discussion throughout their assigned week. I send students a personal reminder a few days before the week they are assigned to lead the discussion with assignment details, a reminder to send me their outline for feedback, and encouragement about how I am looking forward to their discussion on such an interesting topic.

5. A check-in email around week 9 of a 15-week semester. I send students a personal email a little more than halfway through the course to check in with them on how they are doing and

any adjustments they may need to make to succeed in the class. I give them their specific grade for the discussion boards, for the first two exams (including a comment on whether they improved or declined from one exam to the next), and for the textbook readings and quizzes. I also encourage them to reach out to me to talk about their grade if they have questions or want to improve it. I provide advice on how to do better in the class and assure them that I want them to succeed.

In addition to these five personal emails that every student receives, I reach out extra times to students that I see are struggling or are not engaged. If a student misses an exam or hasn't posted in the discussion board for two weeks, I will send an email to ask if everything is okay and if there is anything that I can do to help. I emphasize to students that I am happy to accept late work and that any grade is better than a zero. Other instructors encourage more flexible deadlines or even ungrading entirely (Blum 2020; Boucher 2016; Eyler 2018; Morris and Stommel 2018). The specific policies that any professor chooses for their course will depend on their course goals, their student population, and their preferences. Each professor should choose the policies that work best for them and their students.

The potential impact we can have through the small act of reaching out to our students is illustrated by a response I received after emailing to check in on a student who hadn't posted in the discussion boards for a while. The student wrote, "I really appreciate you checking in with me, and I think that your interaction with students is wonderful! I want to try harder for the class and for you, so I will see you in the boards!" The effort the student contributed to the class changed based on the effort they saw the professor exerting to reach out. When we show our students that we care about them, it makes them want to work harder and do better in our classes. Research by Dunlap and Lowenthal (2009) concludes, "When faculty stay in touch with students through formal and informal communication and dialogue, students report that it helps them get through the rough times and keep on working" (p. 130).

Students can respond incredibly positively to these proactive emails. When I send emails to check in on students' course progress, I often get responses like this one, "Thanks so much for checking in, so grateful for how interactive you are even though it's an online class!" One transfer student replied with an email that illustrated just how much efforts to reach out to students via personal emails can build rapport with them, saying, "Again, thanks for reaching out. It's something my other school/professors didn't really do so I feel very cared about." When I reached out to one student who had missed a couple of deadlines, she quickly replied with a grateful email because, as a new online student, she hadn't realized she had missed those assignments: "I just want to thank you again for reaching out because I know some teachers might have dropped me for missing assignments so I really appreciate you!" Reaching out to students through personal emails can make a difference in how they feel about the course and it can make a difference in their success in the class.

Of course, the downside to sending a lot of personal emails to students is the amount of time it takes. In a class of 30 online students, writing five emails per student each semester is 150 extra personalized emails. If those emails include detailed information on course grades and personalized encouragement, it could take up to 20 minutes per student to write each email, overwhelming already harried instructors with 50 extra hours of work—more than an entire extra week of work in a semester. And that's only for one online class! Importantly, research shows that sending generic emails to the entire class does not significantly improve student outcomes (Leeds et al. 2013) and "lighter touch" emails with less personalization have less of an impact (Carrell and Kurlaender 2020). Building rapport takes a personal touch—the kind of personal touch that can add up to 50 extra hours of email time per class.

For those readers thinking that 50 extra hours sending emails is too much to ask of online instructors, I agree. Luckily, technology can greatly reduce the time and logistical burden of writing personalized emails, while still getting students information that can help them succeed in the class and making them feel like they matter to the instructor.

My favorite tool to facilitate personalized emails is using an email "mail merge" application. I personally use a Google Sheets add-on called Mail Merge for Gmail with Attachments, but you can accomplish the same thing with Microsoft Word and Excel. With a mail merge tool, you can add student names and email addresses to a spreadsheet and then add in any other information you want to merge into your email to students. I copy over entire columns from my gradebook so I can easily share grade information with students. Just put the information specific to each student in a row corresponding to that student's name and put a field in the email that corresponds to the header of that column.

For instance, if I wanted to share a student's discussion grade with them, I would have a column in my Google Sheets spreadsheet for Discussion and I would have a field in my email text for {{Discussion}}. When the merge program sees the field {{Discussion}} in the email, it will fill in the number in the spreadsheet under the column Discussion for each student. An example unmerged check-in email with the merge fields offset by brackets is displayed in table 4.4.

The email mail merge application can connect this email with the spreadsheet I upload to Google Sheets and fill in the merge fields indicated by brackets, which correspond to the column headings in the spreadsheet. This way, I can send personal emails to students giving them details on their grades, how they are doing in the class, and encouragement to improve, without the time and hassle of writing individual emails. An example of what a spreadsheet might look like (using fictional student data) is in table 4.5 below. Once the emails are merged, each student will receive a personal email like the one to Alicia in table 4.6.

The great thing about the email mail merge is that you can put any information you want in the merge fields. You can put entire sentences of feedback or encouragement into the merge fields. My example spreadsheet in table 4.5 contains both simple numeric scores and

Table 4.4. Example Unmerged Check-in Email

To:
From: raglazier@ualr.edu
Subject: POLS 2303 Online: Checking in 2/3 of the way through the semester!

Hi {{First Name}},

I hope that this email finds you well. I just wanted to check in with you now that we are about 2/3 of the way through the semester. You have had two exams now. You scored a {{Exam 1}} on the first one and a {{Exam 2}} on the second one. {{Exam Comment}} We have one more Exam and then the final, so there are plenty of points left in the semester.

Speaking of points, doing the textbook readings and comprehension quizzes are an easy way to earn points—it makes up 15% of your total grade for the class! Right now, your Online Textbook grade is {{Online Textbook Grade}}. {{Online Textbook Comment}} Your next textbook reading assignment is due by Monday, so be sure to get it turned in!

But the easiest points of all come from participating in discussions. Your discussion grade is {{Discussion Grade}}. {{Discussion Comment}} Our new discussion starts on Monday, so you just need to post on two days next week to earn full points.

Please also make sure that you are putting the time you need to into your annotated bibliography, which is due Friday, November 8. There is an example in the Assignments folder to help you get there.

Keep working hard as we turn the corner on our last 1/3 of our class together! Just let me know if there is anything I can do to help you.

Take care,
Dr. Glazier

Dr. Rebecca A. Glazier | Associate Professor
University of Arkansas at Little Rock | School of Public Affairs
501.813.xxxx (cell) | raglazier@ualr.edu | twitter.com/rebeccaglazier
research.ualr.edu/lrcs | rebeccaglazier.net

---

sentence-long comments about how students are doing (the full sentences in the spreadsheet aren't shown due to limited space).

I know of writing instructors who use this method to provide feedback on writing. Instead of telling students "you made mistakes 3, 5, and 9 in the attached rubric" the students get a personalized email addressed to them by name that walks them through exactly what those mistakes were, tells them how they can do better, and encourages them to improve on the next assignment. Just think of what a difference that can make from a student perspective!

Remember the suggestion to send student surveys at the beginning of the semester and keep that information in a spreadsheet? Refer back to it when you are sending check-in emails. If you have it to remind

Table 4.5. Example Spreadsheet for Email Mail Merge

First Name	Exam 1	Exam 2	Exam Comment	Online Textbook Grade	Online Textbook Comment	Discussion Grade	Discussion Comment
Alicia	76	86	You did much better on the second exam . . .	90.11	You are doing really well here! I know textbook readings can get boring, but you . . .	73.29	I think you can do a lot better here. You can earn more points. . . .
Robert	50	65.5	You did much better on the second exam . . .	14.48	I would like to see you do better here. It seems like you have thrown in the towel on . . .	65.32	I think you can do a lot better here. You can earn more points. . . .
Andrew	94	97	You are doing great on the exams . . .	98.16	You are doing really well here! I know textbook readings can get boring, but you . . .	100.59	You are literally doing better than perfect here (extra point . . .
Morgan	86	86	You are pretty consistent in your exam . . .	88.97	You are doing pretty good here! I know textbook readings can get boring, but keep . . .	81.76	I think you can earn some more points here. You can earn more . . .
Juan	88	81	You are doing pretty good on the exams . . .	84.60	You are doing pretty good here! I know textbook readings can get boring, but keep . . .	92.35	You are doing great, but you can earn more points by posting early . . .

Table 4.6. Example Merged Email

To: axsmith@ualr.edu
From: raglazier@ualr.edu
Subject: POLS 2303 Online: Checking in 2/3 of the way through the semester!

Hi Alicia,

I hope that this email finds you well. I just wanted to check in with you now that we are about 2/3 of the way through the semester. You have had two exams now. You scored a 76 on the first one and a 86 on the second one. You did much better on the second exam. Nice work! I hope you are using the study guide and please feel free to email me if you have any questions. We have one more Exam and then the final, so there are plenty of points left in the semester.

Speaking of points, doing the textbook readings and comprehension quizzes are an easy way to earn points--it makes up 15% of your total grade for the class! Right now, your Online Texbook grade is 90.11. You are doing really well here! I know textbook readings can get boring, but you are doing a great job. Keep up the good work! Your next textbook reading assignment is due by Monday, so be sure to get it turned in!

But the easiest points of all come from participating in discussions. Your discussion grade is 73.29. I think you can do a lot better here. You can earn more points by posting early and often--at least twice on at least two different days in each thread. That will get you 10/10 points every time. Our new discussion starts on Monday, so you just need to post on two days next week to earn full points.

Please also make sure that you are putting the time you need to into your annotated bibliography, which is due Friday, November 8. There is an example in the Assignments folder to help you get there.

Keep working hard as we turn the corner on the last 1/3 of our class together! Just let me know if there is anything I can do to help you.

Take care,
Dr. Glazier

Dr. Rebecca A. Glazier | Associate Professor
University of Arkansas at Little Rock | School of Public Affairs
501.813.xxxx (cell) | raglazier@ualr.edu | twitter.com/rebeccaglazier
research.ualr.edu/lrcs | rebeccaglazier.net

---

you that someone is going to give birth in the middle of the semester, or they have a big project at work in October, it can help you understand why they might be participating less. Mentioning these challenges in a personal email to a student when you reach out to check in on them can be really meaningful. It sends the students a strong signal that you know who they are and you care about their success.

Beyond just email, there are other ways to reach out to students. One option is calling students on the phone. Some universities make student phone numbers available to faculty for just this reason, but some faculty might not be comfortable with calling their students.

Honestly, results are mixed with this one. A personal phone call with each student at the beginning of the semester could help build rapport (Franklin 2015), but it is also pretty resource intensive. The vast majority of college students have cell phones and use them for coursework, research, texting, and Tweeting—almost everything but actual phone calls (Pew Research Center 2019). A phone call from a professor may be ignored, along with any other call from an unknown number, or it may be viewed as charming and quaint. The willingness to have an open line of communication to talk about course concerns is something that students appreciate, though (Kilburn, Kilburn, and Cates 2014). Just the offer of a phone call—if you are of course willing to follow through with it at the students' request—may be enough. On the other hand, professors may be better off texting or just sticking to emails, which are where students are most likely to expect faculty contact.

Research that has included phone calls to students has usually treated them as one-shot interventions, for instance, calling students at the start of courses in an attempt to improve retention rates (Leeds et al. 2013). However, to truly build rapport, efforts to reach out to students should be continuous, from before classes even start to just before grades are turned in. Building rapport is really about building relationships—and that is not done in a single shot. When it comes to connecting with students, the classes that I have had the highest rapport with have been the classes that I have had the most contact with, and those are undoubtably travel courses. In those courses, we have set up group messages on WhatsApp to keep in contact as a group while traveling. I'm not sure that is a level of contact I would recommend for most courses, but the students in those courses definitely know they can reach out to me if they need anything.

I flip the phone call script and actually share my personal cell phone number with my students, listing it in the syllabus with a request that they "use it judiciously." I would encourage instructors to think carefully about their student populations before going this route. The university that I teach at has a student population that includes a lot of first-generation students, is located in the Southern United States, where there is a strong norm of deference to authority, and where I am regularly referred to as "ma'am." In short, I don't have a lot of entitled students and they don't call my cell phone very often. There are definitely some student populations that I could imagine abusing that phone number and I would not share it with them. Use your judgment. There are technological solutions to that privacy problem, as well. Apps like Remind, often used by K–12 educators to keep in touch with parents, allow for texts without using your own phone number, so instructors can get creative if they want to connect with students over text while maintaining some professional distance (Minero 2017).

If all of this availability to online students sounds like too much, it may be time to recalibrate expectations for online teaching. Online teaching isn't the same as in-person teaching—every effort we make to connect with our online students can make an outsized difference for them. Jones and Davenport (2018) go so far as to say, "Effective online instructors embrace personal intrusion" (p. 71). I prefer to frame it as a decision to choose human connection over a forcible intrusion by students, but the end result is pretty much the same. When online instructors choose to build rapport with their students, they choose to make themselves available and to be responsive to them. High-rapport professors respond quickly to emails, answer questions directly, reach out to those who are struggling, and may even call and text with their students. This is what it takes to build connections across the distance imposed by technology. It is not always easy, but the result is greater student success and retention.

Helping Students Build Rapport with Each Other

Our primary rapport focus as instructors should be on connecting with our students, and that has been the focus of this chapter. But students also benefit when they have an educational experience that is filled with a multitude of relationships (Felten and Lambert 2020); friendship networks can improve both their academic and their social success (McCabe 2016). There are pedagogical choices that we can make as professors that will help students build rapport with their peers while also building rapport with us. Following the Community of Inquiry literature, this type of pedagogical approach would emphasize both social presence and teaching presence (Garrison, Anderson, and Archer 1999; Garrison and Cleveland-Innes 2004).

What might this look like in practice? Putting students into groups to work on projects and receive feedback from the professor as a group is one idea. Giving students tasks that they can complete by working together in a shared Google document is another way that they can collaborate, get to know each other, and build rapport with one another. As professors enter the documents, leave comments, and join the conversations—either synchronously or asynchronously—they will build rapport with the students as well. Because human beings love to create and identify with groups (Tajfel and Turner 1979), something as simple as having randomly assigned groups come up with group names, colors, or mottos can help them build rapport with each other (Burke 2011; Carron and Spink 1993). Research has also shown that when online students connect with others who are in geographic proximity to them, it can make relationships more meaningful (Boyette 2008; Rovai and Gallien Jr. 2005).

In my online classes, I like to assign one or two students each week to be the discussion leaders in one of the discussion threads. This not only gives students a good opportunity to develop important skills in leading respectful political discussions, it also gives them an incentive to participate in the student-led discussions, as they know that their turn to lead is coming up and they want to rack up some good karma. In some of my upper-division online classes, I also give a few students each week the opportunity to select current events readings that we will discuss as a class. There is an assignment that goes along with their selection, so that students get to exercise some critical media evaluation skills, but they also get to connect with their fellow students as they talk about their pick for the week and why they selected it.

As an extra credit question on their final exam, I ask students what their favorite current events reading was for the semester. Almost every response includes the name of the student who selected the reading. So, students will give responses like, "I really liked Miguel's reading about the EU border crisis" or "my favorite was the article Katie picked about the nuclear standoff on the Korean peninsula." The student-selected current events readings are one way that students are able to connect with each other and build rapport in my class. By inviting them into the curriculum and telling them that I trust them enough to let them pick readings for the class, I'm also building rapport with them through this assignment.

Building Rapport Your Way

Using these three broad strategies to build rapport with students—humanizing the instructor, providing personal feedback, and reaching out to students—faculty can significantly improve retention rates in online classes. Within these three categories, there is plenty of room for instructors to adapt the techniques to their individual personalities, teaching styles, or student populations. And if we can find opportunities to help students build rapport with one another along the way, that is a bonus.

An example of an institution using these principles to build rapport and help their students succeed is Oakton Community College and its "Persistence Project." Faculty who participate in this project commit to do four things in their classes: (1) learn students' names, (2) return assignments with meaningful, helpful feedback in the first few weeks of class, (3) communicate both high standards and support resources, and, most challenging of all, (4) meet one-on-one with each student in their class for a ten-minute conversation (Felten and Lambert 2020). Data from 1,200 students in the classes of 132 faculty who participated in the Persistence Project demonstrate that their rate of persistence—returning to the university the next semester—was 24% higher than for students who did not take classes taught by faculty in the Persistence Project (Barnett 2018). Although this effort did not focus on online classes, it does show that when rapport building is put into action, it makes a real difference for students.

The key to building rapport is to find a strategy that fits your personality and teaching philosophy. Building relationships with students means letting them see some of who you really are. Trying to perform the role of a high-rapport professor as seen on the pages of this book without bringing your own personality to the interactions is unlikely to come across as authentic and, ultimately, will not build rapport. The keys to making real human connections with students are to be yourself and demonstrate that you care. Even for those of us who have been purposefully working to build rapport in our online classes for years, there is always room for improvement. At the end of my multiyear Online Rapport-Building Experiment, described in chapter 3, I had increased retention in my introductory classes from 57% to 70%. This experiment wrapped up in 2015, but I continued working hard to build rapport with the students in my introductory classes and to come up with innovative ways to connect with them. In the two years leading up to the COVID-19 pandemic, the average retention rate in my online intro courses was 78%.

Remember, when we are talking about building rapport with students, we are not talking about getting students to *like* us—this is not a popularity contest. We are talking about making human connections that will engage students in the class, support their learning, and show them that we care about their success. If we are able to connect with our students, those interactions will have consequences beyond just a single class. Especially when we are teaching students who are new to college, the tone we set will influence how they interact with other professors and whether or not they seek them out or ask for help (Graunke and Woosley 2005; Juillerat 2000; Kezar and Maxey 2014a; Reason, Terenzini, and Domingo 2007). This is all the more reason to support students with high-rapport courses as early and often as possible. As we will see in the next chapter, for students on the margins in particular, having rapport in online classes can make all the difference.

FIVE

Students on the Margins

The promise of online education is that it can provide access to college for students who otherwise wouldn't be able to be there. For many of these students, they would love to sit in a traditional college classroom and learn face-to-face, but that just isn't an option. If they want a college education, they have to figure out another way. Take, for instance, the nontraditional student who wrote, "I'm in an all-online program, but some classes it would be nice to be in class, but I have a busy work and family life too, so all-online is really my only option" or the one who told us, "I work full time during the day and I'm a full time single mom. So I take online classes, it's easier for us that has to work for a living." For these students and so many others, online classes are their only path to a college degree. As we saw in chapter 2, all too often, these online students are treated as second-class.

The result is that success can be precarious for many of our students taking online classes. Students of color, first-generation students, and lower-income students are exactly the demographic that online classes are supposed to be reaching with expanded access to college. But repeated studies show that these populations are less likely to successfully complete online classes (Bennett, McCarty, and Carter 2019;

Figlio, Rush, and Yin 2013; Kaupp 2012; McCarty, Bennett, and Carter 2013; Xu and Jaggars 2014). Higher education continues to be stratified by class and race; the achievement gaps that plague face-to-face college classes are only exacerbated by the online environment (Carnevale and Strohl 2013; Sublett 2020). What can we do to help support these students whose success is the most tenuous? While rapport building is a good practice for all of our online students, it is particularly helpful in retaining these students on the margins.

In this chapter, I first present data to illustrate how students who have traditionally been on the margins of higher education—lower-income students, nontraditional students, and students of color—now represent the future. Recognizing the reality of the changing face of higher education, I then use research and student quotes to take a close look at the experience of online classes from the perspective of these students. Next, using original survey data from the Rapport Impact Study, I demonstrate how rapport building can make an especially meaningful difference for underserved student populations. I close with recommendations for an empathetic approach to our online students, addressing some of the key concerns of online instructors around cheating, trauma, and second chances.

The Changing Face of Higher Education

Take the "traditional" college student in the United States. They graduate from high school and move directly into a residential dorm on a campus where they begin a four-year college degree. In 2011, there were about 2.6 million of these students enrolled in college in the United States, and faculty tend to think of them first when we design our classes and our curriculum. But at the same time, there were 14.9 million "nontraditional" students enrolled in college in the United States—more than five times as many as the "traditional" students (National Adult Learner Coalition 2017). The model of going to college full-time at 18, living on campus, taking all of your classes face-to-face, and graduating in four years is followed by a diminishing number of students, probably less than 20% and falling, according to the National Center for Education Statistics (King and Alperstein 2014, 13).

Instead, many more college students today are what we would consider nontraditional; 37% are 25 or older (Lumina Foundation 2019). They are parents, veterans, and employees. They may have delayed going to college and are usually financially independent, even if they are financially stressed. They often face different demands on their time—many struggling to balance family, work, and education (Layne, Boston, and Ice 2013). They make up the vast majority of college students in the United States today and they are significantly more likely to take online classes (Rabourn, BrckaLorenz, and Shoup 2018).

The racial and ethnic dynamics of higher education enrollments are also shifting. Although the percentage of high school completers who have enrolled in college has steadily climbed over time—from around 49% in 1980, to 63% in 2000, to almost 70% by 2016—these gains have not been evenly distributed across race/ethnicity. Census data from the 2017 Digest of Education Statistics Report illustrate how Asian and white students consistently enroll in college at numbers above the average, while Black and Hispanic students (they track Hispanic rather than Latinx populations) consistently enroll at below-average levels, with some gains over time (see figure 5.1).

One promise of online higher education is the ability to close these racial gaps. Some studies indicate that Black and Latinx students enroll in online classes at higher rates than other racial/ethnic groups (Classes & Careers 2011; Fry and Cilluffo 2019), although other research shows that this varies by institutional sector and that Black students may be less likely than white students to take an online class in their first year of college (Sublett 2020). If students who have historically been underrepresented in college classrooms are using online classes to access higher education, then the hope is that online classes can help close racial gaps in higher education attainment (Killion, Gallagher-Lepak, and Reilly 2015; Kronk 2017). But Black and Latinx students also tend to fail and drop out of online classes at higher rates than other racial and ethnic groups (Kaupp 2012; Xu and Jaggars 2014). Although racial and ethnic achievement gaps exist in many col-

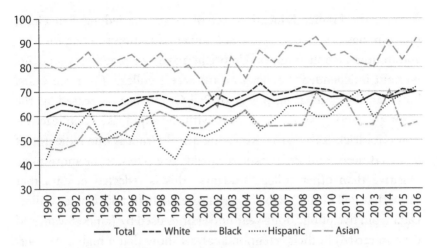

Figure 5.1. Recent High School Completers Enrolled in College, by Race/Ethnicity, in Percentages

lege classes, research shows that they are exacerbated in online classes (Figlio, Rush, and Yin 2013; Johnson and Mejia 2014).

As nontraditional students and students of color have begun to access college in greater numbers, we have also seen a shift in the socioeconomic status of college students. In fact, when we look at overall enrollment growth in colleges and universities in the United States over the past 20 years, we find that it is fueled by an influx of students from lower-income backgrounds (Fry and Cilluffo 2019). In 1996, 21% of undergraduates were in poverty, but this number rises to 31% by 2016. Because the national poverty rate in the United States for adults age 18 to 64 remained steady at about 12% during this same period, this trend suggests that much of the recent growth in higher education has come from lower-income students who were previously unable to access a college education (Fry and Cilluffo 2019). One reason they may be able to finally break through is because of online classes. When we look at independent undergraduates (i.e., those who are 24 and older) as well as younger students who are not receiving financial support from parents, they are much more likely to be poor today than in prior years. In 2016, a full 42% of them were living in poverty, compared to 29% in 1996 (Fry and Cilluffo 2019).

Since the Higher Education Act of 1965, the federal Pell Grant program has been a cornerstone of higher education funding for low- and middle-income families (Umbricht 2016), helping many students without independent financial means access college. Over the years, however, the purchasing power of Pell Grants has decreased, as the grant amounts have not kept pace with the rapid rise of college tuition (Goldrick-Rab 2016). Receiving a Pell Grant is one indicator of financial need, and Pell Grant recipients are likely to be more price sensitive than other college students—this is reflected in data that show that Pell Grant recipients are more likely to take classes online. Data from five public, four-year universities used by James, Swan, and Daston (2016) in their retention analysis show that a higher percentage of students taking fully online course loads receive federal Pell Grants—about 9% more than students taking all of their classes face-to-face. Even in successful and prestigious programs, Pell Grant status is consistently about 5 percentage points higher among students in online classes, compared to students in face-to-face classes (Bailey et al. 2018).

Lower-income students are also drawn to for-profit programs. For-profit institutions saw a 13 percentage point increase in lower-income students from 1996 to 2016, whereas public nonprofit universities only saw 6% growth and private nonprofit universities 3% growth from the same population over the same time period (Fry and Cilluffo 2019). This lopsided growth is likely because private for-profit institutions have explicitly reached out to lower-income students seeking to complete their degrees online (Angulo 2016; Cottom 2017; Schade 2014).

Expanding access to college through online classes has also meant more first-generation students attending. Although there are no national statistics on whether first-generation college students are more likely to enroll in online classes, we do know that they are more likely to enroll in for-profit universities, which skew heavily online. Data from the National Center for Education Statistics shows that 19% of first-generation college students choose a for-profit school, compared to only 8% of college students with at least one parent with a bachelor's degree (Snyder, de Brey, and Dillow 2019).

Although some of our most underserved students are more likely to enroll in online classes, those classes don't always serve them well. Nontraditional and underrepresented college students struggle in online classes at higher rates than traditional university students (Kaupp 2012; Wladis, Conway, and Hachey 2015; Xu and Jaggars 2014). They take on higher rates of student debt and are less likely to graduate, too (Scott-Clayton and Li 2016). When the US Department of Education released data on earnings and student loan payments in 2017, it flagged 803 programs as saddling students with debt they can't afford to repay (defined as loans that exceed 12% of earnings)—and 787 of them were for-profit institutions (US Department of Education 2017). These types of institutions have a history of explicitly reaching out to students who lack traditional paths to a college degree and are seeking to complete their degrees online, but they also have a history of producing worse long-term outcomes for them (Appel and Taylor 2015; Cottom 2017; Deming, Goldin, and Katz 2012; Sridharam 2012).

The face of higher education is changing. These changes are in part attributable to online courses making higher education more accessible, and they provide an opportunity for reflection on how far short we are falling of the promises we have made to our students. Instead of the expanding availability of online classes leading to more students from disadvantaged populations earning college degrees, research indicates that taking more online classes actually leads to lower persistence in a given field and a lower likelihood of graduating (Huntington-Klein, Cowan, and Goldhaber 2017).

Nontraditional, first-generation, lower-income students, and students of color are the future of higher education in the United States. And they are enrolling in online classes. If we want to retain these students and help them graduate, we owe them more of our time and consideration. Because although they represent the future of higher education, right now they are teetering on the edge.

A Mile in Their Shoes

Looking beneath the statistics, what is it like to be an online student? Few faculty members have had the experience of taking a class as an online student. And even fewer have done it as a lower-income, first-generation, student of color who was also working two jobs and raising kids on their own. Can we even imagine how precarious the academic lives of our students are? It's worth trying. Research, together with quotes from real students, can give us a glimpse into what it might be like to be a student in our classes. Taking on the perspective of our students can make us better teachers (Veletsianos 2020).

Let's start with the challenges of being a first-generation college student. If you don't have close relatives to model college and career, enrolling in college at all is often a hurdle, not to mention succeeding once you are there, and persisting to graduation (Cataldi, Bennett, and Chen 2018; Choy 2001; Ishitani 2006; Pascarella et al. 2004; Stephens et al. 2012; Woosley and Shepler 2011). University life includes a "hidden curriculum," beyond the visible curriculum covered in class, which students without college-educated parents don't even know they are missing (Collier and Morgan 2008). For instance, whereas some entering students may have parents with graduate degrees who read over the syllabus with them and encourage them to attend office hours, many of the first-generation students in our online classes may have never had a face-to-face conversation with someone with a PhD before. They may not even know what "office hours" are (Chatelain 2018; Collier and Morgan 2008). Academic preparedness can't make up for not knowing that it is okay to ask for an extension on an assignment if a personal emergency comes up, or that coming to department events to get in "face-time" with faculty is a good idea. Even if more privileged students don't know the specifics of a particular university, they are more comfortable asking questions and demanding answers—it's how affluent, white parents teach their children to interact with institutional authorities from the time they are young (Calarco 2014, 2018; Lareau 2011). Missing this hidden curriculum, and the resulting self-doubt these students struggle with, can thwart their academic success (Cataldi, Bennett, and Chen 2018; Cox 2009).

Even if our students do know what office hours are, and ours are clearly posted, we may need to make an effort to overcome the typical first-generation mindset of self-sufficiency to get them to attend. Interviews with first-generation students reveal that they often default to a view of faculty as antagonistic gatekeepers. As one first-year, first-generation student at a four-year research university said,

> When I go to class, that is our time. It is time for us students. And outside of that it just seems weird and I don't want to bug them. I just have this idea in my head that if I do go to their office, they are going to harangue me. They will say, "What are you doing here? You are a failure. Get out of here. What do you want?" And that is not something that I want to hear. And that is a big reason for me not to see them. (Quoted in Longwell-Grice and Longwell-Grice 2008, 416)

Faculty set the tone for our classes in dozens of small ways that affect how students perceive our accessibility—remember the study referenced in chapter 3 about how students read into when and how office hours are posted (Hurtado et al. 2011)? Many first-generation college students begin from a place of assumed indifference from professors, if not outright antipathy. They may be afraid to speak up and ask questions because they don't want to be judged by their professors as needy or struggling (Calarco 2020; Jack 2016).

Layer onto these challenges those faced by lower-income students. Does your campus have a food pantry? If not, it probably should. A survey of more than 86,000 students at 100 institutions across the country revealed that 45% of students had been food insecure in the last 30 days. The survey also showed that 17% had been homeless in the previous year (Goldrick-Rab et al. 2019). These are students who worry about the cost of gas to drive to campus, who try to share textbooks with their roommates, and who are eager to pick up an extra shift whenever they can. When we take the financial concerns of our students seriously, we see both why they are drawn to online classes and also how online classes can be tenuous for them.

A student of mine told me about one semester when she was taking an online class and her laptop died. In the two weeks it took to get it fixed, she'd lost notes, missed quizzes, and fell behind on lectures. Keeping up with the coursework by accessing public computers on campus was difficult, she told me, because "I was going to school full-time, and working nights to pay rent. Unfortunately . . . [the professor] was unforgiving." The COVID-19 pandemic in 2020 revealed many of the deep inequities in our colleges and universities as classes moved online and many students had to return home—where some had no reliable internet connections or computers, not to mention no incomes without their campus jobs, and no consistent food sources without campus meal plans (Patel 2020).

Now consider what it might be like to be a student of color. In 2017, nearly three-quarters of college faculty were white, while only 55% of students were; Black students make up 14% of our college-going population, but only 6% of faculty; 20% of students are Hispanic, but only 5% of faculty are (Espinosa et al. 2019). Students of color are often taught by white faculty, and they may encounter discrimination, microaggressions, or assumptions about affirmative action, from faculty and from other students, which can have a negative effect on their mental health and sense of self-worth (McCabe 2009; Nadal et al. 2014; Ong et al. 2013).

Not only do our campus climates matter, but our students are also affected by the world outside our classrooms. Research by Desmond Ang (2020) using hyperlocal variation in how close students live to the site of police killings, found that exposure to police violence led to lower GPAs, lower high school completion rates, and lower levels of college enrollment for students in Los Angeles public high schools. The effects are driven almost entirely by Black and Hispanic students. Our students are powerfully affected by the world beyond our courses. We are rarely able to measure those effects in such clear and direct ways, but we should never forget that they are there.

Especially for students of color at Predominantly White Institutions

(PWIs), college can be both isolating and exhausting. Research has demonstrated that Black students put forth more effort but achieve less gain, compared to white students (Greene, Marti, and McClenney 2008; Kugelmass and Ready 2011). Even as universities made statements in support of Black Lives Matter, Black faculty, and Black students in the summer of 2020, those same faculty and students were telling stories of discrimination with the hashtag #BlackInTheIvory (Diep 2020). The surveys my colleagues and I have done regularly return with comments about classes like, "One of the instructors would make offensive and racist comments" and "lack of cultural sensitivity and racist remarks made by professor towards me." Imagine trying to learn in an environment like that.

Some have suggested that online courses may be a way to mitigate the intercultural effort that students of color have to put forth at PWIs. For instance, Stanley (2014) examines students at four-year PWIs and finds greater learning gains for African American students online, compared to African American students in face-to-face classes, arguing, "Absent an environment that creates intercultural effort, African-American students can direct their energy into educationally purposeful activities that translate into learning gains" (p. 106). Taken one step further, imagine online classes that are not simply neutral spaces that approach pedagogy in a colorblind way (Killion, Gallagher-Lepak, and Reilly 2015), but online classes that actively invite and engage all students to be part of the community of the class, to connect with the professor, and to interrupt the reproduction of past inequities (Humiston et al. 2020; Journell 2007; Zembylas 2008). Such classes might result in even greater learning gains and stronger rapport.

Building Rapport to Center Students on the Margins

In the midst of all the demands students have on their time—families, jobs, learning disabilities, navigating college as first-generation students—imagine the outsized impact even a little human connection from an instructor can make. Data drawn mostly from in-person classes show that first-generation students benefit enormously from personally connecting with an individual faculty member (Amelink 2005; Ishiyama 2002). Mentorship also has a significant impact for students of color (Anaya and Cole 2001; Lee 1999), who tend to feel more isolated in online classes and view asynchronous interactions especially negatively (Ashong and Commander 2012; Merrills 2010; Rovai and Wighting 2005). We have seen study after study demonstrate that students want a deeper connection with their professors (e.g., Kezar and Maxey 2014a).

Many students, especially the kinds of marginalized students I have been focusing on in this chapter, may start college with fear and anxiety about their ability to succeed. A study of community college students demonstrates that the ones who were able to overcome these fears and thrive were the ones who had a professor who came to their level and related to them (Cox 2009). These professors reassured them of their competence and ability to succeed. They believed in them. When students believe they can succeed in a class, they are more likely to do just that (Miller 2014). Perhaps no one can have a stronger influence over a student's belief about their ability to succeed in a class than the professor. That doesn't mean that we need to lie to students who are struggling and tell them that everything is fine, but a kind word of encouragement can go a long way.

No matter where our students are academically, we can believe in their ability to learn. Meeting our students where they are and supporting their learning is sometimes called "scaffolding." The idea is that we can support students exactly where they are and, with some help, enable them to climb a little higher. Especially for first-generation students, or students taking online classes for the first time, they may need some scaffolding around the basics of how to navigate an online course and find the appropriate assignments and learning modules (Stavredes 2011; Stavredes and Herder 2013). For these students who are new to college or may feel like outsiders, professors can be a comforting presence to let them know that they belong. The welcome and encouragement from a professor—the rapport and human connection that is at the heart of this book—is exactly what marginalized students need in their online classes to help them succeed.

Measuring the Impact of Rapport on Our Most Vulnerable Students

Having seen the positive impact of rapport building in my own classes through the multiyear Rapport Teaching Experiment discussed in chapter 3, I got together with my colleague Heidi Skurat Harris in 2016 to expand the research. We were interested in knowing more about the impact that rapport could have on student retention rates. We surveyed students in 35 different online classes at the University of Arkansas at Little Rock for our Rapport Impact Study. We asked the students a series of questions to determine the level of rapport in their relationship with their professor. For instance, we asked them the extent to which they agreed or disagreed with statements like "my professor cares about students" and "I felt the instructor was approachable to discuss class-related issues." Using responses from 318 students, we summed a total of nine questions into a single rapport scale and calculated a rapport score for each of the 35 classes, by averaging the scores from all of the responding students in each class. Thus, the average of all of the responding students' evaluations of the rapport in the class was used to give a single score to the class as a whole. This approach smooths out the outlying students who might have been mad about a low grade or who rate every professor highly.

With nine total rapport questions, each using a five-point Likert scale, our rapport measure ranges from 9 to 45 (M = 38.73, SD = 6.21, Min = 23, Max = 44, Alpha = 0.92). We brought these course scores together with anonymous student-level demographic and academic data (GPA and course grade) from all 910 students enrolled in the 35 classes to statistically determine the extent to which being in a class with a higher average rapport score would influence student success. Were students in classes with higher average rapport scores more likely to pass the class successfully? Because many factors can influence retention, we ran a logit regression model to account for GPA, age, transfer status, gender, and race/ethnicity. The short answer of the Rapport Impact Study is yes—rapport matters. Students in classes with higher rapport scores were less likely to fail or drop out, even when all these other variables are considered (Glazier and Skurat Harris 2021).

But to more fully understand exactly what our findings mean for students, we used our statistical model to predict the outcome of a hypothetical student pulled from our data, using statistical averages. This student is a woman of color, 28 years old, and coming to the university as a transfer student. We don't know if she is a first-generation college student, but 80% of the student body at the University of Arkansas at Little Rock is, so chances are good in this data set (Quick Facts 2019). Using predicted probabilities, we can set a hypothetical student in our model with these parameters and see what happens. For this first iteration, we also set her to have the average GPA for the sample at 2.79, or about a letter grade of B. Now, keeping all these characteristics the same, we predict her probability of passing the class she is enrolled in with a C or better while changing one key variable: the level of rapport. We move the level of rapport from the lowest level in the sample, a class with an average rapport score of 23, to the highest level, a class with an average rapport score of 44, about as high as possible on our 9 to 45 scale. The outcome of this prediction is depicted graphically in the dashed center line in figure 5.2.

Our hypothetical student gains more than 22 points (displayed in the text box in the center of the dashed line) in terms of her likelihood of passing the class—going from 62.7 to 84.9—just by moving from a low-rapport to a high-rapport class. Imagine if we could really do that for every nontraditional female transfer student of color in our online classes—or better yet, every student! When we are willing to build real human connections with them and believe in their success, it makes a measurable difference in how students do in our classes. For this statistically created student, representing so many very real students out there, that human connection is powerful enough to move retention 22 percentage points.

The two other lines in figure 5.2 represent slight variations in the characteristics of our hypothetical student. In the top line, all of the demographic characteristics remain the same, but we change our hypothetical student to a very high achiever with a GPA of 3.75, or an A aver-

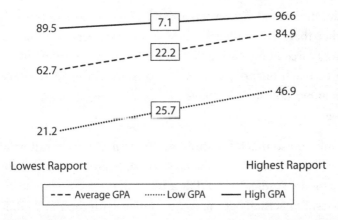

89.5 —————————— 7.1 |—————— 96.6
                              - - - 84.9
62.7 - - - - - - -| 22.2 |- -
                         ········· 46.9
21.2 ·········· | 25.7 |·········

Lowest Rapport   Highest Rapport

--- Average GPA   ······· Low GPA   —— High GPA

Figure 5.2. Probability That a 28-year-old Female Transfer Student of Color Will Pass with a Grade of C or Better

age. In this scenario, the retention gains are smaller: only 7.1 points. At 96.6%, this high-achieving student is almost guaranteed to pass if she is in a high-rapport class.

The bottom line of figure 5.2 tells a very different story. In this scenario, we take the same demographic characteristics again and this time change the GPA downward to 1.75, or the letter grade equivalent of a low C. Now that our student is struggling academically, her potential for success in the class is much lower, but the difference that rapport can make is much higher. In this scenario, moving from a low-rapport to a high-rapport class improves the probability of passing the course by 25.7 percentage points, the largest gain of any of the three scenarios. It is still a difficult road for this student. Even in the highest-rapport class, her probability of passing is below 50%. But it is vastly improved when she believes her professor truly cares about her success.

Guiding Principles for Helping Struggling Students

It can be challenging to pour a lot of time and caring into students who might still drop out of our classes. Knowing that even in a high-rapport class, our hypothetical student would fail or drop out more than 50% of the time can be pretty discouraging. Having spent more than ten years trying to build rapport with a student population that includes many students on the margins, I have come to learn the hard way that there are students whose college careers can't be saved by the sheer force of my caring. When I run into a situation where I keep trying to reach out to a student but am not getting a response, I try to remember the email I received a few years ago from a student who told me:

> Thank you so much for showing concern at my overall wellbeing as well as my success in the classroom. I actually decided that I'm placing my studies on hold at a point that was too late to drop classes. I'm actually going to be content with the F's. Well, I'm going to just not log in to Blackboard or view my transcript and face them. I have, however, received a promotion and raise since I last reached out to you, and am finding myself very fulfilled in a life outside of academics. (Something that my 18 year old self could never conceive). Again, I cannot express how much I appreciate having a teacher that truly cares about her students' success despite their lack of participation. I truly thank you for checking in on me.

I can honestly count on one hand the number of times that I have received this kind of happy-ending closure over a student who disappeared from my online class, but I have to believe that it happens and most students just don't think to send their Introduction to Political Science professor an email update. Remember, institutions of higher education may put student retention as their top goal, but staying enrolled may not always be in a student's best interest.

For this student, she earned a promotion and made a choice not to continue in our class. Far more common, unfortunately, are students who have negative life circumstances that leave them feeling too overwhelmed to do well in class (Beer and Lawson 2017; Fetzner 2013). The loss of a job or a scholarship may make continuing to attend college financially impossible, while the loss of a parent or a child may make it emotionally impossible. In any given semester, our students may experience incredible trauma that can profoundly impact their ability to be successful in our classes. What is the role of an online instructor here?

This is something that each instructor has to decide for themselves. Will you accept late work from a student who has had a death in the family? What about one who has been up all night with a sick child? What about one who hasn't checked in to the online class for the past two weeks because she has been consumed with searching for a new job after being laid off? What about the student who is returning to college after a decade away and just isn't used to online classes yet? A few guiding principles have helped me as I have grappled with these questions over the years.

First, *know your student population*. For me, it makes a difference what kind of institution you are working at and what kind of students you are teaching. This is where the difference between equality and equity comes into play (Gannon 2020). We know that students who take online classes are more likely to be first-generation college students, are more likely to be older, and are more likely to have children and work more hours (Cochran et al. 2014; Frydenberg 2007; Patterson and McFadden 2009). For me, that already builds in a different set of constraints and circumstances. First-generation and lower-income students are likely to need more support and guidance—and less likely to ask for it—especially if they are taking online classes for the first time (Karp 2011; Longwell-Grice and Longwell-Grice 2008; Rosenbaum, Deil-Amen, and Person 2007; Scott-Clayton 2011). The privilege of coming from a community with college experience is not just knowing the "hidden curriculum," it is knowing when and how to ask about the things that you don't know (Calarco 2014, 2020; Lareau 2011).

When the University of California, Los Angeles began a first-generation faculty initiative to raise the visibility of faculty who were the first in their family to graduate from a four-year college, less than 7% of the faculty self-identified as first-generation, compared to nearly half of UCLA's incoming class in fall 2016, when the campaign began (UCLA First to Go 2016). We sometimes wonder why struggling students don't ask for help, but even knowing that asking for help is an option is part of the unwritten rules of academia, which first-generation students might not know. Students from a lower-income background may have been raised with a "no-excuses" approach to problem solving, where figuring out a solution yourself was a sign of respect for the authority figure. Contrast this with a "by-any-means" approach to problem solving, more common among educated, middle-class families, where negotiating with the professor is a learned strategy (Calarco 2014). Faculty and students may have very different backgrounds and life experiences.

As you get to know your students—their cultural backgrounds, their work responsibilities, their goals, their family lives—you can better design your classes with your students in mind (Crosling, Heagney, and Thomas 2009). For instance, if you know some of your students work full-time jobs, you might want to make your deadlines on the weekends, so that they are able to turn things in on time. As one student in the Best/Worst Study said, "Most on-line students, especially older students, work. To have an assignment due mid-week by 5:00 p.m. is a major inconvenience and set-up for failure."

Similarly, having a major assignment due at the end of spring break may not be a great idea for students with families—they likely have not had a lot of free time to work on it with the kids out of school all week. Having an exam open only during 9–5 work hours or only on the weekend is probably not convenient for all of your students. Scheduling exams across a longer time period can make them work for multiple schedules. Because helping students build relationships with one another can be particularly beneficial to students of color in online classes (Ashong and Commander 2012; Rovai and Gallien Jr. 2005), we may want to consider assignments that bring students together to work on projects, even grouping them geographically to further facilitate connections (Boyette 2008) or emphasizing communal over competitive values (Flannery 1995).

These are simple changes, but they can make it easier for students to succeed. One way to get to know your students is through something like the introductory survey mentioned in chapter 4. A sample survey is available in the appendix. If you ask about concerns, challenges, work hours, and similar constraints, you won't have to guess about the difficulties facing your students; you will know.

Whether and to whom to extend grace are judgment calls that each instructor has to make individually. These judgment calls are particularly difficult because many professors have not been in their students' shoes. We may feel uncomfortable making these calls, particularly when we don't have complete information. In these circumstances, I find a second guiding principle especially helpful: *be compassionate*. I have never regretted being kind. I have never wished I could take back a deadline extension for a student in crisis. Now, that may be in large part due to the fact that, because of the student population that I work with, I rarely encounter entitled jerks trying to game the system. Instead, my students are most often trying their best in a system where they are learning the rules as they go and I am the closest thing they have to a guide. So, I don't mind giving them a chance to try again. There is certainly an argument to be made for the importance of deadlines and teaching students self-sufficiency (Zatynsk 2013), but sometimes learning that takes a few iterations. Just knowing to ask for a deadline extension can come from a place of privilege. Recognizing that, and coming from a place of critical pedagogy, some faculty have rolling deadlines, or no late penalties at all (e.g., Mehta and Aguilera 2020; Morris and Stommel 2018), but that approach may not work for all instructors.

One approach is to try to turn "cheating" into an opportunity for learning. For instance, if a student research paper run through plagiarism screening software comes back "matching" with online sources, this presents an opportunity for dialogue instead of a chance to throw the book at the student. The professor can reach out to them, explain that their plagiarism report indicated that their paper had uncited content from online sources, which would be plagiarism and grounds for getting an F for the assignment, and ask if perhaps they accidentally submitted the wrong version of the document. Maybe there was some mistake and they uploaded the document before they entered all of the citations? A student who has never written a research paper before, or perhaps never even taken a college class before, may not entirely understand that reworking some online material into their paper is against the rules. International students or second-language learners may have different expectations about what constitutes plagiarism (Amsberry 2009; Pecorari and Petric 2014); cultural assumptions are part of our understanding of plagiarism and particularly vulnerable students may be harmed by an unthinking application of plagiarism policies (Bayne et al. 2020; Hayes and Introna 2005). An approach that gently suggests the student may have submitted the wrong document and gives them the chance to turn in a correctly cited paper with no penalty at all helps explain what went wrong, lets the student save face, and gives them a chance to make it right.

As more classes have moved online, concerns about academic integrity have increased. In April 2020, a poll of 312 institutions of higher education found that 62% of them were using video surveillance for online proctoring, with an additional 34% considering it (Grajek 2020). Although Watson and Sottile (2010) find that cheating is actually more common in face-to-face classes than online classes, possibly because of social relationships and opportunities for students to cheat off of one another, research does indicate that students are less likely, or able, to cheat when an exam proctor is used (Alessio et al. 2017). The fear of online cheating has led some to advocate for a full student-surveillance approach to online academic integrity, including facial recognition software, video surveillance, and computer restriction software (e.g., Rodchua, Yiadom-Boakye, and Woolsey 2011).

Setting aside the simple practicalities of such an approach—we know that not all of our students have reliable internet access and that facial recognition is racially biased (Bacchini and Lorusso 2019; Folorunso, Busola, and Oluwatosin 2019), so such a system is sure to have some implementation challenges—think of the message it sends to students. We want students to feel like trusted partners, not like criminals-to-be in their own education. These surveillance systems can feel oppressive and authoritarian to students (Andrejevic and Selwyn 2020).

Instead, we should create online classrooms where student learning is centered and rapport is paramount. When students believe they are learning, and learning something meaningful, they are less likely to cheat (Lang 2013). When we build high-rapport relationships with the students in our online classes, they know we are invested in their success and they will be less likely to cheat. As Jesse Stommel puts it, "Cheating is a pedagogical issue, not a technological one" (quoted in Flaherty 2020a). In response to our Best/Worst Study, one student told us about a class where the assignments were tedious busywork and the professor was unresponsive to questions. When a student posted the answers online, many students in the class used them because, "Even good students will cheat if they feel the class is unfair."

If we treat cheating like a technological issue, we will just end up in an arms race with students who find ever more creative means of cheating, like companies willing to take online classes in students' names (Malesky, Baley, and Crow 2016), or ways to yawn or stretch to fool active video surveillance while students glance at notes (Harwell 2020). This doesn't mean that we should abandon all attempts at academic integrity, but we should engage students as our partners in the endeavor and help them understand that their learning and success is the ultimate goal. Every faculty member has to make the call on what the best approach is for their class. In the past, when students have submitted research papers in my online classes, they have had the opportunity to run a draft through the plagiarism screening tool first, to check out their "matching" report and make sure they have cited everything correctly. Thus, the software is used as a teaching tool instead of a "gotcha" trap for catching students. Increasingly, though, I am persuaded that the teacher/student relationship is changed by the presence of surveillance technology meant to catch cheating in the class (Bayne et al. 2020). It sets the tone for the relationship as one that lacks trust, which is antithetical to building rapport.

Assessment design may also play a role here—using the same multiple choice questions in an untimed online exam may lead to more cheating (Harmon, Lambrinos, and Buffolino 2010), but design fixes, like time limits, question randomization, having a limited number of questions selected from a larger test bank, and including a variety of question formats could reduce cheating (Cluskey Jr., Ehlen, and Raiborn 2011). Whatever specific policies we each decide to adopt for our classes, if we "start by trusting students" as Stommel urges (quoted in Flaherty 2020a), we can build rapport that will reduce cheating in our classrooms and make them a place where learning is prioritized.

Our first goal should be to help students learn. Kicking them out of class at the first mistake doesn't meet that goal. Having a little compassion and showing a little kindness can help achieve it. If we decide to be compassionate with all our students, there aren't as many judgment calls to make—just relationships and learning to focus on.

When to Give Up

So, is it ever time to give up on trying to get a student to pass a class? Although college attendance rates have been steadily increasing over the past 40 years, and many people's conception of what it means to live the American Dream includes a college education, college is not a good fit for everyone. Not every student is going to be able to make it through four (or six or eight) years of college courses. Despite my best rapport-building efforts, I still lose about 20 to 25% of students in my online introductory courses. That is heartbreaking, but it is significantly better than the 43% I was losing before I started teaching with rapport, or the 35% average in online courses that meet core requirements at the university where I teach.

My rule of thumb is, as long as the student hasn't told me they are giving up, I am not giving up on them. However, because perseverance may not always be healthy, it may be a good idea to validate for a student that they can take a semester off to deal with a crisis. I have had students go through incredible traumas—from family deaths to hospitalizations to violent attacks—and it can be hard to successfully complete a course in the midst of that. Most universities have policies that allow students to withdraw under such circumstances and that may be the best course of action.

I have found that the biggest problem is students just disappearing when major crises arise, instead of talking with their professors and university staff. Students may think, as one first-generation, working-class student interviewed by Longwell-Grice and Longwell-Grice (2008) did, "I feel like if I told [my professors] about problems I was having, they would say, 'So why are you telling me?'" Not trusting faculty with major life problems, or just being too overwhelmed to reach out, is understandable. Navigating university red tape and arranging to extend course deadlines may be the last thing on a student's mind if their father is dying of cancer, if they just got laid off from their job, or if they were raped last week. When facing life problems like this, students say, like this one did in our Best/Worst Study, "This was enough for me to want to leave the university." And for first-generation students and students with less privilege, it may not even cross their minds that they can ask for help (Calarco 2014). They may think that their life problem just means that they won't get to do college after all.

Part of building rapport is communicating to students that they can come to us if they are struggling in the class—whether it is because of the course material or because of a life problem. We aren't social workers, but we almost always know more about campus and its resources than they do. For instance, we know about counseling services, the writing center, and (if we have one) the campus food pantry. We know when the last day to withdraw from a class is and where to find the right form. We know the number to the financial aid office and that there is a hardship scholarship available for seniors. When we build rapport with them, students can see us as partners in helping them succeed, instead of as obstacles to overcome on their way to a college degree (Longwell-Grice and Longwell-Grice 2008).

We can communicate our willingness to help through the policies we set and by the information we share in our syllabi (Knight 2020). For example, Stommel (2020) recommends "ungrading" policies, where students self-evaluate their work, reflect on the process, and receive qualitative feedback from the professor. Nilson (2015) suggests giving students tokens or passes, which they can trade in for a missed assignment or a redo on an exam. Gannon (2018) recommends including information on campus counseling services, academic support services, and student organizations in syllabi to send a message of inclusion. Putting these things in writing is one step in building rapport. It signals caring to students—about them as complete people beyond the grades they earn in the class. When syllabi are inviting, approachable, and focused on learning, students have more positive perceptions of the course and the professor (Palmer, Wheeler, and Aneece 2016).

When we try to build rapport with students, they notice the difference. Take this email I received from a student in response to a reminder about an assignment deadline: "I can't thank you enough for always keeping me updated and replying to my emails so fast. You are the one teacher I have had so far in my college career that really made me feel like you truly care that your students succeed. Online classes tend to feel as if they are run on auto-pilot, but yours most definitely does not. Thank you for this."

After giving a student a second chance to make up an exam that they missed, I received this email in return, "I woke up this morning, read this email, and burst into tears. I don't know how else to say. Thank you!" The small things we do in our classrooms can make a huge difference for our students (Lang 2016).

The Power of Empathy

The 2020 global COVID-19 pandemic brought into sharp relief for many faculty members what it is like to teach students in crisis. Suddenly, our classes were filled with nothing but students dealing with various levels of trauma and crisis—and we had to teach them all online. Many professors and institutions reacted in student-centered ways, extending grace through flexible deadlines, providing options to take classes for credit/no credit, and offering emergency aid funds. I did everything I could think of to help and support my students during that traumatic first semester as we transitioned to "emergency remote learning," but sometimes a crisis is just too overwhelming. Looking back, retention in my online intro class was only 66% in spring 2020 (down from 82% in fall 2019). The pandemic presented an incredible challenge for all of us, but the reality is that trauma and crisis strike at least some of our students every semester. They lose jobs, their family members get sick and even die, and they have overwhelming caregiving responsibilities. The task of responding to those individual crises with grace and empathy falls on the shoulders of each individual instructor.

After the first pandemic semester ended in May 2020, the University of Arkansas at Little Rock surveyed students and asked them what professors did to help them the most, in the midst of the COVID-19 pandemic (Slagle et al. 2020). Over a thousand students responded (n = 1,052) and, presented with the following four options, this is how their choices broke down:

- Be available to answer questions and respond to emails (n = 410): 38.9%
- Be flexible in assignments and deadlines (n = 395): 37.5%
- Make sure the lectures and content are really interesting (n = 125): 11.8%
- Refer you to university and community resources where you can get help for things beyond classes (n = 122): 11.5%

More than three-quarters of responding students named high-rapport behaviors—availability and flexibility—as the most helpful things their professors did. Survey research from the University of Wisconsin–Whitewater similarly shows that, when students reflected on their experiences during the pandemic spring semester of 2020, what they valued most was a good professor—one who was compassionate and communicated well (Loepp 2020). In times of trauma (and always), our students need us to be flexible, compassionate, and to show up for them.

For context, in the same University of Arkansas at Little Rock survey, 77% of students reported that they worried about paying their bills, 68% reported that they worried about accessing and successfully using the technology they needed for their classes, 41% told researchers that they worried about having enough to eat day-to-day, and 32%

said that they worried about having a safe and secure place to sleep. This is what Sara Goldrick-Rab means by #RealCollege (Goldrick-Rab et al. 2019). Another survey of more than 15,000 students at 21 different institutions in April and May of 2020 found that about a third of students strongly agreed that they were concerned about their mental health during the COVID-19 pandemic (Blankstein, Frederick, and Wolff-Eisenberg 2020). When we see our students as whole people facing challenges beyond our classes, we can be better prepared to meet them with empathy.

Although some may critique an empathetic approach as coddling, the data show that empathy favors learning (Holmberg 2003). Relationships are central to teaching and learning; building rapport with students improves their grades and their graduation rates. When students feel like they belong and like they are understood, they want to try hard and are more committed to learning (Holmberg 2003; Pacansky-Brock 2020). Scholars who focus on developing a "pedagogy of empathy" (Eyler 2018) or "pedagogies of care" (Mondelli and Tobin 2020) center students in the learning process and deliver the message that they are not alone.

For most people, empathy is easier to build face-to-face. Humans are social beings and meeting in person tends to foster stronger connections as a simple byproduct of human nature (Kock 2005) and the availability of more social and emotional cues (Daft and Lengel 1986; Marín-López et al. 2019). But, unfortunately, that fact works to the detriment of our online students and represents another way that they are second-class students at our universities. Listen to the experience of one student with disabilities, who left this anonymous comment on a survey describing why they try to take face-to-face classes whenever possible: "I have a disability that limits when I can go, for me to succeed. So if the classes I need are in a time frame where I'm able to go, I'd much rather go in person. The teachers are a lot more relaxed and able to connect better to the students. It's easier for the teachers to be understanding when they can put a face with the name." The ability for this student to get the accommodations they need depends on the empathy and understanding of their professor, and that is easier to get in a face-to-face class. This situation is difficult (and possibly even illegal; we don't have the full details from these few comments, but students have rights to accommodations under the Americans with Disabilities Act that should not be subject to whether or not the teacher is understanding). Students should be able to connect with considerate and accommodating professors no matter the medium of the course they are enrolled in.

Yet, open-ended comments from survey research Skurat Harris and I have done show time and again that students are frustrated when they encounter online faculty who are not understanding of medical or family emergencies. As one student in our Best/Worst Study said, "This instructor has no sympathy for sick people in which they thought I had a stroke and I asked if I could make up my exam the following day or when I felt better and she said no. So yeah probably going to fail this class because I made a zero." Sometimes students, like any other humans, make mistakes. One student told us, "Some professors are willing to help and some don't care one bit. I have a class that I did this week's homework last week instead of last week's homework on accident. I'm waiting for a big fat zero." You can just feel how dejected and discouraged these students are. We don't know if they were able to pass these classes or if they stayed enrolled at the university. But a little rapport and understanding could have gone a long way to encouraging them on that path.

Many of our students, especially in online classes, are teetering on the edge of success or failure. The thing that can make the difference for them is an instructor who cares about their success and believes in their ability to learn. In the online classroom, the instructor sets the temperature of the class (Lassitter 2009, 55) and can make it a place where all students are welcome and invited to participate, a place where the smallest mistakes are criticized, or a lonely wasteland where they will find little interaction at all. Students in our online classes are human beings. All but the most strongly self-motivated need to experience a real human connection to encourage them to participate and complete the coursework (Artino and Ioannou 2008; Whipp and Chiarelli 2004). We can be that for our students—and dramatically increase their ability to succeed in the process.

So many of our students have plenty of voices—in their lives and in their own heads—telling them that they can't succeed. So long as they are trying in my classes, I want to be a voice that tells them they can do it and I am here to help.

PART III WHAT IT WILL TAKE

Prioritizing retention will require students, faculty,
administrators, and supporters working together

If the university had a better format and better trained faculty to make
online courses more engaging, I'd choose online more often.

Online student at the University of Arkansas at Little Rock

SIX

The Tradeoffs

Building rapport with students takes thought and intentionality. But it also takes time—a resource that is often in short supply. Rapport is built one-on-one by individual faculty members connecting with students. And when we take the time to make those real human connections with our students we are necessarily giving up that time to do other things. There are opportunity costs to building rapport, and they are often paid directly by faculty who may have little left to give. This chapter is about the tradeoffs that rapport building requires and the decisions that faculty members and administrators must make in weighing whether those tradeoffs are worth it.

The benefits of building rapport have been repeatedly documented in previous chapters. The results of the teaching experiment I ran in my introductory classes, presented in chapter 3, demonstrate that using rapport-building measures increased retention by 13% (Glazier 2016). The predicted probabilities presented in chapter 5, drawn from data from 35 different online classes in the Rapport Impact Study, demonstrate how at-risk students in particular benefit from high-rapport classes, with retention increases as high as 27% (Glazier and Skurat Harris 2021). Student comments add meaning to these statistics, helping us see what a difference rapport can make in the lives of our students. When students in high-rapport classes talk about their professors, their comments are effusive. For instance, students in our Best/Worst Study provided comments like these about their best online instructors: "She is an excellent and enthusiastic teacher who genuinely wants her students to excel in her class. Her lectures are thorough and she reaches out to students to ensure they get the material." Another student said, "Best online teacher I've had. No other teacher interacts or tries to help us stay on task like this one does."

Yet rapport building has costs as well. As instructors read through chapter 4 and the various rapport-building strategies, they may think that some of the techniques coddle students too much and would turn out less-well-prepared adults. Or they may think that the techniques sound like way too much work. Both of these reactions get at a key question: We know that there are significant benefits to rapport building in terms of student retention, but are those benefits worth the potential costs to our students and the almost certain costs to ourselves? In other words, does rapport building ask too much of professors? Does it not ask enough of students? And does it distract us from other, more technological, solutions that would be more efficient?

In this chapter, I address these challenging questions head on; first, taking the perspective of faculty and examining the additional burden rapport building places on them. Rapport building has high payoffs, but universities are not generally structured to facilitate and incentivize it. I present the results of the Minimum Rapport Experiment to demonstrate how little rapport building it actually takes to have a positive impact on students. Next, I take the perspective of students to look at whether rapport building removes some important "hard-knock" life lessons of college. Finally, I argue that, although technology might look like an easy fix to lighten the burden on everyone involved, it won't save us. Real human connections are needed to make a difference and reverse the online retention crisis.

How Much Should We Ask of Instructors?

Faculty are often overwhelmed and underpaid, with an increasing number not even certain of employment from one academic year to another (Kezar, DePaola, and Scott 2019). The percentage of the faculty workforce that is full-time has steadily declined over the past 50 years and just keeps falling—from 77% in 1970 to 64% in 1991 to only 52% in 2016 (Snyder, de Brey, and Dillow 2019, 492, table 315.10). Research by Kezar, DePaola, and Scott shows that, in 2019, non-tenure-track instructors made up 70% of college faculty (2019). This insecure majority teaches a heavy instructional load—eight courses a year at an average pay of $22,400, or less than the annual salary of most fast-food workers (Kezar, DePaola, and Scott 2019, 1). As the COVID-19 pandemic raged in 2020, some universities announced an even greater shift toward contingent faculty, as a cost-saving measure. The University of Colorado at Boulder announced plans to replace 50 tenured faculty with 25 lecturers (Flaherty 2020c). Online faculty are especially likely to be on the margins of their universities and are more likely to be contingent (Chapman 2011; Franklin 2015). Building real human relationships with online students takes emotional energy and time, both of which are likely to be in short supply for this faculty population.

Are we asking too much of online instructors if we ask them to build rapport with their students? Teaching online can be a heavy lift. Faculty who teach online classes are already worn out by the online workload, concerned about course evaluations, and missing the energy of the in-person teaching experience. Asking them to dedicate additional time and effort to building rapport with their students is adding a lot to an already full plate.

Faculty who have taught both online and face-to-face can testify that teaching online often takes more time and effort than teaching in person, especially when a class is new (Bolliger and Wasilik 2009; Spector 2005). Even for online classes that are well designed and have all the kinks worked out, teaching online can take more emotional energy, even if the time spent per student is about the same (Hislop and Ellis 2004), because online students might expect greater responsiveness. One instructor in a faculty focus group commented, "I had to log in a couple of times a day, or sometimes more than that. I had to respond to them immediately, otherwise they wouldn't have done their assignments, they would have said, 'Oh, you didn't answer my emails'" (Hiltz, Kim, and Shea 2007, 8). This need to be constantly available for students can be draining.

And online faculty may be worried about poor evaluations if they aren't always on their email. Evaluations for online courses tend to be lower than evaluations for face-to-face courses, and low course evaluations can have negative consequences in terms of promotion, tenure, and merit raises (Lowenthal, Bauer, and Chen 2015; Wingo, Ivankova, and Moss 2017). These downsides may lead some faculty to be wary of teaching online classes at all (Jaschik and Lederman 2018; Lin 2002; Nelson 2003; Shattuck 2013; Shea, Pickett, and Li 2005).

Even when faculty can be persuaded to teach online, many miss the human element in online classes in the same way that students do (Shea, Pickett, and Li 2005). It is simply harder to connect with students online. Many researchers have found that faculty feel disengaged from their students and don't find online communication tools like discussion boards sufficient (Arend 2009; Haber and Mills 2008; Mazzolini and Maddison 2007; Ward, Peters, and Shelley 2010). Faculty concerns about online teaching became particularly acute when virtually all college instructors were forced to suddenly move their courses online as a result of the COVID-19 pandemic in 2020. Many opinion pieces were published voicing the common complaint that online classes just weren't the same, for either faculty or students, recommending that we lower our collective expectations, and providing advice on how to "recover the joy of teaching" after having to move online (Darby 2020; Lang 2020; Zimmerman 2020). According to a survey of more than 3,500 faculty at over 1,500 institutions of higher education in August 2020, the pandemic actually saw a 10% increase in faculty who agreed that "online learning is an effective method for teaching" (49% agreed) (Fox et al. 2020, 13), but many faculty (66%) are rightly concerned about equity gaps (Fox et al. 2020, 34).

Even before adding the additional expectation of rapport build-ing, many online faculty members are already bearing a lot of costs. The good news is that rapport building can actually help. Taking a rapport-driven approach to online teaching can improve the experi-ence for both instructors and students (Glazier 2020). When it comes to missing the joy of teaching students in the classroom, building rap-port can help faculty recover that and create something even more rewarding as we make authentic connections with our students online.

As we have seen in student comments throughout the book, our students notice when their professors reach out. And a rapport-filled course returns better course evaluations, as well. My course evalu-ations significantly improved when I started teaching with rapport-building techniques. When I compare the way students responded to the rapport and non-rapport conditions from the experiment presented in chapter 3, the scores from the rapport conditions are significantly higher in terms of instructor accessibility, instructor engagement, and instructor positivity,* as presented in table 6.1 (Glazier 2016).

Having better course evaluations seems like a small thing in the face of an online retention crisis but, even with persistent and doc-umented problems with gender and racial biases in course evalua-tions (MacNell, Driscoll, and Hunt 2015; Mitchell and Martin 2018; Smith and Hawkins 2011), they remain important at many institu-tions for tenure and promotion decisions. It doesn't hurt to see our additional efforts reflected back to us in higher evaluation scores and comments like this one that I received: "Professor who goes beyond what is required to engage with her students, provide a positive learn-ing environment and attitude, and consistently offer help to students. She is actively engaged in this online course."

Yet no matter how many heartwarming student comments we get at the end of the semester, the fact remains: building rapport with stu-dents takes time and effort. Faculty are right to be skeptical that their

---

* The accessibility (six questions, M = 26.16, SD = 3.22), engagement (ten questions, M = 45.27, SD = 5.01), and positivity (seven questions, M = 29.28, SD = 2.68) scores are each aggregate scores made of up multiple survey questions, each of which was coded on a 1 to 5 Likert scale. Their summary statistics are provided in parentheses.

Table 6.1. Comparison of Student Course Evaluations across Rapport and Non-rapport Online Sections of Introduction to Political Science

Quantitative Questions	Non-rapport	Rapport
Mean Instructor Accessibility Score*	24.7	26.7
Mean Instructor Engagement Score*	42.0	46.3
Mean Instructor Positivity Score*	27.3	29.7
Student n	38	93
Response Rate	43.2%	65.0%

*$p < .05$

efforts will be recognized beyond the kind words of their appreciative students (Hiltz, Kim, and Shea 2007; King and Alperstein 2014). Chapter 7 contains specific recommendations for how administrators can help change the culture of their campuses to incentivize and identify excellent online teaching so that great online teachers get the recognition they deserve.

But as we are waiting for the powers that be to do their part in making structural changes, we can make a difference right now, as individual instructors, for the students who pass through our classes. Knowing that instructors almost always feel pressed for time, we should make it our goal to maximize the effect of rapport, while minimizing the burden on faculty. In the next section, I demonstrate, through the Minimum Rapport Experiment, how faculty can still have impact even if they start with small rapport-building efforts.

The Minimum Rapport Experiment

Are we asking too much of online faculty if we ask them to build rapport with their students? For many overworked, contingent, underpaid, or junior faculty—reading through the extensive rapport-building strategies outlined in chapter 4—the answer may be a resounding yes! Recognizing that those rapport-building recommendations might be a bit overwhelming for some, I partnered with my colleague Heidi Skurat Harris to design an online course experiment to see if we could get positive results through minimum rapport-building effort. Essentially, could we build rapport and retain students without putting in a whole lot of work?

We began our Minimum Rapport Experiment by creating two very similar Google Classroom courses for a fake Philosophy 2000: Ethics and Technology course that we invented. We wanted to present students with a course that was unlikely to be in their major (sorry, philosophy professors) but was the sort of course that might fulfill a core requirement for the university. If a student had to take this Philosophy 2000 course to meet a requirement, and came upon our online course setup, would some minimal efforts to build rapport make a difference for retention?

The fake course came complete with an initial lecture and reading assignment. For the experiment, we wanted students to spend a little bit of time in the course and let us know how likely they would be to stay enrolled, if it was a real class they were taking. We wanted to give them a taste of the experience of that course, so we asked them to complete a series of tasks:

1. Read the syllabus and answer a question about the late work policy.
2. Access the PowerPoint in Unit 1 and then take a short quiz on the content.
3. Complete a short reading and then write a one- to two-sentence summary of it.
4. Write an email to the professor asking about the date of the final exam.

Completing all of these tasks is pretty onerous (sometimes we can't even get students to do them in a course they are enrolled in for credit), so each participant received a $10 gift card that they could spend at the university bookstore.

Students who participated in this experiment were recruited from our own university campus, the University of Arkansas at Little Rock, and were randomly assigned to either the rapport or the non-rapport condition. In the non-rapport condition, we made no efforts to establish an instructor presence, whereas in the rapport condition, we invented a fake professor, Dr. Dave Smith, complete with a picture of a middle-aged white man (because students tend to think that white men are the most knowledgeable instructors) (MacNell, Driscoll, and Hunt 2015; Mendez and Mendez 2018). In the rapport condition, Dr. Smith welcomed students to the class, described the course a bit in his own words, assured them it would be interesting and engaging, and told them exactly what they needed to do to get started. The non-rapport course just listed the course description from the catalog and told students to complete Unit One.

Additional differences between the two courses, including immediate and encouraging feedback in the rapport condition, along with a narrated PowerPoint, and email responses that are respectful and call students by name, are laid out in table 6.2. The table illustrates the many small ways instructors communicate to students that their success is important to us. Through class policies, through feedback, and through personal interactions, we are either building rapport or sending students the message that they are a bother.

Students participating in the experiment also completed a short demographic and attitudinal survey before entering the online course and then completed another short survey about the course afterward. The average time it took our 218 participants to complete both surveys and the tasks in the course was about 27 minutes, meaning they spent about 15 minutes or less in the course itself (with the rest of the time completing the pre- and postsurveys).

Just to revisit, in chapter 3, I describe a rapport-building experiment in which I spent hours per student, for an entire semester, building personal relationships. These intensive efforts yielded a significant increase in retention and inspired me to apply rapport-building techniques in all of my classes. But in this Minimum Rapport Experiment, students completed tasks in a fake Philosophy and Technology course for just 15 minutes. When we asked them whether they would stay enrolled, if this was a real class they were taking, would we see a significant difference between the rapport and non-rapport conditions in this short amount of time?

Table 6.2. Rapport vs. Non-rapport Conditions in the Minimum Rapport Experiment

Course Element	Non-rapport Condition	Rapport Condition
Directions regarding the syllabus	Read the syllabus to get started in the class.	Read the syllabus posted below. This document will provide our required text list, an overview of our assignments in the class, and other helpful information and policies.
Directions regarding Unit One	Then complete the assignments in Unit One.	Then, go to Unit One to see the activities for the first week! To get to Unit One, click on the menu in the top left of this page (three little lines in a box), and go to the Unit One link.
PowerPoint for Unit One	PowerPoint alone with no voice over or screen capture.	Video with screen capture of PowerPoint and voiceover.
Welcome message in the syllabus	No welcome message in the syllabus.	Welcome to this online course in ethics and technology! If you own a smartphone or a computer (please do for this class!), have (or want to have) a job, or interact with others through any kind of digital technology, then you should find this class will benefit you! Please read this syllabus to understand how our class works! A few minutes of reading now will prevent headaches later.
Comment on the course	No additional comment on the course.	I know that some of you are taking this class because it is required, and you might not be looking forward to studying something as "boring" as "ethics." But this class will help to connect ethics to how you use technology in your everyday life and your future career.
Feedback on quiz	Your response has been recorded.	Thanks for completing this quiz!
Timeliness of quiz grade	Quiz grade is not released.	Quiz grade is released immediately.
Feedback on reading response	Your response has been recorded.	You did it! Your first reading summary is done! I will grade your answer by Friday.
Late work policy	All work should be submitted by the deadlines on the syllabus. No late work will be accepted.	I understand that life happens. You can submit one assignment late for any reason (with the exception of the final because I have to have final grades in on time!). Please arrange alternative due dates for your late submission with me in advance. I do not take late work submitted after the deadline if you have not contacted me in advance.

(continued)

Table 6.2. continued

Course Element	Non-rapport Condition	Rapport Condition
Home page instructor accessibility	No photo, listed email, or prompt to contact faculty member.	Photo, email, and message that reads: Please email me at dxsmith33@ualr.edu if you have any questions. I generally respond to emails the first week of class within 12 hours.
Office hours	Office Hours: MWF 8:00–9:00 a.m.	I can meet with you online by appointment through Skype, Google Hangouts, or Zoom. Email me at dxsmith33@ualr.edu to set up an appointment.
Email accessibility	dxsmith33@ualr.edu	dxsmith33@ualr.edu (I respond to all emails within 24 hours during the week and within 48 hours on weekends and holidays. If you haven't heard from me within these times, please email again.)
Email response to question about the final exam	See the syllabus for information about your final exam. Dr. Smith	Hello, [student name]! Thank you for your email. As you could tell from the syllabus, the date for the final exam has not yet been posted. I will have that information available as soon as possible. Looking forward to a great semester! Dr. Smith

With such a small exposure to rapport-building, we were honestly surprised to find a statistically significant increase in students' intent to stay in the course for the rapport condition (from 4.11 to 4.41, on a five-point Likert scale, p = 0.014). The greatest shift in attitudes is from those who were unsure in the non-rapport condition to those who were very likely to stay in the rapport condition, as the distribution in figure 6.1 illustrates.

The open-ended responses students gave also indicate that the instructor presence made a big impact in their evaluation of the course. Students in the rapport condition said that they appreciated the good communication from the professor: "He seems to be very active with students and willing to work with people in his class." Just hearing the professor's voice seemed to make a big difference for the students, who left comments like this one, "I like how Dr. Smith records himself talking about the content instead of just leaving the students to read everything without any actual interaction." Other students com-

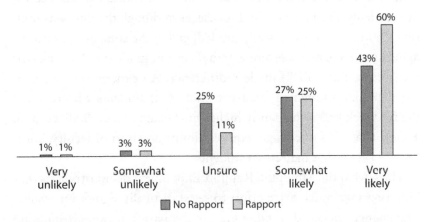

Figure 6.1. Students' Self-Reported Likelihood of Staying Enrolled in the Class, by Condition

mented, "Dr. Smith seemed very understanding" and one wrote, "The instructor is responsive and willing to help."

In the non-rapport condition, on the other hand, students left comments identifying the interaction (or lack thereof) with the professor as a problem with the course. One student said, "Not seeing the teacher face-to-face to explain certain things a little better would be an issue" and another commented, "There needs to be a more personal aspect to it. Some direct teacher involvement via video chat or screencast lessons would be great at achieving this." In the non-rapport condition, the automated response to the student email inquiry about the final exam date was a very short reply telling them to check the syllabus. One student commented that what they didn't like about the course was "the way he responded back to my email from what I could make out. That if you ask a question if you're genuinely lost, he'll get upset."

Though online classes can be time-intensive to teach under any circumstance, the Minimum Rapport Experiment shows that a few simple rapport-building elements can make a surprising impact in a very short amount of time. Students notice when our email responses are abrupt or when our courses lack personality. They are grateful when we communicate clearly and provide quick feedback. Even very simple efforts to build rapport can make a significant difference for our students. For instance, in this case, even though the quiz was multiple choice and automatically graded, giving the students an encouraging automatic message along with their quiz grade (i.e., "Thanks for completing this quiz!") made a difference. An experiment that provided similar automated feedback found that students who received the feedback had significantly higher final exam scores (Wallace et al. 2006). That kind of change requires almost no effort of faculty, but it sends a signal that matters to students.

Thus, what the Minimum Rapport Experiment demonstrates is that it doesn't take much extra effort to see statistically significant results. The changes outlined in table 6.2 are the basics of rapport-building that online instructors can adapt with a minimum amount of work.

How Much Should We Ask of Students?

There are a certain number of people I have encountered over the years who, by this point in the conversation, have decided that rapport is synonymous with overprotecting students. They see building rapport with students as doing them a disservice by not teaching them how the "real world" works. They would like to see a more prominent role for student responsibility. If we add rapport to our courses, are we necessarily making a tradeoff for student responsibility? As each professor contemplates the appropriate role of student responsibility in the equation of their own online course, there are two key things I would encourage them to consider.

First, what are the goals of the course? If it is a course on calculus, the main learning objectives may be to master certain equations and their application. If it is a course on conversational Spanish, the main learning objectives may be to give and receive information in Spanish. If it is a course on professional and technical writing, the main learning objectives may include writing professional emails. Professionalism and responsibility may be more central to the learning objectives in some courses than in others.

Throughout the process of completing a college degree, students learn a number of "soft skills" that employers particularly value. These include things like professionalism, interpersonal skills, communicating well, even coming to work on time (Robles 2012; Stewart, Wall, and Marciniec 2016). Some faculty members and administrators may fear that, by implementing the rapport-building strategies proposed in chapter 4, like sending email reminders or allowing deadline extensions, students will lose out on these soft skills and will be less prepared to succeed in the real world.

The question each instructor must consider for each course is: How central is this to the learning objectives of my course? For instance, is deadline management a key course learning objective? I would venture that for most courses, most of the time, the answer would be no. There are far more important things that the students are meant to be learning, and they won't be able to learn those things if they miss an assignment, get discouraged, and drop the class altogether. Deadline management and professionalization may be an underlying part of the curriculum, but mastering those skills shouldn't overtake everything else a student is trying to learn.

This leads directly to the second question to consider: How can we best help students learn? Strict policies that kick students out of class at the first infraction, or put them in such a deep hole as to make passing the class impossible, are unlikely to foster an environment where they can learn. Instructors who want to help students learn by exposing them to what life is like in the real world might say that your boss won't send you an email to remind you that the report is due, offer to answer your questions, or be willing to cut you a break if you have a crisis and need to turn something in late. Thus, they would conclude, we shouldn't do so now. The world is full of hard knocks and the sooner our students learn that, the better. There is some truth in these critiques. Sometimes failure is the best teacher. If we don't let our students fail, by missing an assignment deadline, for instance, they may not develop the skills it takes to keep track of deadlines themselves.

But if the assumption is that our job is to prepare students for the harsh real world some professors describe, then what we should do is *prepare* them for it, not replicate it. We can best prepare them by giving them the tools to succeed, and for many of our students that starts with helping them not fail out of our classes.

In fact, I would gently suggest that the real world is not always as harsh and cruel as some instructors describe. Although there are some bosses who are jerks, there are also many who do send emails reminding employees that they need the report by Friday. Almost all supervisors—virtually by definition—should be willing to provide information that their subordinates don't have. Most human beings are understanding when crises arrive. To draw on a concept from rational choice theory, in most work environments, the employees are playing an "iterated game," meaning they are going to be interacting with one another repeatedly. It doesn't make for a productive work environment or for positive social interactions to impose harsh penalties at the slightest mistake. For most companies, even when we are talking about entry-level hourly employees, hiring and training an employee is an investment (O'Connell and Kung 2007). There is a strong incentive not to fire someone the first time they turn in a report late. In short, the real world is not always as unforgiving as some instructors are.

When we compare the way we treat our online students to the way we treat our face-to-face students, the issue of equity comes up as well. Rapport is often easier to build in person; humans just connect better that way (Kock 2005; Marín-López et al. 2019). We heard a student in chapter 5 describe being more likely to get the disability accommodations they need in face-to-face classes, compared to online classes, because professors are more understanding in person. This is a question we should all ask ourselves: Are we more compassionate and understanding with our face-to-face students? Are we more likely to give extensions, allow make-up exams, or share our lecture notes when a student makes the request in person? This may be yet another way our online students are treated as second-class students.

It's important to remember that rapport and responsibility are not zero-sum. We don't necessarily give up student responsibility when we introduce rapport. Instead, we can thoughtfully consider how best to help our students learn while also taking into account the constraints they are facing and our own privilege as professors. In chapter 5, we tried to put ourselves in the shoes of our online students to understand what their experiences in our classes might be like and why it might be a good idea to give second and third chances when students falter. When we think about opportunities to try again as opportunities to learn, building rapport becomes a way to encourage responsibility that also supports students.

Thus, building rapport is not coddling students; it is creating relationships to support their learning, which in turn helps professionalize them for the world beyond college. In a sense, building rapport with disadvantaged students in particular is one way to try to give them some of the preparation—over the course of a single class—that other students may have received over the course of a lifetime. That may seem like a high bar. But, if by the end of an online class that uses rapport-building techniques, the students in the class feel like they are important enough to the instructor that they aren't wasting the instructor's time by asking a question, we will have made a positive difference for those students.

Technology without Humanity

Because faculty and universities all have limited time, money, and agenda space when it comes to online teaching, if we choose to prioritize rapport building and focus on human relationships, we must necessarily trade off something else. Currently, a great deal of the online teaching energy in higher education is focused on technology. If we instead invest in people and relationships, will we be giving up something better and more efficient in technology?

When Skurat Harris and I asked students at the University of Arkansas at Little Rock about the worst online classes they had ever taken for our Best/Worst Study, they rarely complained about technology or course navigation. Instead, they told us about classes where they felt totally disconnected from the professor and felt like they weren't getting a full learning experience. As one student put it: "The teacher did not provide any instruction. It was basically self-taught through the publisher's website. There was no need for a professor." Another student similarly said, "I don't feel that the professor was very present in this course. While the class was easy, I don't think I took anything from my experience that I couldn't have gained just simply buying a book and reading it on my own." Given these kinds of experiences, students may even go into online classes expecting that they will have to "teach themselves" through technology with very little human contact (Jaggars 2014; Woodyard and Larson 2018).

In face-to-face classes, technology is viewed as a helpful add-on, but in online classes, it is the means by which the class is communicated and so it can sometimes overshadow the class itself. The result is that technology can become the focus—teacher training centers on how best to utilize the Learning Management System, and advice to students is all about course navigation (King and Alperstein 2014, 68). But when the technology is the center of attention, the importance of the relationship between the professor and student falls by the wayside. While Learning Management Systems and EdTech are busy focusing on design and technology, students are hungry for human connection.

When Jaggars and Xu (2016) systematically studied online course elements in order to create a rubric of quality online instruction, they concluded that, although "well-organized courses with well-specified learning objectives are certainly desirable, these design features do not significantly predict student learning outcomes" (p. 271). In fact, out of all of the factors they examined, the only one to have a positive and significant impact on student grades was the quality of instructor-student interaction in a course. A well-organized course that links assignments and learning objectives is great, and it is certainly helpful if an online instructor knows how to upload videos, but once you master the basics of online literacy and organization, you will get much further with an engaged instructor that students believe truly cares about them than you will with more technological know-how.

At many institutions, there is a gap between the models and their application (Huang et al. 2019). For instance, when in 2015, California Community Colleges implemented self-directed learning support services for math, the intervention had no significant impact on retention in math classes (Chatteinier 2016), because math students weren't looking for an electronic interface—they wanted real human connection. Similarly, when college classes suddenly moved to emergency remote teaching in response to the COVID-19 pandemic in 2020, many professors tried to replicate the in-person classroom environment with synchronous video lectures via platforms like Zoom. But both professors and students soon found that watching hours of lectures on a computer screen was not particularly edifying (Supiano 2020); students joined the class from noisy kitchens, while wearing their pjs, or they just turned their cameras off entirely. For many, it didn't feel like a community at all (Hogan and Sathy 2020). There's nothing wrong with a noisy kitchen, pjs, or taking a class with your camera off. But it's not the same thing as a face-to-face meeting on campus. That's why we need to change our expectations. We need to stop searching for a technological tool that will replicate the physical experience of being together in a face-to-face class and realize that the most important element is the pedagogical tool of human connection, which can exist in online, hybrid, face-to-face, or hyflex formats. Anywhere you have professors caring about their students you can have high-rapport classes and successful students. The solution is not technological—it's human.

Just increasing interaction in an online class is not going to increase retention (Stavredes and Herder 2013). We are social beings—connecting with other humans makes us want to stay around them. Technological solutions are tempting. Every university administrator would love to buy a shiny new piece of software if it could solve their retention problems. But technology without human connection won't solve the problem (although it will cost a lot!). A robot responding systematically to every student post will not make students feel seen and cared about. What matters is not the number of interactions but that the interactions communicate a deeper message about the value of each student to the class and the instructor. That can only be achieved by real human connection.

Making students turn on their cameras or berating students or faculty about on-camera professionalism will not create connection and engagement in online classes. Cameras should be optional any time we hold synchronous class (Davidson 2020), but if we are going to ask students to be in the same place at the same time, we should do it with a purpose. Make it a time when students can contribute, interact, and connect with the professor and with each other. If the instructor is the only one who is going to be talking, that does not need to be a synchronous event. That can be a video or even a written lecture. Students have busy, complicated lives, just like we do. If we are going to ask them to be available for our classes at a specific time, make that a time when they are active in learning and participating through discussions, questions, activities, office hours, and so on. Or, because students don't actually use office hours all that often (Cho and Kim 2013; Hrastinski 2006; Jaasma and Koper 1999; Nadler and Nadler 2000), cut them out all together and add semistructured small group meetings where students ask questions instead (Nadler and Nadler 2000). The key is to use synchronous time to connect, not to talk at students, or to sit in an empty Zoom room waiting for students who never drop by.

We can sometimes become blinded by technology when it comes to online teaching and forget that what really matters is human connection. When technology mediates virtually every aspect of communication (Allen and Seaman 2011), the technology can become primary and the communication becomes secondary. Under these circumstances, the critical relationship between faculty and student drops off the radar. If we want to retain students, we need to focus less on technology and more on relationships.

SEVEN

Building a Support Network

The picture presented here, through the data and the stories of students taking online classes, can be a challenging one to look at straight on. Although more students than ever before are now able to access college through online classes, the retention gap between online and face-to-face courses bears witness to the fact that we are not doing enough to help them succeed. Changing the way instructors approach online teaching and the way students experience online classes on a large scale is going to require a culture shift. In the last chapter, we looked at how this shift can start with very simple changes instructors can implement right now. This chapter pans out to a much larger scale. When we bring everyone in to contribute to structural changes in online higher education, we will enable it to live up to its promises.

So far, this book has focused on the critical role that online instructors play in building rapport with students and closing the online retention gap. But this is not the entire solution. The retention crisis in online higher education is a major problem, and instructors can't solve it alone. Building rapport in online courses can significantly improve retention, but if the impact is going to be more than piecemeal, we need to put together a coalition of people to support online teaching and learning. This practical chapter presents concrete recommendations for a rapport-centric approach to student retention for all those who care about student success—from the students themselves all the way to university presidents.

In this final chapter, I first describe how students, parents, teachers, mentors, and university administrators can each contribute to an online higher education revolution that puts human connection at the center of learning and prioritizes students over technology. I then present three short case studies of different institutions that are each having success through policies that center rapport-building, human connection, and student learning on a broad scale. Because these may feel like ambitious efforts to individuals who are just starting down the path of rapport building at their own institutions, I conclude with a series of increasingly involved recommendations for those who want to start building rapport and improving retention from the ground up.

Students

Perhaps it is almost too obvious to say, but students are the key to their own success. All too often, I find myself reaching out to a student who has stopped logging in to our online course, isn't participating in discussions, and isn't turning in assignments. When a student disappears like this, and doesn't respond to emails or even phone calls, professors hit a brick wall in terms of what we can do to help. When a student turns in a poorly written paper, I can give them feedback, an opportunity to revise, and work with them in office hours to improve. But when they don't turn in a paper at all, I have no choice but to give them a zero. Similarly, when a student just doesn't respond, there's not much professors can do to help them.

Sometimes, students have very legitimate reasons for ghosting on our classes—just disappearing with no notice. They may be going through something so traumatic that the class has fallen completely off their priority list. But most of the time, I have found that they are simply overwhelmed and don't think that asking for help is an option. For many first-generation or lower-income students especially, their life experience may have taught them that second chances just aren't a thing. So, if they make a mistake in the class, they may think they have blown their shot and they have to take the F (Jack 2016). The goal of all of the other players in this equation—professors, parents, mentors, staff, and administrators—should be to equip students with the tools, skills, and resources they need to succeed in online classes so that just disappearing never seems like the best alternative. Students need to know that asking for help is always an option.

So, if you are a student reading this book, I have to say that you have interesting taste in reading material. I am guessing maybe a parent or mentor handed you this section. I am glad you have someone looking out for you. If you are a faculty member or someone who cares about a college student, hopefully there will be something in the following pages that you may find useful enough to pass along. Here is my very best advice to students for what you can do to contribute to your own success in online classes.

Treat your online class like a face-to-face class. The most important way to do this is to schedule time to work on each of your online classes. This is especially important if you are taking an asynchronous online class, one that doesn't have set meeting times for the whole class. Every single semester, I lose students because they forget to check in to our online class, get behind, and then get too discouraged to try to find a way out of the hole they are in. Look at your schedule and decide when you want your online class to be—maybe every Tuesday and Thursday night from 8 to 10? Put it on your calendar and make sure you make it to class. Put all the class due dates on your calendar, too, so you are sure not to miss them. You are using a calendar, right? If not, get on that. You can even use an electronic one that syncs to your phone and dings at you when class is about to start and alerts you when your assignments are due. Pro tip: if you set those alerts the day *before* the assignment is actually due, you may have a better chance of getting it in on time.

If you haven't taken an online class before, know that your fellow students have told my colleagues and me in surveys that "online is very hard to keep up with." One student wrote, "For some classes I do not need the structure of a face-to-face classroom but for others I do need it and it helps me get my work done on time." If you can replicate the structure of a face-to-face class yourself, you will be a step ahead of the game.

Try to take a few classes on campus. I know this can be difficult, but research shows that once you cross a threshold of about 40% of your course load online, the more online courses you take, the less likely you will be to graduate (Glazier et al. 2019b; Johnson and Mejia 2014; Shea and Bidjerano 2018; Wavle and Ozogul 2019). Online classes are challenging in a unique way, and there is a cumulative effect of taking a lot of them. If you are able to add a couple of face-to-face classes to your course load, it will probably increase your success in the end. I know there are a lot of reasons why you may not be able to take classes on campus. A student who lived far from campus once said in a survey, "I would hate to have to drive an hour and a half each way just for one or two classes," and another who was taking an online class wrote, "This class was a great fit for me due to my kids and my health." It may not be possible to take a class on campus. If not, think carefully about how many classes you are enrolling in. A full load of five online classes is very challenging for anyone to complete successfully.

Read the syllabus very carefully. No really, read every word. Professors spend a shocking amount of time crafting those documents, and they tend to think of each syllabus as a detailed plan for that course. They really schedule out exactly what you need to do to be successful in the class, what assignments you will need to turn in, when they will be due, what you will be required to read, when the final will be, and so on. It is like a snapshot of the whole semester in one handy document. Take it seriously and refer back to it often. If you want to stay on your professor's good side, always check the syllabus first before asking a question.

Connect with other students in the class. Making friends in college can be one of the highlights of the experience, so get to know the other students in the class. Research shows that it not only makes the class more enjoyable, but it can actually help you do better academically, as well (Bernard et al. 2009; McCabe 2016). You don't have to wait for the professor to assign a dreaded group project; you can reach out to some of the other students in the class and get together for a virtual study session before an exam. If there is an introductions thread in the early weeks of your online class, use that as an opportunity to look for similarities and connections with other students. Maybe there is someone who has the same major as you do? Or lives in the same city? Maybe another student in the class also wants to study environmental law or hopes to work for a nonprofit? Send them a message and start a conversation! Connecting with other students can help you do better in the class, but it can also help you build a web of relationships that will make your college experience richer (Felten and Lambert 2020).

Ask your professor for help when you need it. And don't be afraid to ask early and often. I know that it might be intimidating to approach the person who is the expert teaching your class, but it is literally their job to answer your questions. You may run into the occasional grumpy professor, but I think this advice will serve you well with most of them. If you want them to give you the most helpful response and have a positive opinion of you, I suggest first looking in the syllabus for the answer to your question (see my recommendation about reading the syllabus above) and, if you don't find it there, try crafting a polite email that begins with "Dear Professor [last name here]." You may also want to try posting a question in an online discussion board or chatting with some of the other students you have connected with—you could even use your question as an opportunity to make some connections and meet some of your fellow students in the class! Many classes have general Q&A discussion boards and, if you have a question, it is probably a safe bet that other students in the class have the same question. Posting your question where the whole class can see it can be a helpful way to clear up confusion for everyone.

Another thing you might try is visiting your professor during office hours. Professors are generally happy to see students and answer sincere questions during office hours. This time is specifically set aside to talk to students! But professors are also generally overworked and very busy, so if you pop by outside of office hours just to shoot the breeze, it is possible they may get annoyed. I would come with a specific question in mind. If you can't come to campus, you can always suggest a meeting via Zoom or Google Meet, or even a phone call.

Getting to know your professor will help you do better in the class and will make it so you are less scared to ask for help if something comes up. You don't have to take my word for it. A student volunteered this advice in a research study we did on online classes: "I have found that it is SO important to communicate with your professors as a student. By communicating, you get to know your professor well, and it seems to help learn information better."

It's (almost) never too late to turn things around. It can be all too easy for online classes to get away from you. If you put the deadline in your calendar wrong, or do next week's assignment this week, or just forget to check in to the class because life gets busy, you may find yourself behind before you know it. This is the time to reach out to your professor, apologize, and ask if you can make a plan with them to turn your assignment in and get back on track. Mathematically, turning in an assignment late and getting even 50% of the points is SO much better than getting 0% of the points. Really, getting *any* points is better than getting zero points. I hate giving students zero points. Even the most unfriendly of professors might write you a cranky email, but they will probably give you partial credit for late assignments, and that can help you get back on track in the class. It is always better to ask instead of thinking that it's too late. The earlier you ask, the better. The further past the original deadline you wait to turn something in, the more likely it is that the professor will write you a cranky email. Avoid cranky emails and stay on track by reaching out early if you think you are in trouble—or even just a little bit off course.

Parents, Friends, and Mentors

Generally speaking, by the time a student gets to college, there have been a lot of people helping, encouraging, teaching, mentoring, cajoling, and even browbeating to get them there. These supporters are a critical part of a student's network and can also play a key role in reversing the retention crisis. Unfortunately, online students may find themselves with fewer of these supporters than students in traditional face-to-face classes. Many online students are categorized as "nontraditional" students, usually defined as over the age of 24 (National Center for Education Statistics 2020). They may have delayed enrollment and may have full-time jobs and kids of their own. They may feel like solid adults who don't require the nurturing support of a network of people that college students fresh out of high school might. But if you know and care about a college student, especially one who is taking online classes, there are things you can do to help support their success, whether or not they think they need your support. It doesn't matter if a student is 18 or 38 or 78, having a community of people to cheer them on and support them will make their graduation more likely.

Ask students how their classes are going. And really listen to the answer. It is easy to forget about or fall behind in online classes. Ask them about what's going on in their online classes, what assignments they have, when they are due, if they know their professor, what they think of their classmates, what the course material is like, and so on. Make sure that their online class stays on their mind and they can't forget about it. One student respondent told my colleagues and me in a survey, "I was a new mom and didn't know what to expect with online class. I had too many online courses and could not keep up with the work load. Online classes are more work." Taking online classes, especially for the first time, can be overwhelming. Check in with the students you care about and see how they are doing. Help them stay accountable. But just because online classes are challenging, doesn't mean students should be discouraged. Another student survey respondent said, "In any online class it really pulls out a person's capability to do the work on their own, with some help of the instructor. For me, online classes make me feel more responsible and more in charge of my grades." Online classes can be a great opportunity for growth and learning, but only if students stay engaged.

Take something off their plate. Rapport is a two-way street. Professors can try to connect with students, but students have to be willing to respond. Making sure students have the resources to stay engaged so that rapport building is possible is a task that supporters can really help with. The students who enroll in online classes usually choose them because they have a lot of other things going on in their lives. The flexibility of online classes allows these students to maintain a full- or part-time job, an unpredictable work schedule, or balance a family while still going to college. We heard this time and again from students, like the student who told us, "I enjoy face to face classes because I learn faster I think, but I am working full time and it is really convenient to manage your own schedule with online classes."

Data from my own university, the University of Arkansas at Little Rock (shared in figure 2.1 in chapter 2), indicates that when students take a small number of online classes—but less than 50% of their course load—their retention actually increases. For our student population, and many others, online classes add flexibility and help students be more successful. Even for students who may be defined as "traditional" and live on campus, online classes can be helpful. One student athlete wrote, "I love face-to-face classes but sometimes you need to take online classes. For me as an athlete I get overwhelmed with taking a lot of credit hours and having one or two online classes helps me with time management and getting them done in my own time."

These busy students are balancing work, family, athletics, and school. They definitely have a lot going on! If you want to help them do well in college, try to take something off their plate. Could you watch the kids for the afternoon while they catch up on homework? Are they taking on the bulk of the caretaker role for a sick or aging relative that you could help with? Could you schedule them for more accommodating work hours? It might make all the difference in the world if you bring over dinner one night during midterms.

Help students get access to a computer. This may come as a shock, but online students may not have regular access to a computer. Eighty percent of the students at the University of Arkansas at Little Rock are first-generation college students, meaning neither of their parents have college degrees (Quick Facts 2019). Data from the American Community Survey reveals that in households where the parents have a bachelor's degree or higher, 97% have a desktop or laptop computer. This number is only 70% for households where the parents have a high school degree and 54% where the parents did not graduate from high school (Snyder, de Brey, and Dillow 2019, 767, figure 30). Some of our students are growing up in homes without computers and are trying to take online classes without consistent access to a computer. Data from community college students indicate only about 85% of these students have access to a laptop (Gierdowski 2019).

Indeed, for many students, the main way that they access their online classes is through their smartphones. In 2018, 67% of college students reported doing some of their online coursework on their mobile phones, and 20% of those students said that they did *all* of their online coursework on their phones (Magda and Aslanian 2018). In 2020, 74% of students reported that they *want* to use their mobile device for online classes (Magda, Capranos, and Aslanian 2020). This is our students' preferred way of accessing online classes. Using a smartphone is manageable for some course content, like posting on discussion boards or watching videos, but there are students who are typing out research papers on their phones. That is a highly inefficient and ineffective way to write a research paper, and they are unlikely to do well on that assignment. Just imagine trying to add citations, connect back to ideas earlier in the paper, or insert a table comparing data, all using a smartphone. University campuses have computer labs, but students in online classes may live far away from campus. Public libraries may be a good resource for those needing to access computers, but reaching them takes time and gas, and sometimes the wait time for computers is long or the library closes before the student gets off work.

If a student is going to take online classes, I strongly recommend that they use a computer, preferably one that works well. Many of our lower-income students are working with older technology that breaks down, doesn't hold a charge, or has trouble connecting (Gonzales, McCrory Calarco, and Lynch 2020). Relying on poorly functioning laptops is associated with lower GPAs (Gonzales, McCrory Calarco, and Lynch 2020), and that effect can only be exacerbated when more of the coursework is online. Students should also be socialized to back up their work in online storage, like Google Drive or Dropbox, as faculty are less likely to be understanding of computer crashes as late-work excuses in the age of cloud storage. There are bare-bones laptops available for a few hundred dollars, which may be an extravagant holiday or graduation gift for some families but may be out of reach for many others. If you as a parent, friend, or mentor are able to gift, hand down, or share a computer with a student taking online classes, it can make a big difference.

Help students get access to high-speed internet. In addition to muddling through on a smartphone, many students are taking online classes using inadequate or inconsistent internet access. Some of these students are using data plans on their smartphones, with no consistent Wi-Fi connection at home. Some students may only have high-speed internet while at work. Some students may stop at the local public library to get access to the internet, or Starbucks, or McDonald's. The limitations of our students' Wi-Fi access became startlingly and abundantly clear in the rush to move all of our classes online in response to the COVID-19 pandemic in 2020. A survey of 1,764 students at the University of Arkansas at Little Rock in March 2020 revealed that only 85% of our student population had access to the internet at home. The rest used the internet on campus, at work, or somewhere else. Not surprisingly, nearly 20% of our students were concerned about being able to access technology needed to complete their schoolwork during the pandemic. Other surveys conducted during the pandemic showed that up to 44% of students had difficulty with internet connectivity when trying to access course materials or participate in course activities online (Clark 2020; Means, Neisler, and with Langer Research Associates 2020).

Students who live in rural communities are especially at a disadvantage here (Church and Prieger 2016; Perrin 2019; Rosenboom and Blagg 2018). Many of my students in rural Arkansas simply don't have the option of having high-speed internet in their homes. This is a problem that individuals can't solve alone—we need the help of policy makers to tackle it. When rural students do get internet access, they often suffer from poor service or long outages in case of storms or other problems. What can family and friends do to help? Well, if you have good internet at your place, invite online students over to use it while they study. Give them a quiet room to work in and don't bother them. If you don't have good internet either, offer to drive them to the public library or the local McDonald's. If you are in a position to help, consider assisting with a monthly Wi-Fi bill. If they are running out of data at the end of the month, consider letting them hotspot off your phone if you have data to spare. Online students shouldn't be worried about whether they have enough data to stream a lecture video. If and when it is clear that individual-level fixes won't be enough, student advocates can contact elected representatives and ask about universal broadband.

Administrators

There are many wonderful and inspiring online teachers who, right now, are changing lives and doing a great deal of good. And there are many others who are talking with their colleagues, seeing the needs of their students, and even reading this book, and thinking, "I bet I can make some adjustments. There is more I can do for our students." But if we want to see the kind of change that will reverse the terrible retention gaps that have been the norm of online higher education, it is going to take more than individual teachers. It is going to take leadership.

Colleges and universities are in an online retention crisis. Because online enrollments have continued to go up, administrators haven't had to confront this crisis head on. It has been possible for entire universities to bury their metaphorical heads in the sand and pretend it isn't happening. But the online retention crisis *is* happening, and it won't be reversed by individual faculty members picking up this book and deciding to connect with their students. Individual instructors can move the needle in their own classes, but college and university administrators are the ones in the best position to help make institutional change to reverse a structural retention gap between online and face-to-face classes.

University administrators set priorities for budgets, create faculty incentives, and determine what counts for teaching, professional development, and service (Jenkins 2011). Administrative leadership is key to closing the retention gap between online and face-to-face classes. The data presented in the previous chapters provides compelling evidence that the best and quickest way to close the online retention gap is to build rapport in online classes. How can administrators support that effort?

Provide opportunities for faculty training in how to teach with rapport. Although the vast majority of faculty who teach online classes at colleges and universities in the United States right now have had training in online teaching (Allen and Seaman 2011), most campuses focus on the technical aspects of delivering online courses with little or no attention paid to the pedagogical aspects (Cox 2005; King and Alperstein 2014; Millward 2008; Xu and Jaggars 2011b). As one instructor said of their experience with campus training, "It was glaringly obvious from the moment I walked in that the course was taught by someone who knew the technology inside out and backwards, but had no sense of how to communicate that material" (Xu and Jaggars 2011b, 1780).

It is no wonder most professors feel overwhelmed and unprepared when they start teaching online (Lichoro 2015; Shattuck 2013). Whereas all professors have been in classrooms before and may have an idea about what good teaching in a face-to-face class looks like, many have never been online students before and have no idea what good teaching in an online class looks like (Schmidt, Tschida, and Hodge 2016). The training most universities provide is almost entirely logistical and technical, which means student relationships fall by the wayside. In fact, what makes many instructors hesitant to teach online, or feel insecure about their abilities to do so, is a lack of training (Paechter, Maier, and Macher 2010).

Faculty regularly don't feel prepared or supported sufficiently for online teaching (Shattuck 2013; Wray et al. 2008). But once faculty are shown that it is possible to connect with students online, they generally want to do it. As faculty were preparing to teach another pandemic term in the fall of 2020, a major survey of more than 3,500 faculty showed 71% said their top priority was increasing student engagement in class, up from 57% just three months earlier (Fox et al. 2020, 17). The same survey also showed that 91% of responding faculty said that they had engaged with professional development at their institution in preparation for the fall (Fox et al. 2020, 28), so if you want to prioritize rapport and train your faculty on it, you are likely to find some takers!

Faculty want to be there for their students. Talking and brainstorming with other online teachers about rapport-building strategies, like those shared in chapter 4, can be invigorating and inspirational. When I lead faculty workshops on rapport building, faculty leave excited to make adjustments in their courses right away, giving comments like "I hadn't realized just how many places I could add communication that might reassure and engage students" and "I can't wait to learn how to use the Mail Merge with Attachments add-on. It's going to save me so much time and still enable me to send personalized feedback to students." Once faculty have these opportunities, and learn about what an impact they can have by building rapport, they often want to continue to connect with their online students. As one faculty member who completed the "humanizing" training conducted by Michelle Pacansky-Brock and her colleagues put it, "My presence matters so much more than I thought. I was guilty of trying to be a neutral voice with a professional (aka sterile) presentation of content. I see now that being active, responsive, present, and empathetic is so vital to . . . my students" (Pacansky-Brock, Smedshammer, and Vincent-Layton 2020, 23). When faculty start making real human connections in their classes, it is hard to see teaching online any other way.

Training and mentorship can thus make online teaching much more appealing to faculty (Chapman 2011), but this training needs to go beyond just the technicalities of navigating Learning Management Systems. When it comes to familiarizing new online instructors with how online courses are organized, technology-focused programs may be helpful, but they teach faculty nothing about actually interacting with students online. A checklist approach that focuses solely on design can actually end up making courses feel like impersonal cookie-cutter replicas to the students who take them. Faculty can also get bogged down in learning the intricacies and latest features of the newest Blackboard add-on or Canvas app and not stop to think about what pedagogical goal it might meet. When researchers talk to new online faculty, they quickly find out that faculty are desperate to learn about online pedagogy—they want to see more focus on course design and pedagogy and less on technology (Schmidt, Tschida, and Hodge 2016, 5). A training approach like the Technological Pedagogical Content Knowledge Framework (TPACK) that integrates technical knowledge (e.g., recording and uploading videos) with pedagogy (e.g., building rapport or designing engaging assignments) and field-specific content (e.g., political science or biology) is likely to be more effective (Herring, Koehler, and Mishra 2016; Koehler et al. 2014). Instead of an end in itself, technology is the medium through which teaching and learning happen.

An increasing number of faculty voices, like those of Sean Michael Morris and Jesse Stommel of the Digital Pedagogy Lab, are coming forward to argue that we should emphasize teaching over technology (Morris and Stommel 2018). Moore and Fetzner (2009, 8) similarly find that programs that are closing the retention gap are separating pedagogy and technology—teaching centers emphasize pedagogy and work with faculty, while specific support staff are assigned to handle the tedious technology management tasks of checking course links and uploading files. Xu and Jaggars (2011b) argue that faculty need training beyond just how to use the Learning Management System; faculty need training opportunities that allow them to "delve more deeply into issues of online quality and pedagogy" (p. 23). Others argue that "technology, pedagogy, and content are inextricably linked" (Herring, Koehler, and Mishra 2016, 1) and faculty professional development is critically important in each area (Rapanta et al. 2020).

Pedagogical training is especially important for faculty because students aren't the only ones who feel the interpersonal distance in online education. Faculty may be reluctant to teach online because they miss interacting with students (Lin 2002; Nelson 2003; Shattuck 2013). They may see online classes as cold and boring—who would want to teach there when they could teach a face-to-face seminar filled with smart students engaging in thoughtful discussion? Teaching online can be downright isolating for instructors (Duncan and Barnett 2009). They don't have many opportunities to reflect and share best practices with one another (Capra 2011). This is one reason why training can be so helpful. Good administrators will provide their online faculty with opportunities to engage in meaningful pedagogical training, where they can learn and share ideas with fellow faculty members about how to build rapport with their students.

In short, administrators need to offer, incentivize, and even require rapport-based training for online instructors. Administrators help set the culture of their campus when it comes to online teaching and learning. This expectation-setting role leads directly to the next recommendation.

Create a campus culture that values good online teaching. Administrators can't dictate caring about students from the top down, and they can't request the faculty senate pass legislation to do so either. But administrators can have a major impact on the culture of a university, and they can help foster a culture that values and rewards faculty who genuinely care about their students. Vincent Tinto, one of the leading voices in the scholarship of college student success since the 1970s, has not held back in his criticism of institutional-level deficiencies, saying, "Most institutions do not align their reward systems to the goal of enhanced student retention. It is one thing to talk about the importance of increasing student retention, it is another to invest scarce resources and adopt institutional faculty and staff reward systems that promote the behaviors that would reinforce that goal" (Tinto 2006, 9). If administrators care about reversing the online retention crisis, they have to invest resources—time, money, and agenda space—to address it by creating a campus culture that centers relationships and rapport.

The key to creating a campus culture that values good online teaching is having faculty who value good online teaching. Creating a new culture begins by hiring faculty members who have prioritized teaching in their graduate work. If you want to have the kind of faculty who will voluntarily attend training sessions about building rapport to help retain their online students, you need to hire faculty who care about teaching.

The elephant in the room is the question of who teaches online courses. At many universities, online classes are taught by overworked and underpaid part-time faculty (Mandernach, Register, and O'Donnell 2015). These contingent faculty are often either teaching across multiple campuses or teaching in addition to their "day job." For these faculty members, who likely don't participate in departmental peer reviews and don't go up for tenure, the structural incentives to improve online retention through the resource-intensive processes of building rapport are simply not there, although the personal incentives may be. Faculty who are teaching exclusively online, who aren't on campus—and possibly not even in the same city as the university—will be less able to connect with and help students who are taking a mix of face-to-face and online classes (Arnsparger and Drivalas 2016; Kezar, DePaola, and Scott 2019). They are also more likely to be teaching large introductory and prerequisite classes, often known for low retention rates, further compounding the problem (Kezar, DePaola, and Scott 2019; Wladis, Conway, and Hachey 2014).

There is a solid argument to be made that the treatment of contingent faculty in higher education today is unethical (Kezar and Maxey 2014b). This treatment matters not just for contingent faculty but also for students. Research suggests that courses taught by contingent faculty can harm student learning by limiting the ability of faculty to invest in relationships with students and build community in their classes (Kezar, DePaola, and Scott 2019, 97). When students are taught by contingent faculty, the research indicates that it has negative effects on their retention and success, including lower graduation rates (Ehrenberg and Zhang 2005; Jaeger and Eagan 2009), reduced year-to-year retention (Jaeger and Eagan 2011), reduced likelihood of subsequent course enrollments (Ran and Xu 2019), and particularly negative outcomes for lower-income, first-generation, and students of color (Kezar, DePaola, and Scott 2019, 99). Programs should not rely solely or primarily on part-time and adjunct faculty to teach their online classes.

If administrators want faculty who are going to invest in building relationships with students to facilitate their success, they need to invest in full-time, tenure-track faculty to teach in online programs. Underpaid adjuncts who are stretched thin across multiple campuses with little job security do not have the institutional incentives to invest in rapport like tenure-track faculty do. Of course, if those institutional incentives don't exist for tenure-track faculty either, you are unlikely to see a difference. At some research universities, where new faculty are told to focus their energies on securing as many publications as possible in order to build a strong tenure case and to aim for satisfactory teaching, the incentive structure is clearly not aligned toward student success. Research even suggests an additional, gender dynamic at play: women are more likely to win teaching awards, but only in institutional contexts where research is valued more than teaching (Butcher and Kersey 2014). Some studies indicate that contingent faculty are actually better teachers because they are not systematically incentivized to minimize the time they spend on teaching, as some of their research-intensive tenure-track colleagues are—and student evaluation data tend to support that argument (Figlio, Schapiro, and Soter 2015; Lowenthal, Bauer, and Chen 2015). If administrators want good online teaching, they have to incentivize it.

My intent is not to malign either the overworked adjunct faculty member teaching at multiple colleges or the harried junior faculty member feeling the pressure to "publish or perish." My intent is to point out the importance of instructors in online classes. The more present and engaged instructors can be to build rapport with students, the more likely students will be to pass the class and stay enrolled. Any system that makes building rapport between faculty and students difficult—whether because of an increasing reliance on adjuncts who are rushing from one campus to another to make ends meet, or because of tenure-track faculty who are necessarily putting more of their attention on research as tenure expectations continue to mount—runs counter to what students want and to what is most likely to help them succeed, no matter the teaching medium (Arnsparger and Drivalas 2016). The model we currently have—what Kezar, DePaola, and Scott (2019) call the "gig academy"—is not working. We need to reevaluate how we view online teaching and learning, how we recruit and incentivize both contingent and tenured/tenure-track faculty, and how we interact with online students. Administrators are uniquely positioned to help shift their campus cultures.

Institutions of higher education in the United States can be wildly different from one another, but even major research universities are offering more online classes. Additionally, the COVID-19 pandemic changed higher education in ways that will likely be felt for years to come. There are many things administrators can do to show that they value teaching and that they value faculty members who care about their students. Programs that are successfully closing the retention gap between online and face-to-face classes have award and recognition programs to honor excellent online teachers and to encourage innovation. They offer incentives to teach online, ongoing professional development, and support to make sure that faculty are happy teaching online (Bailey et al. 2018; Moore and Fetzner 2009). If administrators care about and prioritize teaching, their priorities will help shift the culture of their institutions toward a more student-centered ethic.

Institutions can also offer support to help reduce the responsibility of building rapport. It should not fall entirely on instructors. If administrators are helping to build a culture of rapport, students should feel supported and connected all over campus. This is what the staff of eCore at the University of Georgia did (Zatynsk 2013). They reached out to struggling students so that the entire burden wasn't on faculty alone. Arizona State University provides 24/7 tech support, as well as online tutoring and support from retention coaches (Bailey et al. 2018).

At my own university, the Department of Rhetoric and Writing has sought to build a culture of rapport that involves both faculty and students in "collaborative mentoring relationship[s] . . ., in which the professors make an effort to get to know their students and also allow themselves to be known as people" (Thomas et al. 2020, 9). From the time students reach out to the department to inquire about a class or program, they receive individual attention from a faculty member and advising that is tailored to their needs, creating what Dr. Heidi Skurat Harris, the graduate coordinator in the department, calls "a continuum of rapport from recruitment through matriculation" (Skurat Harris 2020).

Although administrators tend to think that only more money will get their faculty to teach online, faculty don't rank pay particularly high in importance as a reason for teaching online classes (Allen and Seaman 2008). Instead, most faculty are motivated to teach online for intrinsic reasons—they want to be flexible in helping to meet students' needs and reach diverse students, and they also enjoy the challenge of working in a new medium (Orr, Williams, and Pennington 2009; Shattuck 2013; Shea, Pickett, and Li 2005). Thus, administrators will likely not have to dedicate a great deal of resources to incentivize faculty to be trained in methods to improve retention. A course release is especially useful when developing an online class for the first time (Marek 2009) or significantly revising it to include rapport elements. Other positive incentives could include faculty development grants, a new laptop, support for conference attendance, explicit consideration in tenure and promotion, a small increase in salary for trained faculty, or other benefits (Bettinger and Long 2010; Xu and Jaggars 2011b). Keep in mind that contingent faculty need training and mentoring opportunities as well (Kezar, DePaola, and Scott 2019), which are rarely available to them currently.

Provide an orientation for online students. Beyond helping online instructors do better at teaching online classes, administrators can help online students get better at learning in online classes. There are valuable technical skills and study strategies that can help students succeed in online classes, which they may not develop in their face-to-face classes. The skills needed both to teach an online class and to learn in an online class are different from the skills needed to teach and learn in a face-to-face class. Simply moving face-to-face courses online is not sufficient if we want to actually retain our online students

(Cox 2006; Jaggars and Xu 2016; Xu and Xu 2019). Both instructors and students need to adjust and treat online classes differently.

Some universities have had success with requiring online students to attend face-to-face orientations, as we saw in chapter 2. Making personal contact through an orientation can help students connect with the campus and the support resources there, but it may be a burden on students who live far from campus, don't have the resources to take off work, or don't have reliable transportation to attend. Remember that the promise of online higher education is its ability to expand access to students who would otherwise be unable to attend college. Expecting those students to behave like traditional college students and attend an in-person orientation may not be a fair expectation.

An online orientation or an online readiness assessment is another option (Xu and Jaggars 2011b). Having students complete some kind of online information program can ensure that every student taking online courses has a baseline of knowledge about how to navigate the Learning Management System, the importance of the course syllabus, resources available to support them on campus, and the availability of their professors should they need help. This should be paired with rapport training for professors so that students aren't unpleasantly surprised when they start an online class and find a distant, unavailable instructor who doesn't answer questions.

A self-assessment component to an online orientation program, possibly coming around the time of registration, could be particularly helpful for online students. It could provide students with data on success rates at different online course loads, expected hourly workload commitments, and research on best practices for success. Students could then self-assess how many online classes they are prepared to take, if any, without any automatic gatekeeping by the system. The help of an academic advisor in the process could result in even more informed choices. If the self-assessment included some questions about self-regulation and study skills, as well as computer and internet access, it could help the student determine their level of readiness for the particular challenges of online classes and, if they may not be quite ready to succeed, point the student in the direction of specific support systems at the university, like technology training, laptop checkout, time-management classes, or advising help to find classes that will work better for their schedule and learning style (Xu and Jaggars 2011b).

This approach gives students autonomy over their educational decisions and sends them the message that we trust them to make those decisions. At the same time, it lets students know that we are here with support resources whenever they need them. That is the kind of message our online students—and all of our students—need to hear over and again: "You can do this. If you need help, you've got backup. We are on your side and we'll do whatever we can to help you succeed."

Encourage online students to take some classes on campus. Through the process of taking an online self-assessment, students should see the data that show retention dropping when students take all of their classes online. This will hopefully encourage them to take some classes on campus, if they can. This may not be possible for every student, but research I have published with colleagues from the University of Central Florida shows that any increase in face-to-face courses increases a student's success (Glazier et al. 2019b; Hamann et al. 2020).

Administrators can come in with creative solutions to enable students to take face-to-face classes and improve their chances of graduating. Some students may take all online classes because they live too far away to regularly come to campus. It may be a long commute to campus, but if there were a small scholarship available to pay for the cost of that single face-to-face course, as well as the cost of gas and an on-campus parking permit for the semester, you may be able to get more students on campus. Perhaps a childcare scholarship would be a helpful way to get some additional students on campus for one or two classes. There haven't been many initiatives like this, so there isn't data on their impact on student success, but it may be that helping students get on campus, meet and connect with at least one professor face-to-face, connect with some of their classmates, and reach some campus resources, may increase their chance of success through the rest of their college career. It would be well worth the investment if the payoff were a successfully retained and graduated student.

What Success Looks Like: Case Studies of
Three Different Institutions

As faculty and administrators contemplate how they might implement rapport at their own institutions, it might be helpful to consider examples of specific cases where a rapport-centric focus has yielded positive outcomes for students. Here, I briefly present three such cases, from diverse institutions, as examples of the different ways that prioritizing rapport can benefit students and improve retention. Now, as I noted in chapter 2, my scientific bias is toward peer-reviewed academic studies that control for as many potential intervening variables as possible. These case studies are not that. This book has been filled with citations of those kinds of studies, as well as experimental and survey research I have conducted myself. These case studies are intended to give readers an idea of what the actual application of rapport-building looks like at real colleges and universities.

The first two cases come from community colleges in California, both of which have benefited from placing a strong emphasis on humanizing in their online faculty trainings under the leadership of Michelle Pacansky-Brock. Southwestern College has seen a remarkable improvement in its retention numbers in just two short years. And Modesto Junior College has focused its rapport-building efforts on equity and dramatically improved online retention for Black and Hispanic students.

Unlike the two community college case studies, the third case study is the University of Central Florida, a major research university with a huge student population. Its early investment in rapport-centric faculty development has led to a sustained elimination of the online retention gap and online retention numbers over 90%. Together, these case studies illustrate that there is no one way to build rapport and no single institutional model by which rapport-building improves retention. The strategy of building rapport with students can be implemented with whatever means and level of commitment you can convince your institution to put toward it.

Southwestern College

More than 28,000 students attend Southwestern College, a regional community college in southern California. In recent years, Southwestern has invested in its faculty, placing increased emphasis on training online teachers, including through a five-week, fully online training program called Distance Education Faculty Training (DEFT). Faculty are required to undergo training before teaching online or hybrid classes at Southwestern and the DEFT program in particular emphasizes the importance of humanizing the online classroom and connecting with students.

What is unique about the DEFT program at Southwestern College is that, through the program, faculty participate in a long-term online training course *as students*. As Tracy Schaelen, the Distance Education Faculty coordinator at Southwestern College, explained it, "Facilitators of DEFT model the supportive, humanized approach to instruction that we are teaching our faculty, so participants experience a humanized online course from a student perspective. They tell us that this is eye-opening and leads to greater empathy" (Schaelen 2020). Indeed, faculty who attend the training leave comments showing just how much seeing the class through the eyes of a student changes the way they teach. Schaelen shared some of these comments. For instance, one instructor said, "I am a very encouraging professor, usually, but I never realized how important it was to get those kudos! It makes me feel special, important, valued, and worthy." Another professor who went through the training commented on how doing so helped familiarize them with reaching out through technology: "It was a little nerve-wracking at first, but now I feel completely comfortable with reaching out electronically and seeing myself online through videos and images" (Schaelen 2020).

Faculty are not the only ones becoming better acquainted with online learning at Southwestern College. Students are encouraged to determine if they are ready for online classes through an online readiness quiz; they are invited to attend a free orientation to online learning and Canvas, the Learning Management System the campus uses; and they are encouraged to complete the self-paced Quest for Online Success microcourse to prepare for their first online class (Southwestern College 2020).

Since the DEFT program began, with its emphasis on humanizing online classrooms and seeing the online teaching and learning process through the students' eyes, Southwestern College has significantly improved the percentage of students who are successfully passing their online classes with a C or better, up from 62.1% to 67.8% in just two years (Schaelen 2020). Retention rates in hybrid classes are similarly up from 65.3% to 71.5%.

What is especially noteworthy about the case of Southwestern College is how quickly these numbers moved as a result of rapport-centric faculty training in online teaching. The retention gap between face-to-face and online classes was nearly cut in half, shrinking from 8.1 to 4.6 percentage points, and the gap between face-to-face and hybrid courses was virtually eliminated, dropping from 4.9 all the way to 0.9, in only two years. Not only does making real human connections with students make a difference for their success—it does so remarkably quickly.

The positive impact this rapport-focused professional development is having reaches beyond just the online classes the trained faculty go on to teach. Tracy Schaelen says, "Faculty regularly tell us that learning how to teach online has improved their in-person teaching, too, and that really resonates with me; at its heart, good online teaching is simply good teaching. And good teachers know that it all starts with human connections" (Schaelen 2020).

Modesto Junior College

Modesto Junior College (MJC) is one of the oldest community colleges in California and today serves a diverse student body of over 18,000, only about 32% of whom identify as non-Hispanic white, and more than half of whom receive federal Pell Grants (About MJC 2020). Like many community colleges, Modesto Junior College serves an increasing number of online students—the number of students taking at least one online class increased from 10% in 2013 to 28% in 2018 (Smedshammer et al. 2018). Since 2012, nearly every faculty member who has taught online at MJC has received training, including through the @ONE Project at the California Community College Online Education Initiative (OEI), known for its rigor and focus on humanizing (@ONE Online Network of Educators 2020).

Additionally, since 2016, the online training program for faculty at MJC has explicitly focused on equity, working with the Center for Urban Excellence at USC to offer training, and with Professor Luke Wood from San Diego State University to form the Minority Male Collaborative and offer the open online course Black Minds Matter (Smedshammer et al. 2018, 7). These training programs have explicitly focused on connecting faculty and students, built around principles of "humanizing the online classroom" and "intrusive instruction" (Smedshammer et al. 2018, 7; Kaupp 2012; Pacansky-Brock 2020; Wood and Turner 2010).

Between 2012 and 2017, the retention gap between online and face-to-face classes at MJC shrank from 7 points down to 2. Even more impressive are the gains that MJC has made in closing the racial disparity gaps in online education. In 2010, white students in online classes at MJC were successfully passing their classes with a grade of C or better 56% of the time, while Hispanic students were only successfully passing about 44% of the time. By 2017, those numbers were 68% and 64%, respectively. Not only did MJC make double-digit improvements in retention for both groups of students, but they also narrowed the gap between them, from 12% to only 4%. The data for Black students at MJC are even more impressive. In 2015, the year before their equity training program began, Black students successfully passed their online classes only 30% of the time. Only two years later, in 2017, that number had increased an impressive 25%, to 55%. The dedicated faculty and staff at MJC aren't stopping there, saying, "Training efforts will continue to focus on this area, as more work needs to be done" (Smedshammer et al. 2018, 6). Although this was not a controlled study, the focused equity training and immediate equity gains indicate the work these faculty are doing is having a positive impact.

Modesto Junior College is a great example of how building rapport with underserved students can lead to immediate and positive results. The research is clear: when Black and Hispanic students talk with faculty, have informal conversations with them, and are mentored by them, they are significantly more likely to be successful (Kaupp 2012; Wood 2014a; Wood and Turner 2010; Wood and Williams 2013). And we know faculty contact and relationships are especially important for students of color in online classes (Merrills 2010; Palacios and Wood 2016; Rovai and Wighting 2005). We see this playing out in a very real way at Modesto Junior College. Dr. Michael Smedshammer, the distance education coordinator at MJC, says of their rapportfocused training and approach to online teaching, "Humanizing is our best opportunity to reach the most vulnerable students" (Smedshammer 2020).

The University of Central Florida

With an enrolled student population of nearly 70,000 in 2020, the University of Central Florida (UCF) is one of the largest universities in the United States (UCF Facts 2020). Because UCF has faced the challenge of having more students than classroom space, it invested early on in online classes and online faculty. Today, many students at UCF take a mix of online, hybrid, and face-to-face classes.

UCF is a major research university that attracts an elite student body—and its students are very successful. In spring 2019, 89% of students in face-to-face classes successfully passed with a C or better. Even more impressive, that same semester, 92% of students in hybrid classes and 91% of students in online classes passed with a C or better (Moskal 2020). That means that, at UCF, online and hybrid retention is actually higher than face-to-face retention. UCF has not only closed the retention gap; its online students are succeeding at higher rates than its face-to-face students.

This is not a new development at UCF. Thanks to a long-term investment in faculty professional development, a robust data-collection effort, and an emphasis on learning from rigorous scholarship on online teaching, UCF has had a very small or nonexistent online retention gap for nearly a decade (Dziuban et al. 2012), all while enrolling tens of thousands of students in online classes each semester.

The faculty online training and support infrastructure at UCF is extensive and reflects the university's decision to prioritize high-quality online teaching. All faculty who teach online, whether fully online or through hybrid courses, are required to complete an 80-hour boot camp on digital learning. An administrator there says that this level of training and commitment "sets a cultural expectation" (Bailey et al. 2018, 42). As Dr. Patsy D. Moskal, the director of Digital Learning Impact Evaluation at UCF told me, "The faculty development focuses not only on learning the digital learning 'tools' to teach, but more importantly on quality pedagogy" (Moskal 2020). At UCF, it's not just about moving your course online, but about rethinking the best way to teach in the online medium. Faculty members are individually paired up with instructional designers, and they also work with graphic artists, video teams, animators, and game designers in the Center for Distributed Learning to create engaging and innovative online courses (Center for Distributed Learning 2020a).

The Office of Digital Learning Impact Evaluation at UCF also works with faculty to evaluate the impact of their pedagogical innovations and to publish peer-reviewed articles. Dozens of academic articles on the scholarship of teaching and learning have come out of this office (Center for Distributed Learning 2020b), reflecting a commitment to rigorous scholarship and learning best practices.

The University of Central Florida also pays close attention to the data generated from all of those students, faculty, and classes. Using a proprietary data-mining platform developed by the Center for Distributed Learning, the Executive Information System (EIS), it brings together data from many disparate information streams across campus to inform decision makers (Dziuban et al. 2012). But, as Chuck Dziuban, the director of UCF's Research Initiative for Teaching Effectiveness, and colleagues write in a 2012 publication on the use of data to inform university decision making, "Data do not make decisions, people do" (Dziuban et al. 2012, 27). It's the personal touch that really makes a difference at UCF.

UCF uses its data to improve programs, to help determine which programs might be ready to go fully online, and to alert faculty and mentors to personally reach out to students who may be struggling. Faculty who have high-rapport relationships with their students are critical to the success of the data-collection effort. As Dziuban and colleagues write, "Engaged faculty are much more likely to use analytics for helping students achieve success, in some cases, by additional personal intervention when possible" (Dziuban et al. 2012, 27). This approach capitalizes on an institutional culture that values personal connections and rewards engaged faculty.

The model at UCF may represent an ideal that seems almost unachievable—an online retention rate over 90%, a completely eliminated online retention gap, and significant, long-term investments in high-quality professional development for online faculty. UCF began with a problem of classroom space and decided that it was going to provide its students with excellent online courses. It got there through a focus on people and pedagogy. Although the scale of the online program at UCF is one that most institutions don't even dream of, the notion that administration sets the cultural expectations for the campus holds, even if the budgetary and time constraints are different. It is imminently possible to scale UCF's rapport-centric approach down to the size and budget of your own institution.

Where to Begin?

If you are ready to change the culture of your institution and move toward a greater focus on building rapport with students, but you aren't sure where to begin, here are a series of increasingly involved steps to get you started.

1. *Start a faculty rapport group.* Get a group of faculty together— it could be just a few friends or it could be your entire college—and talk about some of the ideas in this book. You could read the whole

book together. But, if you are short on time, you could get a faculty rapport group together just to discuss chapter 4, or even just table 4.1 (the one with the ideas about building rapport). Share what you are already doing in your online classes to build rapport and brainstorm new ideas together. Come back together after you have tried a few things in your classes and talk about how they went. Share some of the nice emails you get from students and talk about how to support the students who are struggling. Beyond discussing a single book, creating a faculty book group can be a useful professional development resource, bringing together diverse faculty for what can be powerful experiences learning and sharing (Burbank, Kauchak, and Bates 2010; White 2016). Some have even had success with asynchronous online book groups (Porath 2018). Administrators can use professional development funds to buy copies of the book for faculty, supply refreshments for group meetings, and even provide a small stipend for the discussion leaders. As an added bonus, faculty in a rapport group will be building rapport with each other, while they learn about building rapport with their students, and they exchange ideas about how to build rapport. It's like the rapport trifecta!

2. *Find the rapport builders on your campus.* There are already faculty on your campus who are making real human connections with students and helping them succeed. Maybe you are one of them! If you don't know who they are, ask the students. They can tell you. And there are likely other people on campus (e.g., your university might have instructional design staff or other administrators focused on pedagogy, online and/or offline) who have already been thinking about rapport building in its many forms. Once you find them, invite these rapport builders to share what they are doing in their classes. This can be at informal brown bag lunches or roundtable conversations. These less-formal professional development opportunities can be really valuable to faculty (Schmidt, Tschida, and Hodge 2016). Administrators should be looking for the rapport builders on their own campuses and drawing on their expertise. Use professional development funds to support them in providing formal online teacher trainings. Consider sending them to more advanced trainings and then teaching others

what they learned when they come back. Value the time and expertise of your faculty. Bake them cookies or give them a small gift card. Use professional development funds to pay them an honorarium for training or for taking on new or challenging online classes.

3. *Look at your data.* Nearly every campus has internal data-collection operations, usually through an office of institutional research, or something similar. Talk to your data office about where your online retention numbers are the lowest. Where are you losing the most students? There are probably some large first-year courses being taught online that have low retention rates, but the retention gap may be the widest in upper-division classes (Mensch 2017; Wladis, Conway, and Hachey 2017). Consider putting some high-rapport teachers into those courses and/or prioritize training the faculty who are teaching those classes in how to teach with rapport. Talk to faculty about how to access their own retention data. They will probably be shocked to see how much lower their numbers are for their online classes compared to their face-to-face classes. As you make changes, either on an individual or an institutional level, collect data! That way, you can know what effect your rapport-building efforts are having, faculty can publish in peer-reviewed journals, and you can appeal for more funding for rapport-based initiatives based on the evidence of your success.

4. *Start a campus-wide rapport-building movement.* If you really want to change things for the better for your students and see significant improvements in retention across the board, you likely need a culture shift. You need a campus-wide movement toward building rapport. This is bigger than any single professor and can include all kinds of creative ways of getting the entire campus excited about making connections and building rapport. Your movement might include things like: a student-selected online rapport builder award, department-level retention improvement grants, a campus-wide big read, holding trainings, bringing in speakers, funding travel to teaching conferences, publicizing kind student comments about online professors who went the extra mile, and so on. A movement like that would likely take a big investment and a commitment from leader-

ship—the funding and organization for many of these ideas would need to come from administrators—but it could result in a campus with an entirely different attitude about online education.

Living Up to the Promise of Online Higher Education

There is a great deal of promise in online higher education, but we will miss our opportunity to realize this promise if we allow our online students to keep failing and dropping out at such high rates. It is unacceptable to continue to see such a yawning gap between online and face-to-face retention rates as the norm. We owe it to our online students to do better. Even if it takes more work on our part. Even if it's hard.

The higher education system we have now is suffering from an online retention crisis, but the system we can create—through prioritizing faculty-student relationships in online classes and building rapport—can lead to more students graduating and improving life for themselves and their families, more fulfilling teaching experiences for online instructors, and more stable enrollment numbers for colleges and universities. This is a future we can start creating right now. Every professor teaching an online course has the ability to connect with their students and let them know that we are pulling for them. It will make a real, measurable difference in their success.

1. First Name
2. Last Name
3. Preferred Name—what do you like to go by?
4. Preferred pronouns (multiple choice: she/her/hers, he/him/his, they/them/theirs)
5. What are you most looking forward to about this class?
6. Is there anything that worries you about this class?
7. Do you have anything going on this semester that might make it difficult for you to succeed in this class?
8. What show are you binge watching right now?
9. If you had $10,000 and two weeks that you had to spend traveling, where would you go?
10. What is your major?
11. How do you feel about online classes?
12. Is there anything else you want me to know?

1. Welcome email—sent about one week before classes start

This is the unmerged version:

Hi {{First Name}},

Welcome to Introduction to International Politics (POLS 2303)! {{First Term}} I hope that you had a great winter break and are looking forward to an exciting class. There are all kinds of interesting political things going on in the world, so we are going to have a lot to talk about.

Our class will officially start with the semester on Tuesday, January 21. Until then, you can't get into Blackboard, but I wanted to write now to touch base and give you a heads up about what to expect. I have attached the course syllabus here for you. It is a really important document, so I wanted to make sure you got a look at it as soon as possible.

Also, I wanted to make sure you know about **our totally online course textbook,** which will be available from our course Blackboard site. I have attached a document here letting you know how this whole online textbook thing works.

The textbook is really important because **you have two textbook sections and short quizzes due by Monday, January 27.** Feel free to get started as soon as the Blackboard course opens so you are sure to have them done before the due date.

Also, {{First Name}}, {{Major}}

If you ever need anything at all, just ask! If you have a preferred name or pronouns you would like me to use, please just let me know that and some other important stuff in this short survey: {{survey link}}. I want you to succeed in our class, so please say the word if I can do anything to help you. Looking forward to a great semester!

Take care,

Dr. Glazier

This is a version that has been merged in Gmail mail merge:

Hi Jaelyn,

Welcome to Introduction to International Politics (POLS 2303)! And welcome back to another semester at UA Little Rock! I hope that you had a great winter break and are looking forward to an exciting class. There are all kinds of interesting political things going on in the world, so we are going to have a lot to talk about.

Our class will officially start with the semester on Tuesday, January 21. Until then, you can't get into Blackboard, but I wanted to write now to touch base and give you a heads up about what to expect. I have attached the course syllabus here for you. It is a really important document, so I wanted to make sure you got a look at it as soon as possible.

Also, I wanted to make sure you know about **our totally online course textbook**, which will be available from our course Blackboard site. I have attached a document here letting you know how this whole online textbook thing works.

The textbook is really important because **you have two textbook sections and short quizzes due by Monday, January 27.** Feel free to get started as soon as the Blackboard course opens so you are sure to have them done before the due date.

Also, Jaelyn, I just wanted to let you know even though political science is not your major and this class is probably just a core requirement for you, I will still do my best to make the class interesting, engaging, and helpful for your life in general. If everything goes as planned, you will develop some research, writing, and critical thinking skills that will serve you well. And you can always declare a political science major if you want to!

If you ever need anything at all, just ask! If you have a preferred name or pronoun you would like me to use, please just let me know that and some other important stuff in this short survey: Intro to International Politics Survey. I want you to succeed in our class, so please say the word if I can do anything to help you. Looking forward to a great semester!

Take care,
Dr. Glazier

2. A check-in email after 3 weeks of a 15-week semester

This is the unmerged version:

Hi {{First Name}},

I hope that you are doing well and that your semester is going smoothly. I know that using a totally online textbook can take some getting used to, so I wanted to check in with you and see how it is going.

I just took a look at the scores and it looks like you are {{score comment}} Your average grade for the first three reading assignments is {{score}}. {{Additional comment}}

The textbook readings and quizzes make up 15% of your total grade, so definitely pay attention to these assignments! Your next reading assignment is due on Monday, February 17. It is the last one before your first exam, so definitely pay close attention!

Do you have any concerns or is there anything I can do to help you succeed? Please let me know!

All the best,

Dr. Glazier

This is a version that has been merged in Gmail mail merge:

Hi Cole,

I hope that you are doing well and that your semester is going smoothly. I know that using a totally online textbook can take some getting used to, so I wanted to check in with you and see how it is going.

I just took a look at the scores and it looks like you are struggling a bit, mostly because you missed this week's deadline. If you need an extension, just let me know. I would hate for you to have a zero. Your average grade for the first three reading assignments is 45. I don't think that score reflects your abilities, so get those quizzes in on time and let's see some higher scores!

The textbook readings and quizzes make up 15% of your total grade, so definitely pay attention to these assignments! Your next reading assignment is due on Monday, February 17. It is the last one before your first exam, so definitely pay close attention!

Do you have any concerns or is there anything I can do to help you succeed? Please let me know!

All the best,

Dr. Glazier

3. An assignment reminder email about their satire assignment

This is the unmerged version:

Hi {{First Name}},

I hope that you are doing well and your semester is going smoothly. I am writing to remind you that your satire presentation is coming up. You are scheduled to share your satire with the class after your satire discussion thread opens on {{Satire Thread Opens}}. I am really looking forward to seeing what you find!

Be sure to turn in your one-page critical analysis through the link in the Assignments folder by Friday, {{Satire Critical Analysis Due}} at 11:59 p.m. I have attached the assignment here for you, in case you need to review it. This little assignment makes up 10% of your grade, so read the assignment carefully and give me some insightful analysis.

Please let me know if you have any questions! I would be happy to chat with you about it over email or in a phone call or video call.

All the best,

Dr. Glazier

This is a version that has been merged in Gmail mail merge:

Hi Spencer,

I hope that you are doing well and your semester is going smoothly. I am writing to remind you that your satire presentation is coming up. You are scheduled to share your satire with the class after your satire discussion thread opens on April 20. I am really looking forward to seeing what you find!

Be sure to turn in your one-page critical analysis through the link in the Assignments folder by Friday, April 24 at 11:59 p.m. I have attached the assignment here for you, in case you need to review it. This little assignment makes up 10% of your grade, so read the assignment carefully and give me some insightful analysis.

Please let me know if you have any questions! I would be happy to chat with you about it over email or in a phone call or video call.

All the best,

Dr. Glazier

4. An assignment reminder email about their discussion leadership assignment

This is the unmerged version:

Hi {{First Name}},

I am just writing to touch base and remind you that we are discussing {{Topic}} next week. This should be a really interesting discussion! And, as you know, you are scheduled to be one of our discussion leaders. You are assigned to Side {{Side}} for the discussion, so you will be defending the position: "{{Side Description}}."

The discussion thread opens at 8:00 a.m. on Monday, {{Date}} and you are responsible for leading the discussion through the close of the thread on Sunday night at 11:59 p.m. I would love to give you feedback on your discussion outline (per the attached assignment details—just to be clear, this isn't optional) so please send it to me as soon as possible (48 hours in advance is ideal for me to give you feedback). There is an example discussion outline in the Assignments folder you can check out to get some ideas.

Don't forget that your annotated bibliography on the same topic of {{Topic}} is due on Friday, April 17.

This is a really big part of your grade, so take the time to do a good job on it and let me know if there is anything I can do to help you along the way. You are going to do great!

All the best,

Dr. Glazier

This is a version that has been merged in Gmail mail merge:

Hi Jasmine,

I am just writing to touch base and remind you that we are discussing "Is Terrorism Ever a Justifiable Form of Political Violence?" next week. This should be a really interesting discussion! And, as you know, you are scheduled to be one of our discussion leaders. You are assigned to Side 2 for the discussion, so you will be defending the position: "All Terrorism Is Indefensible."

The discussion thread opens at 8:00 a.m. on Monday, April 27 and you are responsible for leading the discussion through the close of the thread on Sunday night at 11:59 p.m. I would love to give you feedback on your discussion outline (per the attached assignment details—just to be clear, this isn't optional) so please send it to me as soon as possible (48 hours in advance is ideal for me to give you feedback). There is an example discussion outline in the Assignments folder you can check out to get some ideas.

Don't forget that your annotated bibliography on the same topic of "Is Terrorism Ever a Justifiable Form of Political Violence?" is due on Friday, April 17.

This is a really big part of your grade, so take the time to do a good job on it and let me know if there is anything I can do to help you along the way. You are going to do great!

All the best,

Dr. Glazier

5. A check in email around week 9 of a 15-week semester.

This is the unmerged version:

Hi {{First Name}},

I hope that this email finds you well. I just wanted to check in with you now that we are about 2/3 of the way through the semester. You have had two exams now. You scored a {{Exam 1}} on the first one and a {{Exam 2}} on the second one. {{Exam Comment}} We have one more Exam and then the final, so there are plenty of points left in the semester.

Speaking of points, doing the textbook readings and comprehension quizzes are an easy way to earn points—it makes up 15% of your total grade for the class! Right now, your Online Textbook score is {{Online Textbook Score}}. {{Textbook Comment}} Your next textbook reading assignment is due by Monday, so be sure to get it turned in!

But the easiest points of all come from participating in discussions. Your discussion grade is {{Discussion}}. {{Discussion Comment}} Our new discussion starts on Monday, so you just need to post on two days next week to earn full points.

Please also make sure that you are putting the time you need to into your annotated bibliography, which is due Friday, April 17. There is an example in the Assignments folder to help you get there.

Keep working hard as we turn the corner on the last 1/3 of our class together! Just let me know if there is anything I can do to help you.

Take care,

Dr. Glazier

This is a version that has been merged in Gmail mail merge:

Hi Jake,

I hope that this email finds you well. I just wanted to check in with you now that we are about 2/3 of the way through the semester. You have had two exams now. You scored a 85 on the first one and a 91 on the second one. You improved on the second exam. Nice work! I hope you are using the study guide and please feel free to email me if you have any questions. We have one more Exam and then the final, so there are plenty of points left in the semester.

Speaking of points, doing the textbook readings and comprehension quizzes are an easy way to earn points—it makes up 15% of your total grade for the class! Right now, your Online Textbook score is 82.29. You are doing pretty good here, but make sure you aren't missing out on any of these easy points. If for some reason you can't make the deadline one week, just email me and let me know and I can extend it. I want to see you do well here, so please let me know how I can help. Your next textbook reading assignment is due by Monday, so be sure to get it turned in!

But the easiest points of all come from participating in discussions. Your discussion grade is 44.70. I am pretty concerned with how low your score is here. I think you can do a lot better. You can earn more points by posting early and often—at least twice on at least two different days in each thread. That will get you 10/10 points every time. Our new discussion starts on Monday, so you just need to post on two days next week to earn full points.

Please also make sure that you are putting the time you need to into your annotated bibliography, which is due Friday, April 17. There is an example in the Assignments folder to help you get there.

Keep working hard as we turn the corner on the last 1/3 of our class together! Just let me know if there is anything I can do to help you.

Take care,
Dr. Glazier

REFERENCES

@ONE Online Network of Educators. 2020. "Humanizing Online Teaching & Learning." California Virtual Campus—Online Education Initiative (CVC-OEI). https://onlinenetworkofeducators.org/course-cards/humanizing-online-teaching-learning/.

About MJC. 2020. "About MJC." Last modified February 25, 2020. https://www.mjc.edu/general/aboutmjc.php.

Ackerman, David S., Curt J. Dommeyer, and Barbara L. Gross. 2017. "The Effects of Source, Revision Possibility, and Amount of Feedback on Marketing Students' Impressions of Feedback on an Assignment." *Journal of Marketing Education* 39 (1):17–29. Doi: 10.1177/0273475316628293.

Ackerman, David S., and Barbara L. Gross. 2010. "Instructor Feedback: How Much Do Students Really Want?" *Journal of Marketing Education* 32 (2):172–81. Doi: 10.1177/0273475309360159.

Alessio, Helaine M., Nancy Malay, Karsten Maurer, A. John Bailer, and Beth Rubin. 2017. "Examining the Effect of Proctoring on Online Test Scores." *Online Learning* 21 (1):146–61.

Alexander, Austin. 2014. "Fixing For-Profit Failures: Why Student Loans for For-Profit Schools Should Be Dischargeable in Bankruptcy." *Mississippi Law Journal* 83 (189–210).

Alfred State. 2020. "How Online Classes Work." Alfred State College. Accessed July 29, 2020. https://www.alfredstate.edu/academics/online/online-learning.

Alfred State News. 2017. "Alfred State Online Recognized for Quality." Alfred State College. Accessed July 29, 2020. https://www.alfredstate.edu/news/2017-08-09/alfred-state-online-recognized-quality.

Ali, Radwan, and Elke M. Leeds. 2009. "The Impact of Face-to-Face Orientation on Online Retention: A Pilot Study." *Online Journal of Distance Learning Administration* 12 (4).

Allen, I. Elaine, and Jeff Seaman. 2008. *Staying the Course: Online Education in the United States, 2008.* Newburyport, MA: Sloan Consortium.

———. 2011. *Going the Distance: Online Education in the United States.* Newburyport, MA: Sloan Consortium.

———. 2012. *Conflicted: Faculty and Online Education, 2012.* Babson Park, MA: Babson Survey Research Group and Inside Higher Ed.

———. 2016. *Online Report Card: Tracking Online Education in the United States.* Babson Park, MA: Babson Survey Research Group.

Allen, Walter. 1992. "The Color of Success: African-American College Student Outcomes at Predominantly White and Historically Black Public Colleges and Universities." *Harvard Educational Review* 62 (1):26–45. Doi: 10.17763 /haer.62.1.wv5627665007v701.

Alman, Susan W., Barbara A. Frey, and Christinger Tomer. 2012. "Social and Cognitive Presence as Factors in Learning and Student Retention: An Investigation of the Cohort Model in an iSchool Setting." *Journal of Education for Library and Information Science* 53 (4): 290–302.

Alpert, William T., Kenneth A. Couch, and Oskar R. Harmon. 2016. "A Randomized Assessment of Online Learning." *American Economic Review* 106 (5):378–82. Doi: 10.1257/aer.p20161057.

Altman, Irwin. 1990. "Conceptualizing 'Rapport.'" *Psychological Inquiry* 1 (4):294–97.

Amelink, Catherine T. 2005. "Predicting Academic Success among First-Year, First Generation Students." PhD diss., Educational Leadership and Policy Studies, Virginia Tech.

Amsberry, Dawn. 2009. "Deconstructing Plagiarism: International Students and Textual Borrowing Practices." *Reference Librarian* 51 (1):31–44. Doi: 10.1080/02763870903362183.

Anaya, Guadalupe, and Darnell G. Cole. 2001. "Latina/o Student Achievement: Exploring the Influence of Student-Faculty Interactions on College Grades." *Journal of College Student Development* 42 (1):3–14.

Andrejevic, Mark, and Neil Selwyn. 2020. "Facial Recognition Technology in Schools: Critical Questions and Concerns." *Learning, Media and Technology* 45 (2):115–28. Doi: 10.1080/17439884.2020.1686014.

Ang, Desmond. 2020. "The Effects of Police Violence on Inner-City Students." *Quarterly Journal of Economics.* Doi: 10.1093/qje/qjaa027.

Angelino, Lorraine M., Frankie Keels Williams, and Deborah Natvig. 2007. "Strategies to Engage Online Students and Reduce Attrition Rates." *Journal of Educators Online* 4 (2):1–14.

Angulo, A. J. 2016. *Diploma Mills: How For-Profit Colleges Stiffed Students, Taxpayers, and the American Dream.* Baltimore, MD: Johns Hopkins University Press.

Appel, Hannah, and Astra Taylor. 2015. "Education with a Debt Sentence: For-Profit Colleges as American Dream Crushers and Factories of Debt." *New Labor Forum* 24 (1):31–36. Doi: 10.1177/1095796014562860.

Aragon, Steven R., and Elaine S. Johnson. 2008. "Factors Influencing Completion and Noncompletion of Community College Online Courses." *American Journal of Distance Education* 22 (3):146–58.

Arbaugh, J. Ben. 2001. "How Instructor Immediacy Behaviors Affect Student Satisfaction and Learning in Web-Based Courses." *Business Communication Quarterly* 64 (4):42–54.

Arbaugh, J. Ben, and Raquel Benbunan-Fich. 2005. "Contextual Factors that Influence ALN Effectiveness." In *Learning Together Online: Research on Asynchronous Learning Networks,* edited by Starr Roxanne Hiltz and Ricki Goldman, 123–44. Mahwah, NJ: Lawrence Erlbaum.

Arend, Bridget. 2009. "Encouraging Critical Thinking in Online Threaded Discussions." *Journal of Educators Online* 6 (1):n11.

Arnold, Kimberly E., and Matthew D. Pistilli. 2012. "Course Signals at Purdue:

Using Learning Analytics to Increase Student Success." Proceedings of the 2nd International Conference on Learning Analytics and Knowledge, New York.

Arnsparger, Arleen, and Joanna Drivalas. 2016. "Students Speak about Faculty: What Students Need, What They Want, and What Helps Them Succeed." In *Envisioning the Faculty for the Twenty-First Century: Moving to a Mission-Oriented and Learner-Centered Model,* edited by Adrianna Kezar and Daniel Maxey. New York: Rutgers University Press.

Artino, Anthony, and Andri Ioannou. 2008. "Promoting Academic Motivation and Self-Regulation: Practical Guidelines for Online Iinstructors." Society for Information Technology & Teacher Education International Conference, Las Vegas, NV, March 3, 2009.

Ashong, Carol Y., and Nannette E. Commander. 2012. "Ethnicity, Gender, and Perceptions of Online Learning in Higher Education." *MERLOT Journal of Online Learning and Teaching* 8 (2).

Aslanian, Carol B., and David L. Clinefelter. 2012. *Online College Students 2012: Comprehensive Data on Demands and Preferences.* Louisville, KY: The Learning House, Inc.

Astleitner, Hermann. 2000. "A Review of Motivational and Emotional Strategies to Reduce Dropout in Web-Based Distance Education." In *Neue Medien in Unterricht, Aus-und Weiterbildung,* edited by Detlev Leutner, 17–24. Münster: Waxmann.

ASU Online. 2020. "A Look at Today's College Student: The Growth of Online Learning." Accessed September 4, 2020. https://asuonline.asu.edu/newsroom /online-learning-tips/look-todays-college-student-growth-online-learning/.

Atchley, Thomas Wayne, Gary Wingenbach, and Cynthia Akers. 2013. "Comparison of Course Completion and Student Performance through Online and Traditional Courses." *International Review of Research in Open and Distributed Learning* 14 (4).

Aversa, Elizabeth, and Steven MacCall. 2013. "Profiles in Retention Part 1: Design Characteristics of a Graduate Synchronous Online Program." *Journal of Education for Library and Information Science* 54 (2):147–61.

Bacchini, Fabio, and Ludovica Lorusso. 2019. "Race, Again: How Face Recognition Technology Reinforces Racial Discrimination." *Journal of Information, Communication and Ethics in Society* 17 (3).

Bacow, Lawrence S., William G. Bowen, Kevin M. Guthrie, Matthew P. Long, and Kelly A. Lack. 2012. *Barriers to Adoption of Online Learning Systems in US Higher Education.* New York: Ithaka S+R Consulting.

Bahr, Peter Riley. 2010. "Making Sense of Disparities in Mathematics Remediation: What Is the Role of Student Retention?" *Journal of College Student Retention: Research, Theory & Practice* 12 (1):25–49. Doi: 10.2190 /CS.12.1.c.

Bailey, Allison, Nithya Vaduganathan, Tyce Henry, Renee Laverdiere, and Lou Pugliese. 2018. *Making Digital Learning Work—Success Strategies from Six Leading Universities and Community Colleges.* Boston, MA: Boston Consulting Group.

Bailey, Thomas, Dong Wook Jeong, and Sung-Woo Cho. 2010. "Referral,

Enrollment, and Completion in Developmental Education Sequences in Community Colleges." *Economics of Education Review* 29 (2):255–70.

Baker, Credence. 2010. "The Impact of Instructor Immediacy and Presence for Online Student Affective Learning, Cognition, and Motivation." *Journal of Educators Online* 7 (1):1–30.

Baker, Rachel, Thomas Dee, Brent Evans, and June John. 2018. "Bias in Online Classes: Evidence from a Field Experiment." *Stanford Center for Education Policy Analysis*. CEPA Working Paper No. 18–03.

Baker, Rachel, Brent Evans, Qiujie Li, and Bianca Cung. 2019. "Does Inducing Students to Schedule Lecture Watching in Online Classes Improve Their Academic Performance? An Experimental Analysis of a Time Management Intervention." *Research in Higher Education* 60 (4):521–52. Doi: 10.1007 /s11162-018-9521-3.

Bali, Maha, Maureen Crawford, Rhonda Jessen, Paul Signorelli, and Mia Zamora. 2015. "What Makes a cMOOC Community Endure? Multiple Participant Perspectives from Diverse cMOOCs." *Educational Media International* 52 (2):100–115. Doi: 10.1080/09523987.2015.1053290.

Bambara, Cynthia S., Clifford P. Harbour, Timothy Gray Davies, and Susan Athey. 2009. "Delicate Engagement: The Lived Experience of Community College Students Enrolled in High-Risk Online Courses." *Community College Review* 36 (3):219–38.

Barnett, Elisabeth. 2018. "Faculty Leadership and Student Persistence—A Story From Oakton Community College." Community College Research Center. Last modified May 9, 2018. https://ccrc.tc.columbia.edu/easyblog/faculty -leadership-student-persistence-oakton-community-college.html.

Bassett, Penny. 2011. "How Do Students View Asynchronous Online Discussions as a Learning Experience?" *Interdisciplinary Journal of E-Learning and Learning Objects* 7 (1):69–79.

Bawa, Papia. 2016. "Retention in Online Courses: Exploring Issues and Solutions—A Literature Review." *SAGE Open* 6 (1):1–11. Doi: 10.1177 /2158244015621777.

Bayne, Sian, Peter Evans, Rory Ewins, Jeremy Knox, and James Lamb. 2020. *The Manifesto for Teaching Online.* Cambridge, MA: MIT Press.

Beer, Colin, and Celeste Lawson. 2017. "The Problem of Student Attrition in Higher Education: An Alternative Perspective." *Journal of Further and Higher Education* 41 (6):773–84.

Bell, Paul D., and Duane Akroyd. 2006. "Can Factors Related to Self-Regulated Learning Predict Learning Achievement in Undergraduate Asynchronous Web-Based Courses?" *International Journal of Instructional Technology and Distance Learning* 3 (10):5–16.

Bennett, Doris, Cynthia McCarty, and Shawn Carter. 2019. "Teaching Graduate Economics: Online vs. Traditional Classroom Instruction." *Journal for Economic Educators* 11 (2):1–11.

Bennett, Sue, and Lori Lockyer. 2004. "Becoming an Online Teacher: Adapting to a Changed Environment for Teaching and Learning in Higher Education." *Educational Media International* 41 (3):231–48.

Benson, Trisha A., Andrew L. Cohen, and William Buskist. 2005. "Rapport: Its

Relation to Student Attitudes and Behaviors toward Teachers and Classes."
Teaching of Psychology 32 (4):237–70.

Bernacki, Matthew L., Lucie Vosicka, and Jenifer C. Utz. 2020. "Can a Brief, Digital Skill Training Intervention Help Undergraduates 'Learn to Learn' and Improve Their STEM Achievement?" *Journal of Educational Psychology* 112 (4):765–81. Doi: 10.1037/edu0000405.

Bernard, Robert M., Philip C. Abrami, Eugene Borokhovski, C. Anne Wade, Rana M. Tamim, Michael A. Surkes, and Edward Clement Bethel. 2009. "A Meta-Analysis of Three Types of Interaction Treatments in Distance Education." *Review of Educational Research* 79 (3):1243–89. Doi: 10.3102 /0034654309333844.

Berzenski, Sara R. 2019. "The When and Who of Graduation and Dropout Predictors: A Moderated Hazard Analysis." *Journal of College Student Retention: Research, Theory & Practice.* Doi: 10.1177/1521025119875104.

Bettinger, Eric P., and Bridget Terry Long. 2010. "Does Cheaper Mean Better? The Impact of Using Adjunct Instructors on Student Outcomes." *Review of Economics and Statistics* 92 (3):598–613.

Blackner, Deborah M. 2000. "Prediction of Community College Students' Success in Developmental Math with Traditional Classroom, Computer-Based On-Campus and Computer-Based at a Distance Instruction Using Locus of Control, Math Anxiety and Learning Style." PhD diss., University of North Texas.

Blankstein, Melissa, Jennifer K. Frederick, and Christine Wolff-Eisenberg. 2020. *Student Experiences during the Pandemic Pivot.* New York: Ithaka S+R Consulting.

Blocher, J. Michael, L. Sujo De Montes, Elizabeth M. Willis, and Gary Tucker. 2002. "Online Learning: Examining the Successful Student Profile." *Journal of Interactive Online Learning* 1 (2):1–12.

Blum, Susan D., ed. 2020. *Ungrading: Why Rating Students Undermines Learning (and What to Do Instead).* Morgantown: West Virginia University Press.

Bolliger, Doris U., and Oksana Wasilik. 2009. "Factors Influencing Faculty Satisfaction with Online Teaching and Learning in Higher Education." *Distance Education* 30 (1):103–16.

Bond, Niya. 2019. "Pedagogies of Online Welcome." *Faculty Focus,* December 18. https://www.facultyfocus.com/articles/online-education/pedagogies -of-welcome/?st=FFdaily;s=FF191218;utm_term=FF191218&utm_source= ActiveCampaign&utm_medium=email&utm_content=Pedagogies+of+ Online+Welcome&utm_campaign=FF191218.

Bonnel, Wanda, Charlene Ludwig, and Janice Smith. 2008. "Providing Feedback in Online Courses: What Do Students Want? How Do We Do That?" *Annual Review of Nursing Education* 6:205.

Boston, Wally, Sebastián R. Díaz, Angela M. Gibson, Phil Ice, Jennifer Richardson, and Karen Swan. 2009. "An Exploration of the Relationship between Indicators of the Community of Inquiry Framework and Retention in Online Programs." *Journal of Asynchronous Learning Networks* 13 (3):67–83.

———. 2014. "An Exploration of the Relationship between Indicators of the Community of Inquiry Framework and Retention in Online Programs." *Journal of Asynchronous Learning Networks* 13 (3):67–83.

Boston, Wally, Phil Ice, and Melissa Burgess. 2012. "Assessing Student Retention in Online Learning Environments: A Longitudinal Study." *Online Journal of Distance Learning Administration* 15 (2):1–6.

Boston, Wally, Phil Ice, and Angela M. Gibson. 2010. "Comprehensive Assessment of Student Retention in Online Learning Environments." *Online Journal of Distance Learning Administration* 14 (1):1593–99.

Botsch, Robert E., and Carol S. Botsch. 2012. "Audiences and Outcomes in Online and Traditional American Government Classes Revisited." *PS: Political Science & Politics* 45 (3):493–500. Doi: 10.1017/S104909651200042X.

Boucher, Ellen. 2016. "It's Time to Ditch Our Deadlines: Why You Should Stop Penalizing Your Students for Submitting Work Late." *Chronicle of Higher Education.* Last modified August 22, 2016. https://o-www-chronicle-com .library.ualr.edu/article/its-time-to-ditch-our-deadlines/.

Bowen, William G., Matthew M. Chingos, Kelly A. Lack, and Thomas I. Nygren. 2014. "Interactive Learning Online at Public Universities: Evidence from a Six-Campus Randomized Trial." *Journal of Policy Analysis and Management* 33 (1):94–111. Doi: https://doi.org/10.1002/pam.21728.

Bowen, William G., Matthew M. Chingos, and Michael S. McPherson. 2009. *Crossing the Finish Line: Completing College at America's Public Universities.* Princeton, NJ: Princeton University Press.

Bowers, James, and Poonam Kumar. 2015. "Students' Perceptions of Teaching and Social Presence: A Comparative Analysis of Face-to-Face and Online Learning Environments." *International Journal of Web-Based Learning and Teaching Technologies* 10 (1):27–44.

Boyette, Marie Adele. 2008. "An Investigation of the Online Learning Environment in Higher Education through the Observations and Perceptions of Students of Color." PhD diss., Adult, Career, and Higher Education, University of South Florida.

Boyington, Briana, and Emma Kerr. 2019. "20 Years of Tuition Growth at National Universities." *US News & World Report,* September 19. https:// www.usnews.com/education/best-colleges/paying-for-college/articles/2017 -09-20/see-20-years-of-tuition-growth-at-national-universities.

Bozarth, Jane, Diane D. Chapman, and Laura LaMonica. 2004. "Preparing for Distance Learning: Designing an Online Student Orientation Course." *Journal of Educational Technology & Society* 7 (1):87–106.

Braxton, John M., Nathaniel J. Bray, and Joseph B. Berger. 2000. "Faculty Teaching Skills and Their Influence on the College Student Departure Process." *Journal of College Student Development* 41 (2):215.

Burbank, Mary D., Don Kauchak, and Alisa J. Bates. 2010. "Book Clubs as Professional Development Opportunities for Preservice Teacher Candidates and Practicing Teachers: An Exploratory Study." *New Educator* 6 (1):56–73.

Burke, Alison. 2011. "Group Work: How to Use Groups Effectively." *Journal of Effective Teaching* 11 (2):87–95.

Bush, Edward C., and Lawson V. Bush. 2010. "Calling Out the Elephant: An Examination of African American Male Achievement in Community Colleges." *Journal of African American Males in Education* 1 (1).

Butcher, Charity, and Timothy Kersey. 2014. "When Winning Is Really Losing:

Teaching Awards and Women Political Science Faculty." *PS: Political Science & Politics* 48 (1):138–41. Doi: 10.1017/S104909651400167X.

Buzzetto-Hollywood, Nicole, Kathy Quinn, Wendy Wang, and Austin Hill. 2019. "Grit in Online Education." *Journal of Education, Society and Behavioural Science* 30 (4):1–11.

Calarco, Jessica McCrory. 2014. "Coached for the Classroom: Parents' Cultural Transmission and Children's Reproduction of Educational Inequalities." *American Sociological Review* 79 (5):1015–37.

———. 2018. *Negotiating Opportunities: How the Middle Class Secures Advantages in School*. New York: Oxford University Press.

———. 2020. *A Field Guide to Grad School: Uncovering the Hidden Curriculum*. Princeton, NJ: Princeton University Press.

Campbell, Nittaya. 2007. "Bringing ESL Students Out of Their Shells: Enhancing Participation Through Online Discussion." *Business Communication Quarterly* 70 (1):37–43. Doi: 10.1177/1080569907070000105.

Cano, Alberto, and John D. Leonard. 2019. "Interpretable Multiview Early Warning System Adapted to Underrepresented Student Populations." *IEEE Transactions on Learning Technologies* 12 (2):198–211. Doi: 10.1109 /TLT.2019.2911079.

Capra, Theresa. 2011. "Online Education: Promise and Problems." *Journal of Online Learning and Teaching* 7 (2):288–293.

Carini, Robert M., George D. Kuh, and Stephen P. Klein. 2006. "Student Engagement and Student Learning: Testing the Linkages." *Research in Higher Education* 47 (1):1–32.

Carnevale, Anthony P., and Jeff Strohl. 2013. *Separate & Unequal: How Higher Education Reinforces the Intergenerational Reproduction of White Racial Privilege*. Georgetown University: Georgetown Public Policy Institute: Center on Education and the Workforce.

Carnevale, Dan. 2000. "'Boot Camp' Helps New Online Students at Boise State U." *Chronicle of Higher Education* 46 (24):A48.

Carr-Chellman, Alison, and Philip Duchastel. 2000. "The Ideal Online Course." *British Journal of Educational Technology* 31 (3):229–41.

Carrell, Scott E., and Michal Kurlaender. 2020. "My Professor Cares: Experimental Evidence on the Role of Faculty Engagement." Working Paper No. 27312. Washington, DC: National Bureau of Economic Research. Doi: 10.3386/w27312.

Carron, Albert V., and Kevin S. Spink. 1993. "Team Building in an Exercise Setting." *Sport Psychologist* 7 (1):8–18.

Cataldi, Emily Forrest, Christopher T. Bennett, and Xianglei Chen. 2018. "First-Generation Students: College Access, Persistence, and Postbachelor's Outcomes." Statistics in Brief. Washington, DC: National Center for Education Statistics.

Cavanaugh, Terence W., and Cathy Cavanaugh. 2008. "Interactive Maps for Community in Online Learning." *Computers in the Schools* 25 (3–4):235–42.

Center for Distributed Learning. 2020a. "Instructional Design Services." University of Central Florida. Accessed July 28, 2020. https://cdl.ucf.edu/services /instructional/instructional-design/.

———. 2020b. "Our Publications." University of Central Florida. Accessed July 28, 2020. https://cdl.ucf.edu/about/cdl/publications/.

Chamberlin, Lisa, and Tracy Parish. 2011. "MOOCs: Massive Open Online Courses or Massive and Often Obtuse Courses?" *Elearn* 2011 (8).

Chambers, Timothy E. 2002. "Internet Course Student Achievement: In Ohio's Two-Year Community and Technical Colleges, Are Online Courses Less Effective Than Traditional Courses?" PhD diss., Bowling Green State University.

Chambliss, Daniel F., and Christopher G. Takacs. 2014. *How College Works.* Cambridge, MA: Harvard University Press.

Chapman, Diane D. 2011. "Contingent and Tenured/Tenure-Track Faculty: Motivations and Incentives to Teach Distance Education Courses." *Online Journal of Distance Learning Administration* 14 (3).

Chatelain, Marcia. 2018. "We Must Help First-Generation Students Master Academe's 'Hidden Curriculum.'" *Chronicle of Higher Education.* Accessed April 23, 2020. https://www.chronicle.com/article/we-must-help-first -generation-students-master-academes-hidden-curriculum/.

Chatteinier, Nancy. 2016. "Self-Regulated Learning and Success in an Online Developmental Math Community College Course." PhD diss., Education, Northcentral University.

Chen, Pu-Shih Daniel, Amber D. Lambert, and Kevin R. Guidry. 2010. "Engaging Online Learners: The Impact of Web-Based Learning Technology on College Student Engagement." *Computers & Education* 54 (4):1222–32. Doi: https://doi.org/10.1016/j.compedu.2009.11.008.

Chickering, Arthur W., and Zelda F. Gamson. 1987. "Seven Principles for Good Practice in Undergraduate Education." *AAHE Bulletin,* March:3–7.

Chingos, Matthew M., Rebecca J. Griffiths, Christine Mulhern, and Richard R. Spies. 2017. "Interactive Online Learning on Campus: Comparing Students' Outcomes in Hybrid and Traditional Courses in the University System of Maryland." *Journal of Higher Education* 88 (2):210–33.

Cho, Moon-Heum, and B. Joon Kim. 2013. "Students' Self-Regulation for Interaction with Others in Online Learning Environments." *The Internet and Higher Education* 17:69–75.

Choy, Susan P. 2001. "Students Whose Parents Did Not Go to College: Postsecondary Access, Persistence, and Attainment." *The Condition of Education:* xviii–xliii. U.S. Department of Education. Washington, DC: National Center for Education Statistics.

Church, Thomas V., and James E. Prieger. 2016. "An Update on Mobile Broadband Availability in the United States." In *Encyclopedia of E-Commerce Development, Implementation, and Management,* edited by In Lee, 1518–31. Hershey, PA: IGI Global.

Clark, Ashley. 2020. "Today's Students Need Access to Affordable and Reliable Broadband Services." Last modified May 11, 2020. https://medium.com /higher-learning-advocates/todays-students-need-access-to-affordable-and -reliable-broadband-services-f9c39068a96b.

Classes & Careers. 2011. "Student Demographics." Last modified May 26,

2011. https://blog.classesandcareers.com/education/infographics/student
-demographics-infographic/.

Clay, Melanie N., Stacey Rowland, and Abbot Packard. 2008. "Improving
Undergraduate Online Retention through Gated Advisement and Redundant
Communication." *Journal of College Student Retention: Research, Theory &
Practice* 10 (1):93–102. Doi: 10.2190/CS.10.1.g.

Clinefelter, D. L., and C. B. Aslanian. 2016. *Online College Students: Comprehensive Data on Demands and Preferences.* Louisville, KY: The Learning
House.

Cluskey Jr., G. R., Craig R. Ehlen, and Mitchell H. Raiborn. 2011. "Thwarting
Online Exam Cheating without Proctor Supervision." *Journal of Academic
and Business Ethics* 4 (1).

Cochran, Justin D., Stacy M. Campbell, Hope M. Baker, and Elke M. Leeds.
2014. "The Role of Student Characteristics in Predicting Retention in Online
Courses." *Research in Higher Education* 55 (1):27–48.

Cokley, Kevin. 2000. "Perceived Faculty Encouragement and Its Influence on
College Students." *Journal of College Student Development* 31 (3):348–52.

Cole, Darnell. 2007. "Do Interracial Interactions Matter? An Examination of
Student-Faculty Contact and Intellectual Self-Concept." *Journal of Higher
Education* 78 (3):249–81. Doi: 10.1080/00221546.2007.11772316.

College Board. 2019. "Trends in College Pricing 2019." In *Trends in Higher
Education Series.* New York: College Board.

Collier, Peter J., and David L. Morgan. 2008. "'Is That Paper Really Due
Today?': Differences in First-Generation and Traditional College Students'
Understandings of Faculty Expectations." *Higher Education* 55 (4):425–46.

Contreras, Frances, and Gilbert J. Contreras. 2015. "Raising the Bar for Hispanic Serving Institutions: An Analysis of College Completion and Success
Rates." *Journal of Hispanic Higher Education* 14 (2):151–70. Doi: 10.1177
/1538192715572892.

Cooper, Katelyn M., Brian Haney, Anna Krieg, and Sara E. Brownell. 2017.
"What's in a Name? The Importance of Students Perceiving that an Instruc-
tor Knows Their Names in a High-Enrollment Biology Classroom." *CBE—
Life Sciences Education* 16 (1):ar8.

Costa, Karen. 2020. *99 Tips for Creating Simple and Sustainable Educational
Videos: A Guide for Online Teachers and Flipped Classes.* Sterling, VA:
Stylus Publishing.

Cottom, Tressie McMillan. 2017. *Lower Ed: The Troubling Rise of For-Profit
Colleges in the New Economy.* New York: The New Press.

Cox, Rebecca. 2005. "Online Education as Institutional Myth: Rituals and Real-
ities at Community Colleges." *Teachers College Record* 107 (8):1754–87.

———. 2006. "Virtual Access." In *Defending the Community College Equity
Agenda,* edited by Thomas Bailey and Vanessa Smith Morest, 110–31. Baltimore, MD: Johns Hopkins University Press.

———. 2009. *The College Fear Factor.* Cambridge, MA: Harvard University
Press.

Craig, Ryan. 2019. "Prelude to a Pricing Paradigm Shift." *Inside Higher Ed.*

Last modified October 4, 2019. https://www.insidehighered.com/digital
-learning/views/2019/10/04/why-hasn%E2%80%99t-tuition-online
-education-tumbled-and-what-will-it-take.

Creasey, Gary, Patricia Jarvis, and Daniel Gadke. 2009. "Student Attachment
Stances, Instructor Immediacy, and Student-Instructor Relationships as Pre-
dictors of Achievement Expectancies in College Students." *Journal of College
Student Development* 50 (4):353–72.

Crook, Anne, Alice Mauchline, Stephen Maw, Clare Lawson, Robyn Drink-
water, Karsten Lundqvist, Paul Orsmond, Stephen Gomez, and Julian Park.
2012. "The Use of Video Technology for Providing Feedback to Students:
Can It Enhance the Feedback Experience for Staff and Students?" *Computers
& Education* 58 (1):386–96. Doi: https://doi.org/10.1016/j.compedu
.2011.08.025.

Crosling, Glenda, Margaret Heagney, and Liz Thomas. 2009. "Improving Student Retention in Higher Education: Improving Teaching and Learning."
Australian Universities' Review 51 (2):9.

Crosson, Patricia H. 1991. "Environmental Influences on Minority Degree
Attainment." *Equity & Excellence in Education* 25 (2–4):5–15.

Cuba, Lee J. 2016. *Practice for Life*. Cambridge, MA: Harvard University Press.

Czaplewski, Andrew J. 2009. "Computer-Assisted Grading Rubrics: Automating
the Process of Providing Comments and Student Feedback." *Marketing Education Review* 19 (1):29–36. Doi: 10.1080/10528008.2009.11489057.

Daft, Richard L., and Robert H. Lengel. 1986. "Organizational Information
Requirements, Media Richness and Structural Design." *Management Science*
32 (5):554–71.

Daigle, Delton T., and Aaron Stuvland. 2020. "Teaching Political Science
Research Methods across Delivery Modalities: Comparing Outcomes
between Face-to-Face and Distance-Hybrid Courses." *Journal of Political
Science Education* (May 13):1–23. Doi: 10.1080/15512169.2020.1760105.

Daniel, John. 2012. "Making Sense of MOOCs: Musings in a Maze of Myth,
Paradox and Possibility." *Journal of Interactive Media in Education* 2012 (3).

Darby, Flower. 2020. "How to Recover the Joy of Teaching after an Online
Pivot." *Chronicle of Higher Education,* March 24. https://o-www-chronicle
-com.library.ualr.edu/article/how-to-recover-the-joy-of-teaching-after-an
-online-pivot/.

Darby, Flower, and James M. Lang. 2019. *Small Teaching Online: Applying
Learning Science in Online Classes*. San Francisco, CA: Wiley.

Davidson, Cathy. 2020. "Cameras Optional, Please! Remembering Student
Lives as We Plan Our Online Syllabus." HASTAC: Changing the Way We
Teach + Learn. Last modified July 22, 2020. https://www.hastac.org/blogs
/cathy-davidson/2020/07/22/cameras-optional-please-remembering
-student-lives-we-plan-our-online.

Davidson, Cody, and Kristin Wilson. 2013. "Reassessing Tinto's Concepts of
Social and Academic Integration in Student Retention." *Journal of College Student Retention: Research, Theory & Practice* 15 (3):329–46. Doi:
10.2190/CS.15.3.b.

Daymont, Thomas, Gary Blau, and Deborah Campbell. 2011. "Deciding between Traditional and Online Formats: Exploring the Role of Learning Advantages, Flexibility, and Compensatory Adaptation." *Journal of Behavioral and Applied Management* 12 (2):156–75.

De Castro e Lima Baesse, Deborah, Alexandra Monteiro Grisolia, and Ana Emilia Figueiredo de Oliveira. 2016. "Pedagogical Monitoring as a Tool to Reduce Dropout in Distance Learning in Family Health." *BMC Medical Education* 16 (1):213. Doi: 10.1186/s12909-016-0735-9.

De los Santos, Alfredo G., and Farah Sutton. 2012. "Swirling Students: Articulation between a Major Community College District and a State-Supported Research University." *Community College Journal of Research and Practice* 36 (12):967–81. Doi: 10.1080/10668920903182641.

Delaney, Anne Marie. 2008. "Why Faculty-Student Interaction Matters in the First Year Experience." *Tertiary Education and Management* 14 (3):227–41. Doi: 10.1080/13583880802228224.

Deming, David J., Claudia Goldin, and Lawrence F. Katz. 2012. "The For-Profit Postsecondary School Sector: Nimble Critters or Agile Predators?" *Journal of Economic Perspectives* 26 (1):139–64. Doi: 10.1257/jep.26.1.139.

Deming, David J., Claudia Goldin, Lawrence F. Katz, and Noam Yuchtman. 2015. "Can Online Learning Bend the Higher Education Cost Curve?" *American Economic Review* 105 (5):496–501.

DeNavas-Walt, Carmen, Robert W. Cleveland, and Marc I. Roemer. 2001. "Money Income in the United States: 2000." In *Consumer Population Reports*. Washington, DC: US Census Bureau.

Dhilla, Sarah J. 2017. "The Role of Online Faculty in Supporting Successful Online Learning Enterprises: A Literature Review." *Higher Education Politics & Economics* 3 (1):3.

Diaz, David P. 2002. "Online Drop Rates Revisited." *Technology Source* 3 (May/June).

Diaz, David P., and Ryan B. Cartnal. 1999. "Students' Learning Styles in Two Classes: Online Distance Learning and Equivalent On-Campus." *College Teaching* 47 (4):130–35.

Diep, Francie. 2020. "'I Was Fed Up': How #BlackInTheIvory Got Started, and What Its Founders Want to See Next." *Chronicle of Higher Education*, June 9. https://o-www-chronicle-com.library.ualr.edu/article/i-was-fed-up-how-blackintheivory-got-started-and-what-its-founders-want-to-see-next.

Dowd, Alicia C., Misty Sawatzky, and Randi Korn. 2011. "Theoretical Foundations and a Research Agenda to Validate Measures of Intercultural Effort." *Review of Higher Education* 35 (1):17–44.

Duckworth, Angela L., Christopher Peterson, Michael D. Matthews, and Dennis R. Kelly. 2007. "Grit: Perseverance and Passion for Long-Term Goals." *Journal of Personality and Social Psychology* 92 (6):1087.

Duncan, Heather E., and John Barnett. 2009. "Learning to Teach Online: What Works for Pre-Service Teachers." *Journal of Educational Computing Research* 40 (3):357–76.

Dunlap, Joanna C., and Patrick R. Lowenthal. 2009. "Tweeting the Night Away: Using Twitter to Enhance Social." *Journal of Information Systems Education* 20 (2):129–35.

Dutton, John, Marilyn Dutton, and Jo Perry. 2001. "Do Online Students Perform as Well as Lecture Students?" *Journal of Engineering Education* 90 (1):131–36.

Dykman, Charlene A., and Charles K. Davis. 2008. "Part One: The Shift toward Online Education." *Journal of Information Systems Education* 19 (1).

Dziuban, Charles, Patsy Moskal, Thomas Cavanagh, and Andre Watts. 2012. "Analytics That Inform the University: Using Data You Already Have." *Journal of Asynchronous Learning Networks* 16 (3):21–38.

Eby, Lillian T., Tammy D. Allen, Sarah C. Evans, Thomas Ng, and David L. DuBois. 2008. "Does Mentoring Matter? A Multidisciplinary Meta-analysis Comparing Mentored and Non-mentored Individuals." *Journal of Vocational Behavior* 72 (2):254–67. Doi: https://doi.org/10.1016/j.jvb.2007.04.005.

Ehrenberg, Ronald G., and Liang Zhang. 2005. "Do Tenured and Tenure-Track Faculty Matter?" *Journal of Human Resources* 40 (3):647–59.

Ehrman, Madeline. 1990. "Psychology: Psychological Factors and Distance Education." *American Journal of Distance Education* 4 (1):10–24.

Eisenberg, Eli, and Tony Dowsett. 1990. "Student Drop-out from a Distance Education Project Course: A New Method of Analysis." *Distance Education* 11 (2):231–53.

Eliasquevici, Marianne Kogut, Marcos César da Rocha Seruffo, and Sônia Nazaré Fernandes Resque. 2017. "Persistence in Distance Education: A Study Case Using Bayesian Network to Understand Retention." *International Journal of Distance Education Technologies (IJDET)* 15 (4):61–78. Doi: 10.4018 /IJDET.2017100104.

Elliott, Jacquelyn D., and Rodney Parks. 2018. "Latino Students and Degree Attainment." *College and University* 93 (1):10–18.

Engle, Jennifer, and Vincent Tinto. 2008. *Moving beyond Access: College Success for Low-Income, First-Generation Students*. Washington, DC: Pell Institute for the Study of Opportunity in Higher Education.

Eom, Sean B., H. Joseph Wen, and Nicholas Ashill. 2006. "The Determinants of Students' Perceived Learning Outcomes and Satisfaction in University Online Education: An Empirical Investigation." *Decision Sciences Journal of Innovative Education* 4 (2):215–35.

Erichsen, Elizabeth A., and Doris U. Bolliger. 2011. "Towards Understanding International Graduate Student Isolation in Traditional and Online Environments." *Educational Technology Research and Development* 59 (3):309–26.

Espinosa, Lorelle, Robert Kelchen, and Morgan Taylor. 2018. *Minority Serving Institutions as Engines of Upward Mobility*. Washington, DC: American Council on Education.

Espinosa, Lorelle L., Jonathan M. Turk, Morgan Taylor, and Hollie M. Chessman. 2019. *Race and Ethnicity in Higher Education: A Status Report*. Washington, DC: American Council on Education.

Eyler, Joshua. 2018. *How Humans Learn: The Science and Stories behind Effective College Teaching*. Morgantown: West Virginia University Press.

Fagan-Wilen, Ruth, David W. Springer, Bob Ambrosino, and Barbara W. White. 2006. "The Support of Adjunct Faculty: An Academic Imperative." *Social Work Education* 25 (1):39–51.

Felten, Peter, and Leo M. Lambert. 2020. *Relationship-Rich Education: How Human Connections Drive Success in College.* Baltimore, MD: Johns Hopkins University Press.

Ferguson, Christopher J., and Moritz Heene. 2012. "A Vast Graveyard of Undead Theories: Publication Bias and Psychological Science's Aversion to the Null." *Perspectives on Psychological Science* 7 (6):555–61.

Fetzner, Marie. 2013. "What Do Unsuccessful Online Students Want Us to Know?" *Journal of Asynchronous Learning Networks* 17 (1):13–27.

Figlio, David N., Mark Rush, and Lu Yin. 2013. "Is It Live or Is It Internet? Experimental Estimates of the Effects of Online Instruction on Student Learning." *Journal of Labor Economics* 31 (4):763–84.

Figlio, David N., Morton O. Schapiro, and Kevin B. Soter. 2015. "Are Tenure Track Professors Better Teachers?" *Review of Economics and Statistics* 97 (4):715–24.

Flaherty, Colleen. 2020a. "Big Proctor." *Inside Higher Ed,* May 11, 2020. https://www.insidehighered.com/news/2020/05/11/online-proctoring-surging -during-covid-19.

———. 2020b. "Zoom Boom." *Inside Higher Ed,* April 29. Accessed July 31, 2020. https://www.insidehighered.com/news/2020/04/29/synchronous -instruction-hot-right-now-it-sustainable.

———. 2020c. " 'Never Waste a Good Pandemic.' " *Inside Higher Ed,* December 4. Accessed December 11, 2020. https://www.insidehighered.com/news /2020 /12/04/boulder-arts-and-sciences-dean-wants-build-back-faculty-post -pandemic-one-non-tenure.

Flannery, Daniele D. 1995. "Adult Education and the Politics of the Theoretical Text." In *Critical Multiculturalism: Uncommon Voices in a Common Struggle,* edited by B. Kanpol and P. McLaren, 149–63. Westport, CT: Bergin and Garvey.

Folorunso, Orimolade Joseph, Oronti Iyabosola Busola, and Olopade Abdullah Oluwatosin. 2019. "A Control System for Assessing Commercial Face Recognition Software for Racial Bias." *International Journal of Computer Applications* 177 (28).

Fox, K., G. Bryant, N. Srinivasan, N. Lin, and A Nguyen. 2020. *Time for Class— COVID-19 Edition Part 2: Planning for a Fall Like No Other.* Boston, MA: Tyton Partners.

Franklin, Mitchell. 2015. "Keys to Success in the Online Accounting Classroom to Maximize Student Retention." *Journal of Higher Education Theory and Practice* 15 (5):36.

Frankola, Karen. 2001. "Why Online Learners Drop Out." *Workforce* 80 (10):52–61.

Frisby, Brandi N., and Matthew M. Martin. 2010. "Instructor-Student and Student-Student Rapport in the Classroom." *Communication Education* 59 (2):146–64.

Frisby, Brandi N., and Scott A. Myers. 2008. "The Relationships among Perceived Instructor Rapport, Student Participation, and Student Learning Outcomes." *Texas Speech Communication Journal* 33 (1).

Fry, Richard, and Anthony Cilluffo. 2019. *A Rising Share of Undergraduates*

Are from Poor Families, Especially at Less Selective Colleges. Washington, DC: Pew Research Center.

Frydenberg, Jia. 2007. "Persistence in University Continuing Education Online Classes." *International Review of Research in Open and Distributed Learning* 8 (3):1–15.

Gallien, Tara, and Jody Oomen-Early. 2008. "Personalized versus Collective Instructor Feedback in the Online Courseroom: Does Type of Feedback Affect Student Satisfaction, Academic Performance and Perceived Connectedness with the Instructor?" *International Journal on E-Learning* 7 (3):463–76.

Gallup-Purdue Index Report. 2014. *Great Jobs, Great Lives: A Study of More than 30,000 College Graduates across the US.* Gallup, Purdue University, Lumina Foundation.

Gannon, Kevin M. 2018. "How to Create a Syllabus." *Chronicle of Higher Education.* September 12, 2018. https://www.chronicle.com/article/how-to-create -a-syllabus/.

———. 2020. *Radical Hope: A Teaching Manifesto.* Morgantown: West Virginia University Press.

Garrison, D. Randy, Terry Anderson, and Walter Archer. 1999. "Critical Inquiry in a Text-Based Environment: Computer Conferencing in Higher Education." *The Internet and Higher Education* 2 (2–3):87–105.

Garrison, D. Randy, and Marti Cleveland-Innes. 2004. "Critical Factors in Student Satisfaction and Success: Facilitating Student Role Adjustment in Online Communities of Inquiry." In *Elements of Quality Online Education: Into the Mainstream*, edited by J. Bourne, J. C. J. Bourne, and J. C. Moore. Needham, MA: The Sloan Consortium.

Gaytan, Jorge. 2015. "Comparing Faculty and Student Perceptions Regarding Factors that Affect Student Retention in Online Education." *American Journal of Distance Education* 29 (1):56–66. Doi: 10.1080/08923647.2015 .994365.

Gering, Carol S., Dani K. Sheppard, Barbara L. Adams, Susan L. Renes, and Allan A. Morotti. 2018. "Strengths-Based Analysis of Student Success in Online Courses." *Online Learning* 22 (3):55–85.

Gierdowski, Dana C. 2019. *ECAR Study of Community College Students and Information Technology, 2019.* Research Report. Louisville, CO: ECAR, May 2019. https://tacc.org/sites/default/files/documents/2019–06/2018 commcollss.pdf.

Gilmore, Melanie, and Evadna M. Lyons. 2012. "Nursing 911: An Orientation Program to Improve Retention of Online RN-BSN Students." *Nursing Education Perspectives* 33 (1):45–47.

Glazier, Rebecca A. 2016. "Building Rapport to Improve Retention and Success in Online Classes." *Journal of Political Science Education* 12 (4):437–56.

———. 2020. "Making Human Connections in Online Teaching." *PS: Political Science & Politics:*7–8. Doi: 10.1017/S1049096520001535.

Glazier, Rebecca A., Kerstin Hamann, Philip H. Pollock, and Bruce M. Wilson. 2019a. "Age, Gender, and Student Success: Mixing Face-to-Face and Online Courses in Political Science." *Journal of Political Science Education.* 16:2, 142–57. Doi: 10.1080/15512169.2018.1515636.

————2019b. "What Drives Student Success? Assessing the Combined Effect of Transfer Students and Online Courses." *Teaching in Higher Education,* published online November 4, 2019. https://www.tandfonline.com/doi/abs /10.1080/13562517.2019.1686701.

Glazier, Rebecca A., and Heidi Skurat Harris. 2020. "Common Traits of the Best Online and Face-to-Face Classes: Evidence from Student Surveys." American Political Science Association Teaching and Learning Conference, Albuquerque, New Mexico, February 7–9.

————. 2021. "How Teaching with Rapport Can Improve Online Student Success and Retention: Data from Two Empirical Studies." *Quarterly Review of Distance Education,* 21(4).

Goldrick-Rab, Sara. 2016. *Paying the Price: College Costs, Financial Aid, and the Betrayal of the American Dream.* Chicago, IL: University of Chicago Press.

————. 2020. "Beyond the Food Pantry: When It Comes to Caring about Your Students, a Little Can Go a Long Way." The Hope Center: Hope4College. https://hope4college.com/wp-content/uploads/2020/10/BFP_MyProfessor Cares.pdf.

Goldrick-Rab, Sara, Christine Baker-Smith, Vanessa Coca, Elizabeth Looker, and Tiffani Williams. 2019. *College and University Basic Needs Insecurity: A National #RealCollege Survey Report.* Philadelphia, PA: The Hope Center, Temple University.

Gonzales, Amy L., Jessica McCrory Calarco, and Teresa Lynch. 2020. "Technology Problems and Student Achievement Gaps: A Validation and Extension of the Technology Maintenance Construct." *Communication Research* 47 (5):750–70. Doi: 10.1177/0093650218796366.

Goodman, Joshua, Julia Melkers, and Amanda Pallais. 2019. "Can Online Delivery Increase Access to Education?" *Journal of Labor Economics* 37 (1):1–34.

Grajek, Susan. 2020. "EDUCAUSE COVID-19 QuickPoll Results: Grading and Proctoring." *EDUCAUSE Review,* April 10, 2020. https://er.educause .edu/blogs/2020/4/educause-covid-19-quickpoll-results-grading-and -proctoring#fn1.

Granitz, Neil A., Stephen K. Koernig, and Katrin R. Harich. 2009. "Now It's Personal: Antecedents and Outcomes of Rapport between Business Faculty and Their Students." *Journal of Marketing Education* 31 (1):52–65.

Graunke, Steven S., and Sherry A. Woosley. 2005. "An Exploration of the Factors that Affect the Academic Success of College Sophomores." *College Student Journal* 39 (2).

Grawe, Nathan D. 2018. *Demographics and the Demand for Higher Education.* Baltimore, MD: John Hopkins University Press.

Greene, Thomas G., C. Nathan Marti, and Kay McClenney. 2008. "The Effort-Outcome Gap: Differences for African American and Hispanic Community College Students in Student Engagement and Academic Achievement." *Journal of Higher Education* 79 (5):513–39.

Guglielmino, Lucy M., and Paul J. Guglielmino. 2003. "Identifying Learners Who Are Ready for E-Learning and Supporting Their Success." In *Preparing*

Learners for E-Learning, edited by G. Piskurich, 18–33. San Francisco, CA: Jossey-Bass.

Gunawardena, Charlotte N., and Frank J. Zittle. 1997. "Social Presence as a Predictor of Satisfaction within a Computer-Mediated Conferencing Environment." *American Journal of Distance Education* 11 (3):8–26.

Gustafson, Patricia, and Donna Gibbs. 2000. "Guiding or Hiding? The Role of the Facilitator in Online Teaching and Learning." *Teaching Education* 11 (2):195–210. Doi: 10.1080/713698967.

Gütl, Christian, Rocael Hernández Rizzardini, Vanessa Chang, and Miguel Morales. 2014. "Attrition in MOOC: Lessons Learned from Drop-out Students." International Workshop on Learning Technology for Education in Cloud, Santiago, Chile, September 2–5, 2014.

Guzman, Gloria G. 2019. "Household Income: 2018." In *American Community Survey Briefs*. Washington, DC: United States Census Bureau.

Haber, Jennifer, and Michael Mills. 2008. "Perceptions of Barriers Concerning Effective Online Teaching and Policies: Florida Community College Faculty." *Community College Journal of Research and Practice* 32 (4–6):266–83.

Hachey, Alyse C., Claire W. Wladis, and Katherine M. Conway. 2013. "Balancing Retention and Access in Online Courses: Restricting Enrollment . . . Is It Worth the Cost?" *Journal of College Student Retention: Research, Theory & Practice* 15 (1):9–36. Doi: 10.2190/CS.15.1.b.

Hagedorn, Linda Serra. 2012. "How to Define Retention: A New Look at an Old Problem." In *College Student Retention: Formula for Student Success*, edited by Alexander W. Astin, Joseph B. Berger, Erin W. Bibo, Kurt R. Burkum, Alberto F. Cabrera, Gloria Crisp, Ann Gansemer-Topf, Linda Serra Hagedorn, Steven M. LaNasa, and Susan Lyons, 81–100. Lanham, MD: Rowman & Littlefield Publishers.

Hamann, Kerstin, Rebecca A. Glazier, Bruce M. Wilson, and Philip H. Pollock. 2020. "Online Teaching, Student Success, and Retention in Political Science Courses." *European Political Science*, published online July 30, 2020. Doi: 10.1057/s41304-020-00282-x.

Hammond, Danielle E., and Candice Shoemaker. 2014. "Are there Differences in Academic and Social Integration of College of Agriculture Master's Students in Campus Based, Online and Mixed Programs?" *NACTA Journal* 58 (3):180.

Hannans, Jaime, Jill Leafstedt, and Michelle Pacansky-Brock. 2017. "The Power of Choice: Why Online Classes Matter to Students." Digital Learning in Higher Ed. Last modified July 14, 2017. https://www.edsurge.com/news/2017-07-14-the-power-of-choice-why-online-classes-matter-to-students.

Hannay, Maureen, and Tracy Newvine. 2006. "Perceptions of Distance Learning: A Comparison of Online and Traditional Learning." *Journal of Online Learning and Teaching* 2 (1):1–11.

Harmon, Oskar R., James Lambrinos, and Judy Buffolino. 2010. "Assessment Design and Cheating Risk in Online Instruction." *Online Journal of Distance Learning Administration* 13 (3).

Hart, Carolyn. 2012. "Factors Associated with Student Persistence in an Online

Program of Study: A Review of the Literature." *Journal of Interactive Online Learning* 11 (1).

Harwell, Drew. 2020. "Mass School Closures in the Wake of the Coronavirus Are Driving a New Wave of Student Surveillance." *Washington Post*. April 1, Technology. https://www.washingtonpost.com/technology/2020/04/01/online-proctoring-college-exams-coronavirus/.

Hayes, Niall, and Lucas D. Introna. 2005. "Cultural Values, Plagiarism, and Fairness: When Plagiarism Gets in the Way of Learning." *Ethics & Behavior* 15 (3):213–31.

Herbert, Michael. 2006. "Staying the Course: A Study in Online Student Satisfaction and Retention." *Online Journal of Distance Learning Administration* 9 (4):300–317.

Herring, Mary C., Matthew J. Koehler, and Punya Mishra. 2016. *Handbook of Technological Pedagogical Content Knowledge (TPACK) for Educators.* New York: Taylor & Francis.

Hiltonsmith, Robert. 2017. *Small Loans, Big Risks: Major Consequences for Student Debtors.* New York: Demos.

Hiltz, Starr Roxanne, Eunhee Kim, and Peter Shea. 2007. "Faculty Motivators and De-motivators for Teaching Online: Results of Focus Group Interviews at One University." 2007 40th Annual Hawaii International Conference on System Sciences (HICSS'07).

Hirschheim, Rudy. 2005. "The Internet-Based Education Bandwagon: Look Before You Leap." *Communications of the ACM* 48 (7):97–101.

Hislop, Gregory W., and Heidi J. C. Ellis. 2004. "A Study of Faculty Effort in Online Teaching." *The Internet and Higher Education* 7 (1):15–31. Doi: https://doi.org/10.1016/j.iheduc.2003.10.001.

Hodges, Charles, Stephanie Moore, Barb Lockee, Torrey Trust, and Aaron Bond. 2020. "The Difference between Emergency Remote Teaching and Online Learning." *EDUCAUSE Review.* March 27, 2020. Accessed September 1, 2020. https://er.educause.edu/articles/2020/3/the-difference-between-emergency-remote-teaching-and-online-learning.

Hoeschler, Peter, and Uschi Backes-Gellner. 2019. "Shooting for the Stars and Failing: College Dropout and Self-Esteem." *Economics of Education Working Paper Series* (100).

Hogan, Kelly A., and Viji Sathy. 2020. "8 Ways to Be More Inclusive in Your Zoom Teaching." *Chronicle of Higher Education*, April 7. https://o-www-chronicle-com.library.ualr.edu/article/8-ways-to-be-more-inclusive-in-your-zoom-teaching/.

Hollins, Nancy, and Alan R. Foley. 2013. "The Experiences of Students with Learning Disabilities in a Higher Education Virtual Campus." *Educational Technology Research and Development* 61 (4):607–24.

Holmberg, Borje. 2003. "A Theory of Distance Education Based on Empathy." In *Handbook of Distance Education,* edited by Michael Grahame Moore and William G. Anderson, 79–86. Mahwah, NJ: Lawrence Erlbaum.

Horn, Laura. 1998. *Stopouts or Stayouts? Undergraduates Who Leave College in Their First Year.* Edited by Project Officer: C. Dennis Carroll.

Washington, DC: US Department of Education, National Center for Education Statistics.

Hoyt, Jeff E. 1999. "Remedial Education and Student Attrition." *Community College Review* 27 (2):51–72.

Hrastinski, Stefan. 2006. "Introducing an Informal Synchronous Medium in a Distance Learning Course: How Is Participation Affected?" *The Internet and Higher Education* 9 (2):117–31.

Huang, Qing, Nilupulee Nathawitharana, Kok-Leong Ong, Susan Keller, and Damminda Alahakoon. 2019. "Mind the Gap: From Analytics to Action in Student Retention." In *Applying Business Intelligence Initiatives in Healthcare and Organizational Settings,* edited by Shah J. Miah and William Yeoh, 218–36. Hershey, PA: IGI Global.

Humiston, Jon P., Sarah M. Marshall, Nicole L. Hacker, and Luis M. Cantu. 2020. "Intentionally Creating an Inclusive and Welcoming Climate in the Online Learning Classroom." In *Handbook of Research on Creating Meaningful Experiences in Online Courses,* edited by Lydia Kyei-Blankson, Esther Ntuli, and Joseph Blankson, 173–86. Hershey, PA: IGI Global.

Huntington-Klein, Nick, James Cowan, and Dan Goldhaber. 2017. "Selection into Online Community College Courses and Their Effects on Persistence." *Research in Higher Education* 58 (3):244–69.

Hurt, Joyce. 2008. "The Advantages and Disadvantages of Teaching and Learning On-line." *Delta Kappa Gamma Bulletin* 74 (4).

Hurtado, Sylvia, M. Kevin Eagan, Minh C. Tran, Christopher B. Newman, Mitchell J. Chang, and Paolo Velasco. 2011. "'We Do Science Here': Underrepresented Students' Interactions with Faculty in Different College Contexts." *Journal of Social Issues* 67 (3):553–79. Doi: 10.1111/j.1540-4560 .2011.01714.x.

Huss, John A., and Shannon Eastep. 2013. "The Perceptions of Students toward Online Learning at a Midwestern University: What Are Students Telling Us and What Are We Doing About It?" *ie: inquiry in education* 4 (2):5.

Hutchins, Holly M. 2003. "Instructional Immediacy and the Seven Principles: Strategies for Facilitating Online Courses." *Online Journal of Distance Learning Administration* 6 (3):1–11.

Huun, Kathleen, and Andreas Kummerow. 2018. "Student Presence and Faculty Availability in Fully Online Courses: Is Alignment Requisite?" *Journal of Educators Online* 15 (2):n2.

Ishitani, Terry T. 2006. "Studying Attrition and Degree Completion Behavior among First-Generation College Students in the United States." *Journal of Higher Education* 77 (5):861–85.

Ishiyama, John. 2002. "Does Early Participation in Undergraduate Research Benefit Social Science and Humanities Students?" *College Student Journal* 36 (September).

Ivankova, Nataliya V., and Sheldon L. Stick. 2005. "Collegiality and Community-Building as a Means for Sustaining Student Persistence in the Computer-Mediated Asynchronous Learning Environment." *Online Journal of Distance Learning Administration* 8 (3).

Jaasma, Marjorie A., and Randall J. Koper. 1999. "The Relationship of Student-

Faculty Out-of-Class Communication to Instructor Immediacy and Trust and to Student Motivation." *Communication Education* 48 (1):41–47.

Jack, Anthony Abraham. 2016. "(No) Harm in Asking: Class, Acquired Cultural Capital, and Academic Engagement at an Elite University." *Sociology of Education* 89 (1):1–19.

Jaeger, Audrey J., and M. Kevin Eagan. 2009. "Unintended Consequences: Examining the Effect of Part-Time Faculty Members on Associate's Degree Completion." *Community College Review* 36 (3):167–94.

———. 2011. "Examining Retention and Contingent Faculty Use in a State System of Public Higher Education." *Educational Policy* 25 (3):507–37.

Jaggars, Shanna Smith. 2013. "Online Learning in Community Colleges." In *Handbook of Distance Education,* edited by Michael G. Moore, 612–26. New York: Routledge.

———. 2014. "Choosing between Online and Face-to-Face Courses: Community College Student Voices." *American Journal of Distance Education* 28 (1):27–38.

Jaggars, Shanna Smith, and Thomas R. Bailey. 2010. "Effectiveness of Fully Online Courses for College Students: Response to a Department of Education Meta-Analysis." Teachers College, Columbia University: Community College Research Center. https://academiccommons.columbia.edu/doi /10.7916/D85M63SM.

Jaggars, Shanna Smith, and Di Xu. 2010. "Online Learning in the Virginia Community College System." Community College Research Center, Teachers College: Columbia University. https://ccrc.tc.columbia.edu/publications /online-learning-virginia.html.

———. 2014. "Adaptability to Online Learning: Differences across Types of Students and Academic Subject Areas." *American Journal of Distance Education* 28 (1).

———. 2016. "How Do Online Course Design Features Influence Student Performance?" *Computers & Education* 95 (April):270–84.

James, Scott, Karen Swan, and Cassandra Daston. 2016. "Retention, Progression and the Taking of Online Courses." *Online Learning* 20 (2):75–96.

Jaschik, Scott, and Doug Lederman. 2018. "Faculty Attitudes on Technology." Washington, DC: Gallup and Inside Higher Education. https://www.inside highered.com/booklet/2018-survey-faculty-attitudes-technology.

Jenkins, Davis. 2011. "Redesigning Community Colleges for Completion: Lessons from Research on High-Performance Organizations." In *Community College Research Center Brief, Number 48.* New York, NY: Columbia University.

Johnson, Hans P., and Marisol Cuellar Mejia. 2014. *Online Learning and Student Outcomes in California's Community Colleges.* San Francisco, CA: Public Policy Institute of California.

Johnson, Judith L. 1997. "Commuter College Students: What Factors Determine Who Will Persist and Who Will Drop Out?" *College Student Journal* 31:323–32.

Johnson, W. Brad. 2015. *On Being a Mentor: A Guide for Higher Education Faculty.* New York: Routledge.

Johnson, Wendy, Caroline E. Brett, and Ian J. Deary. 2010. "The Pivotal Role of Education in the Association between Ability and Social Class Attainment: A Look across Three Generations." *Intelligence* 38 (1):55–65.

Jones, Patrice W. Glenn, and Elizabeth K. Davenport. 2018. "Resistance to Change: HBCUs and Online Learning." *Thought & Action* Summer:59.

Journell, Wayne. 2007. "The Inequities of the Digital Divide: Is E-Learning a Solution?" *E-Learning and Digital Media* 4 (2):138–49. Doi: 10.2304/elea .2007.4.2.138.

Juillerat, S. 2000. "Assessing the Expectations and Satisfactions of Sophomores." In *Visible Solutions for Invisible Students: Helping Sophomores Succeed,* edited by L. A. Schreiner and J. Pattengale, 19–29. Columbia: University of South Carolina, National Resource Center for the First-Year Experience and Students in Transition.

Karp, Melinda Mechur. 2011. "Toward a New Understanding of Non-Academic Student Support: Four Mechanisms Encouraging Positive Student Outcomes in the Community College." Community College Research Center, Working Paper No. 28, Assessment of Evidence Series, New York.

Katsinas, Steven, Nathaniel Bray, Linda Hagedorn, Skip Dotherow, and Mike Malley. 2019. "From Vertical to Dynamic Transfer: Recognizing Continuous Swirl in American Higher Education." *Change: The Magazine of Higher Learning* 51 (3):44–51. Doi: 10.1080/00091383.2019.1606607.

Kaupp, Ray. 2012. "Online Penalty: The Impact of Online Instruction on the Latino-White Achievement Gap." *Journal of Applied Research in the Community College* 19 (2):3–11.

Kearsley, Greg. 2002. "Is Online Learning for Everybody?" *Educational Technology* 42 (1):41–44.

Kemp, Nenagh, and Rachel Grieve. 2014. "Face-to-Face or Face-to-Screen? Undergraduates' Opinions and Test Performance in Classroom vs. Online Learning." *Frontiers in Psychology* 5 (1278). Doi: 10.3389/fpsyg.2014 .01278.

Kezar, Adrianna, Tom DePaola, and Daniel T. Scott. 2019. *The Gig Academy: Mapping Labor in the Neoliberal University.* Baltimore, MD: Johns Hopkins University Press.

Kezar, Adrianna, and Daniel Maxey. 2014a. "Faculty Matter: So Why Doesn't Everyone Think So." *Thought & Action* 2014:29–44.

———. 2014b. "Troubling Ethical Lapses: The Treatment of Contingent Faculty." *Change: The Magazine of Higher Learning* 46 (4):34–37. Doi: 10.1080 /00091383.2014.925761.

Kilburn, Ashley, Brandon Kilburn, and Tommy Cates. 2014. "Drivers of Student Retention: System Availability, Privacy, Value and Loyalty in Online Higher Education." *Academy of Educational Leadership Journal* 18 (4):1.

Killion, Cheryl M., Susan Gallagher-Lepak, and Janet Reilly. 2015. "Are Virtual Classrooms Colorblind?" *Journal of Professional Nursing* 31 (5):407–15. Doi: https://doi.org/10.1016/j.profnurs.2015.03.006.

Kinder, Molly, and Martha Ross. 2020. "Reopening America: Low-Wage Workers Have Suffered Badly from COVID-19 So Policymakers Should Focus on Equity." Washington, DC: Brookings Institute. https://www.brookings.edu

/research/reopening-america-low-wage-workers-have-suffered-badly-from
-covid-19-so-policymakers-should-focus-on-equity/.

King, Elliot, and Neil Alperstein. 2014. *Best Practices in Online Program Development: Teaching and Learning in Higher Education.* New York: Routledge.

King-Sears, Margaret. 2009. "Universal Design for Learning: Technology and Pedagogy." *Learning Disability Quarterly* 32 (4):199–201.

Kirp, David L. 2019. "The College Dropout Scandal." *Chronicle Review* 65 (38).

Kleinman, Joan, and Eileen B. Entin. 2002. "Comparison of In-Class and Distance-Learning Students' Performance and Attitudes in an Introductory Computer Science Course." *Journal of Computing Sciences in Colleges* 17 (6):206–19.

Knight, Ethan J. H. 2020. "The Syllabus as Establishing Tone." *Syllabus* 9 (1).

Knowles, Malcolm S. 1990. *The Adult Learner: A Neglected Species.* Houston: Gulf Publishing Company.

Kock, Ned. 2005. "Media Richness or Media Naturalness? The Evolution of Our Biological Communication Apparatus and Its Influence on Our Behavior toward E-Communication Tools." *IEEE Transactions on Professional Communication* 48 (2):117–30. Doi: 10.1109/TPC.2005.849649.

Koehler, Matthew J., Punya Mishra, Kristen Kereluik, Tae Seob Shin, and Charles R. Graham. 2014. "The Technological Pedagogical Content Knowledge Framework." In *Handbook of Research on Educational Communications and Technology,* edited by J. Michael Spector, M. David Merrill, Jan Elen, and M. J. Bishop, 101–11. New York: Springer New York.

Kolodner, Meredith. 2016. "Fewer than One in Seven Community College Students Transfer and Get a Bachelor's Degree—But There Is New Hope." *The Hechinger Report,* January 19, 2019. https://hechingerreport.org/how-often-do-community-college-students-who-get-transfer-get-bachelors-degrees/.

Komarraju, Meera, Sergey Musulkin, and Gargi Bhattacharya. 2010. "Role of Student-Faculty Interactions in Developing College Students' Academic Self-Concept, Motivation, and Achievement." *Journal of College Student Development* 51 (3):332–42.

Kramarae, Cheris. 2001. *The Third Shift: Women Learning Online.* Michigan: American Association of University Women Educational Foundation.

Krieg, John M., and Steven E. Henson. 2016. "The Educational Impact of Online Learning: How Do University Students Perform in Subsequent Courses?" *Education Finance and Policy* 11 (4):426–48. Doi: 10.1162/EDFP_a_00196.

Kronk, Henry. 2017. "The Most Diverse U.S. Universities Are Online." Elearning Inside. Last modified September 19, 2017. https://news.elearninginside.com/diverse-u-s-universities-online/.

Kugelmass, Heather, and Douglas D. Ready. 2011. "Racial/Ethnic Disparities in Collegiate Cognitive Gains: A Multilevel Analysis of Institutional Influences on Learning and Its Equitable Distribution." *Research in Higher Education* 52 (4):323–48.

Kuh, George D. 1995. "The Other Curriculum: Out-of-Class Experiences Associated with Student Learning and Personal Development." *Journal of Higher Education* 66 (2):123–55.

Kuh, George D., and Shouping Hu. 2001. "The Effects of Student-Faculty Interaction in the 1990s." *Review of Higher Education* 24 (3):309–32.

Kuh, George D., Jillian Kinzie, Jennifer A. Buckley, Brian K. Bridges, and John C. Hayek. 2006. "What Matters to Student Success: A Review of the Literature." In *ASHE Higher Education Report*. San Francisco: Jossey-Bass.

Kuh, George D., Jillian Kinzie, John H. Schuh, and Elizabeth J. Whitt. 2010. *Student Success in College: Creating Conditions that Matter.* San Francisco, CA: John Wiley & Sons.

Lang, James M. 2013. *Cheating Lessons.* Cambridge, MA: Harvard University Press.

———. 2016. *Small Teaching: Everyday Lessons from the Science of Learning.* San Francisco, CA: Wiley.

———. 2020. "On Not Drawing Conclusions about Online Teaching Now—or Next Fall." *Chronicle of Higher Education,* May 18. https://o-www-chronicle-com.library.ualr.edu/article/on-not-drawing-conclusions-about-online-teaching-now-or-next-fall.

Lareau, Annette. 2011. *Unequal Childhoods: Class, Race, and Family Life.* Berkeley: University of California Press.

Lassitter, Stefanie A. 2009. "Establishing a Relationship between Virtual Instructor and Student in the Online Classroom." *Distance Learning* 6 (1):53.

Layne, Melissa, Wallace E. Boston, and Phil Ice. 2013. "A Longitudinal Study of Online Learners: Shoppers, Swirlers, Stoppers, and Succeeders as a Function of Demographic Characteristics." *Online Journal of Distance Learning Administration* 16 (2):1–12.

Lee, Sang Joon, Sandhya Srinivasan, Trudian Trail, David Lewis, and Samantha Lopez. 2011. "Examining the Relationship among Student Perception of Support, Course Satisfaction, and Learning Outcomes in Online Learning." *The Internet and Higher Education* 14 (3):158–63.

Lee, Wynetta Y. 1999. "Striving toward Effective Retention: The Effect of Race on Mentoring African American Students." *Peabody Journal of Education* 74 (2):27–43. Doi: 10.1207/s15327930pje7402_4.

Lee, Youngju, and Jaeho Choi. 2013. "A Structural Equation Model of Predictors of Online Learning Retention." *The Internet and Higher Education* 16:36–42. Doi: http://dx.doi.org/10.1016/j.iheduc.2012.01.005.

Lee, Youngju, Jaeho Choi, and Taehyun Kim. 2013. "Discriminating Factors between Completers of and Dropouts from Online Learning Courses." *British Journal of Educational Technology* 44 (2):328–37. Doi: 10.1111/j.1467-8535.2012.01306.x.

Leeds, Elke, Stacy Campbell, Hope Baker, Radwan Ali, Dorothy Brawley, and John Crisp. 2013. "The Impact of Student Retention Strategies: An Empirical Study." *International Journal of Management in Education* 7 (1–2):22–43.

Leibold, Nancyruth, and Laura Marie Schwarz. 2015. "The Art of Giving Online Feedback." *Journal of Effective Teaching* 15 (1):34–46.

Leidman, Mary Beth, Mark Piwinsky, and Matthew McKeague. 2010. "Faculty-Student Interaction in the Technological Age: The Perpetual Professor?" Society for Information Technology & Teacher Education International Conference 2010, San Diego, CA.

Leonhardt, David, and Sahil Chino. 2019. "The College Dropout Crisis." *New York Times,* May 23. https://www.nytimes.com/interactive/2019/05/23/opinion/sunday/college-graduation-rates-ranking.html.

Levy, Yair. 2007. "Comparing Dropouts and Persistence in E-Learning Courses." *Computers & Education* 48 (2):185–204.

Lichoro, David Muturia. 2015. "Faculty Preparedness for Transition to Teaching Online Courses in the Iowa Community College Online Consortium." PhD diss., Education, Iowa State University.

Light, Richard J. 2004. *Making the Most of College.* Cambridge, MA: Harvard University Press.

Lin, Hsiao-Ping. 2002. "Motivating and Inhibiting Factors that Affect Faculty Participation in Distance Education at Idaho State University." PhD diss., Idaho State University.

Lindt, Suzanne Fischer, and Stacia Celeste Miller. 2018. "Understanding Factors Leading to College Classroom Engagement for Millennials: Development of the College Classroom Engagement Scale." *Higher Education Research* 3 (3):38–44.

Liu, Simon Y., Joel Gomez, and C. Yen. 2009. "Community College Online Course Retention and Final Grade: Predictability of Social Presence." *Journal of Interactive Online Learning* 8 (2):165–82.

Loepp, Eric D. 2020. "Introduction: COVID-19 and Emergency e-Learning in Political Science and International Relations." *PS: Political Science & Politics* 54 (1): 1–3. Doi: 10.1017/S1049096520001511.

Long, Mark C., and Nicole A. Bateman. 2020. "Long-Run Changes in Underrepresentation after Affirmative Action Bans in Public Universities." *Educational Evaluation and Policy Analysis* 42 (2):188–207.

Longwell-Grice, Rob, and Hope Longwell-Grice. 2008. "Testing Tinto: How Do Retention Theories Work for First-Generation, Working-Class Students?" *Journal of College Student Retention: Research, Theory & Practice* 9 (4):407–20.

Lowenthal, Patrick R. 2010. "The Evolution and Influence of Social Presence Theory on Online Learning." In *Social Computing: Concepts, Methodologies, Tools, and Applications,* edited by Patrick R. Lowenthal, 113–28. Hershey, PA: IGI Global.

Lowenthal, Patrick R., Christine Bauer, and Ken-Zen Chen. 2015. "Student Perceptions of Online Learning: An Analysis of Online Course Evaluations." *American Journal of Distance Education* 29 (2):85–97. Doi: 10.1080/08923647.2015.1023621.

Lumina Foundation. 2019. Today's Student. Indianapolis, IN: Lumina Foundation.

Lundberg, Carol A., and Laurie A. Schreiner. 2004. "Quality and Frequency of Faculty-Student Interaction as Predictors of Learning: An Analysis by Student Race/Ethnicity." *Journal of College Student Development* 45 (5):549–65.

Lundquist, Cara, Rebecca J. Spalding, and R. Eric Landrum. 2002. "College Student's Thoughts about Leaving the University: The Impact of Faculty Attitudes and Behaviors." *Journal of College Student Retention: Research, Theory & Practice* 4 (2):123–33. Doi: 10.2190/flal-7am5-q6k3-l4op.

Ma, Jennifer, Matea Pender, and Meredith Welch. 2016. Education Pays 2016: The Benefits of Higher Education for Individuals and Society. In *Trends in Higher Education Series*. New York: College Board.

MacNell, Lillian, Adam Driscoll, and Andrea N. Hunt. 2015. "What's in a Name: Exposing Gender Bias in Student Ratings of Teaching." *Innovative Higher Education* 40 (4):291–303.

Magda, Andrew J., and Carol B. Aslanian. 2018. *Online College Students 2018: Comprehensive Data on Demands and Preferences*. Louisville, KY: The Learning House.

Magda, Andrew J., David Capranos, and Carol B. Aslanian. 2020. *Online College Students 2020: Comprehensive Data on Demands and Preferences*. Louisville, KY: Wiley Education Services.

Malesky, L. Alvin, John Baley, and Robert Crow. 2016. "Academic Dishonesty: Assessing the Threat of Cheating Companies to Online Education." *College Teaching* 64 (4):178–83. Doi: 10.1080/87567555.2015.1133558.

Mandernach, Jean, Lexi Register, and Carrie O'Donnell. 2015. "Characteristics of Adjunct Faculty Teaching Online: Institutional Implications." *Online Journal of Distance Learning Administration* 18 (1):1–17.

Marek, Kate. 2009. "Learning to Teach Online: Creating a Culture of Support for Faculty." *Journal of Education for Library and Information Science* 50 (4):275–92.

Marín-López, Inmaculada, Izabela Zych, Claire P. Monks, and Rosario Ortega-Ruiz. 2019. "Empathy, Morality and Social and Emotional Competencies in Interpersonal Interactions Online." In *Thriving in Digital Workspaces: Emerging Issues for Research and Practice,* edited by Melinde Coetzee, 217–33. Cham, Switzerland: Springer International Publishing.

Martinez, Margaret. 2003. "High Attrition Rates In E-Learning: Challenges, Predictors, and Solutions." *The E-Learning Developers' Journal* 14:1–8.

Maxfield, R. Jeffery. 2008. "Online Education for Nontraditional Adult Students: Perceptions and Attitudes of Emergency Services Workers in Asynchronous Learning Environments." Doctor of Education, Utah State University.

Mazzolini, Margaret, and Sarah Maddison. 2007. "When to Jump In: The Role of the Instructor in Online Discussion Forums." *Computers & Education* 49 (2):193–213.

McCabe, Janice. 2009. "Racial and Gender Microaggressions on a Predominantly-White Campus: Experiences of Black, Latina/o and White Undergraduates." *Race, Gender & Class* 16 (1/2):133–51.

———. 2016. *Connecting in College: How Friendship Networks Matter for Academic and Social Success*. Chicago: University of Chicago Press.

McCabe, Margaret Foley, and Patricia Gonzalez-Flores. 2017. *Essentials of Online Teaching: A Standards-Based Guide*. New York: Taylor & Francis.

McCarthy, Sally A. 2009. *Online Learning as a Strategic Asset. Volume I: A Resource for Campus Leaders*. A Report on the Online Education Benchmarking Study Conducted by the APLU-Sloan National Commission on Online Learning. Association of Public and Land-grant Universities. https://eric.ed.gov/?id=ED517308.

McCarty, Cynthia, Doris Bennett, and Shawn Carter. 2013. "Teaching College Microeconomics: Online vs. Traditional Classroom Instruction." *Journal of Instructional Pedagogies* 11 (May).

McClendon, Cristie, Robin Massey Neugebauer, and Amanda King. 2017. "Grit, Growth Mindset, and Deliberate Practice in Online Learning." *Journal of Instructional Research* 8:8–17.

McEwen, Beryl C. 2001. "Web-Assisted and Online Learning." *Business Communication Quarterly* 64 (2):98–103.

McLaren, Constance H. 2004. "A Comparison of Student Persistence and Performance in Online and Classroom Business Statistics Experiences." *Decision Sciences Journal of Innovative Education* 2 (1):1–10. Doi: 10.1111 /j.0011-7315.2004.00015.x.

Means, B., J. Neisler, and with Langer Research Associates. 2020. *Suddenly Online: A National Survey of Undergraduates during the COVID-19 Pandemic.* San Mateo, CA: Digital Promise.

Mehta, Rohit, and Earl Aguilera. 2020. "A Critical Approach to Humanizing Pedagogies in Online Teaching and Learning." *International Journal of Information and Learning Technology,* published online April 12, 2020. https:// www.emerald.com/insight/content/doi/10.1108/IJILT-10–2019–0099/full /html.

Mendez, Jeanette Morehouse, and Jesse Perez Mendez. 2018. "What's in a Name . . . or a Face? Student Perceptions of Faculty Race." *Journal of Political Science Education* 14 (2):177–96.

Mensch, Scott. 2017. "Improving Distance Education through Student Online Orientation Classes." *Global Education Journal* 2017 (1):1–6.

Merrills, J. Maria Sweeney. 2010. "Factors Affecting Nontraditional African American Students' Participation in Online World Literature Classes." PhD diss., University of North Carolina at Greensboro.

Meyer, Katrina Anne. 2014. *Student Engagement Online: What Works and Why.* Hoboken, NJ: John Wiley & Sons.

Mikołajewska, Emilia, and Dariusz Mikołajewski. 2011. "E-Learning in the Education of People with Disabilities." *Advances in Clinical and Experimental Medicine* 20 (1):103–9.

Miller, Michelle D. 2014. *Minds Online.* Cambridge, MA: Harvard University Press.

Millward, Jody. 2008. "An Analysis of the National 'TYCA Research Initiative Survey Section III: Technology and Pedagogy' in Two-Year College English Programs." *Teaching English in the Two Year College* 35 (4):372.

Minero, Emelina. 2017. "Parent Engagement in the Digital Age." *Edutopia,* November 22, 2017. https://www.edutopia.org/article/parent-engagement -digital-age.

Mitchell, Kristina M. W., and Jonathan Martin. 2018. "Gender Bias in Student Evaluations." *PS: Political Science & Politics* 51 (3):648–52.

Mondelli, Victoria, and Thomas J. Tobin. 2020. West Virginia University Press. "Pedagogies of Care." Accessed July 20, 2020. https://sabresmonkey.wixsite .com/pedagogiesofcare.

Moody, Josh. 2019. "10 Schools with the Most Online Students." *US News &
World Report,* October 3. https://www.usnews.com/higher-education/online
-education/slideshows/schools-with-the-most-online-students?slide=10.

Moore, Janet C., and Marie J. Fetzner. 2009. "The Road to Retention: A Closer
Look at Institutions that Achieve High Course Completion Rates." *Journal of
Asynchronous Learning Networks* 13 (3):3–22.

Moore, Michael G. 1991. "Distance Education Theory." *American Journal of
Distance Education* 5 (3):1–6.

Morris, Sean Michael, and Jesse Stommel. 2018. *An Urgency of Teachers: The
Work of Critical Digital Pedagogy.* Hybrid Pedagogy, Inc.

Morris, Terry A. 2010. "Anytime/Anywhere Online Learning: Does It Remove
Barriers for Adult Learners?" In *Online Education and Adult Learning: New
Frontiers for Teaching Practices,* edited by Terry T. Kidd, 115–23. Hershey,
PA: IGI Global.

Mortenson, Thomas G. 2012. "Measurements of Persistence." In *College Stu-
dent Retention: Formula for Student Success,* edited by Alexander W. Astin,
Joseph B. Berger, Erin W. Bibo, Kurt R. Burkum, Alberto F. Cabrera, Gloria
Crisp, and Ann Gansemer-Topf, 35–60. Lanham, MD: Rowman & Littlefield
Publishers.

Moskal, Patsy D. 2020. Director of Digital Learning Impact Evaluation, University of Central Florida. Personal communication, July 28, 2020.

Muilenburg, Lin Y., and Zane L. Berge. 2005. "Student Barriers to Online
Learning: A Factor Analytic Study." *Distance Education* 26 (1):29–48.

Muljana, Pauline S., and Tian Luo. 2019. "Factors Contributing to Student
Retention in Online Learning and Recommended Strategies for Improve-
ment: A Systematic Literature Review." *Journal of Information Technology
Education: Research* 18.

Murphy, Elizabeth, and María A. Rodríguez-Manzanares. 2012. "Rapport in
Distance Education." *International Review of Research in Open and Distance Learning* 13 (1):167–90.

Murtaugh, Paul A., Leslie D. Burns, and Jill Schuster. 1999. "Predicting the
Retention of University Students." *Research in Higher Education* 40
(3):355–71.

Nadal, Kevin L., Yinglee Wong, Katie E. Griffin, Kristin Davidoff, and Julie
Sriken. 2014. "The Adverse Impact of Racial Microaggressions on College Students' Self-Esteem." *Journal of College Student Development* 55
(5):461–74.

Nadler, Marjorie Keeshan, and Lawrence B. Nadler. 2000. "Out of Class Communication between Faculty and Sudents: A Faculty Perspective." *Communication Studies* 51 (2):176–88.

Nate' Evans, Tiffany. 2009. "An Investigative Study of Factors that Influence the
Retention Rates in Online Programs at Selected State, State-Affiliated, and
Private Universities." PhD diss., Instructional Management and Leadership,
Robert Morris University.

National Adult Learner Coalition. 2017. "Strengthening America's Economy by
Expanding Educational Opportunities for Working Adults: Policy Opportunities to Connect the Working Adult to Today's Economy through Education

and Credentials." Newburyport: Online Learning Consortium. https://www
.voced.edu.au/content/ngv:76929.

National Center for Education Statistics. 2020. "Who Is Nontraditional?"
National Center for Education Statistics. Accessed April 18, 2020. https://
nces.ed.gov/pubs/web/97578e.asp.

National Science Board. 2020. "Bachelor's Degree Holders among Individuals 25–44 Years Old." National Science Foundation. April 29, 2020. https://
ncses.nsf.gov/indicators/states/indicator/bachelors-degree-holders-per
-25-44-year-olds.

Nelson, Karen J., and Tracy A. Creagh. 2013. *A Good Practice Guide: Safe-
guarding Student Learning Engagement.* Brisbane: Queensland University of
Technology.

Nelson, Susanne J. 2003. "Perceptions of Agricultural Education Teacher Preparation Programs toward Distance Education." PhD diss., Oregon State
University.

Nichols, Mark. 2010. "Student Perceptions of Support Services and the Influence of Targeted Interventions on Retention in Distance Education." *Distance Education* 31 (1):93–113. Doi: 10.1080/01587911003725048.

Nilson, Linda. 2015. *Specifications Grading: Restoring Rigor, Motivating Students, and Saving Faculty Time.* Sterling, VA: Stylus Publishing.

Nistor, Nicolae, and Katrin Neubauer. 2010. "From Participation to Dropout:
Quantitative Participation Patterns in Online University Courses." *Computers & Education* 55 (2):663–72.

North Carolina General Assembly. 2010. *University Distance Courses Cost
More to Develop Overall but the Same to Deliver as On-Campus Courses.*
Raleigh, North Carolina: Program Evaluation Division, North Carolina Gen-
eral Assembly.

O'Connell, Matthew, and Mei-Chuan Kung. 2007. "The Cost of Employee
Turnover." *Industrial Management* 49 (1).

Ong, Anthony D., Anthony L. Burrow, Thomas E. Fuller-Rowell, Nicole M. Ja,
and Derald Wing Sue. 2013. "Racial Microaggressions and Daily Well-Being
among Asian Americans." *Journal of Counseling Psychology* 60 (2):188.

Orellana, Anymir. 2009. "Class Size and Interaction in Online Courses." In *The
Perfect Online Course: Best Practices for Designing and Teaching,* edited by
Michael Simonson, Terry L. Hudgins, and Anymir Orellana, 117–35. Char-
lotte, NC: Information Age Publishing.

Orr, Robert, Mitchell R. Williams, and Kevin Pennington. 2009. "Institutional
Efforts to Support Faculty in Online Teaching." *Innovative Higher Education*
34 (4):257.

Ortagus, Justin C. 2017. "From the Periphery to Prominence: An Examination
of the Changing Profile of Online Students in American Higher Education."
The Internet and Higher Education 32:47–57. Doi: https://Doi.org/10.1016
/j.iheduc.2016.09.002.

Osei, Zipporah. 2019. "Low-Income and Minority Students Are Growing
Share of Enrollments, and 2 Other Takeaways from New Study." *Chronicle
of Higher Education,* May 22. https://www.chronicle.com/article/Low
-IncomeMinority/246346.

Pacansky-Brock, Michelle. 2020. "Humanizing." Accessed March 14, 2020. https://brocansky.com/humanizing.

Pacansky-Brock, Michelle, Michael Smedshammer, and Kim Vincent-Layton. 2020. "Humanizing Online Teaching to Equitize Higher Education." *Current Issues in Education* 12 (2).

Paechter, Manuela, Brigitte Maier, and Daniel Macher. 2010. "Students' Expectations of, and Experiences in E-Learning: Their Relation to Learning Achievements and Course Satisfaction." *Computers & Education* 54 (1):222–29.

Palacios, Angelica M. G., and J. Luke Wood. 2016. "Is Online Learning the Silver Bullet for Men of Color? An Institutional-Level Analysis of the California Community College System." *Community College Journal of Research and Practice* 40 (8):643–55.

Palmer, Michael S., Lindsay B. Wheeler, and Itiya Aneece. 2016. "Does the Document Matter? The Evolving Role of Syllabi in Higher Education." *Change: The Magazine of Higher Learning* 48 (4):36–47. Doi: 10.1080 /00091383.2016.1198186.

Parkes, Mitchell, Sue Gregory, Peter Fletcher, Rachael Adlington, and Nicolas Gromik. 2015. "Bringing People Together while Learning Apart: Creating Online Learning Environments to Support the Needs of Rural and Remote Students." *Australian and International Journal of Rural Education* 25 (1):65.

Parsad, Basmat, Laurie Lewis, and Peter Tice. 2008. *Distance Education at Degree-Granting Postsecondary Institutions: 2006–2007*. Washington, DC: National Center for Education Statistics, Institute of Education Sciences.

Pascarella, Ernest T., Christopher T. Pierson, Gregory C. Wolniak, and Patrick T. Terenzini. 2004. "First-Generation College Students: Additional Evidence on College Experiences and Outcomes." *Journal of Higher Education* 75 (3):249–84.

Pascarella, Ernest T., and Patrick T. Terenzini. 2005. *How College Affects Students: A Third Decade of Research*. Vol. 2. Indianapolis, IN: Jossey-Bass.

Patel, Vimal. 2020. "Covid-19 Is a Pivotal Moment for Struggling Students: Can Colleges Step Up?" *Chronicle of Higher Education*, April 14.

Patterson, Belinda, and Cheryl McFadden. 2009. "Attrition in Online and Campus Degree Programs." *Online Journal of Distance Learning Administration* 12 (2).

Pecorari, Diane, and Bojana Petric. 2014. "Plagiarism in Second-Language Writing." *Language Teaching* 47 (3):269–302.

Perrin, Andrew. 2019. "Digital Gap between Rural and Nonrural America Persists." Accessed April 24, 2020. https://www.pewresearch.org/fact-tank/2019 /05/31/digital-gap-between-rural-and-nonrural-america-persists/.

Peterson, Cynthia L., and Nathan Bond. 2004. "Online Compared to Face-to-Face Teacher Preparation for Learning Standards-Based Planning Skills." *Journal of Research on Technology in Education* 36 (4):345–60.

Pew Research Center. 2019. "Mobile Fact Sheet." Pew Research Center: Internet and Technology. Last modified June 12, 2019. https://www.pewresearch.org /internet/fact-sheet/mobile/.

Pinchbeck, Jessica, and Caroline Heaney. 2017. "Case Report: The Impact of a Resubmission Intervention on Level 1 Distance Learning Students." *Open Learning: The Journal of Open, Distance and e-Learning* 32 (3):236–42.

Polatajko, Mark M., and Catherine H. Monaghan. 2017. "Performance Funding of United States' Public Higher Education: Impact on Graduation and Retention Rates." In *Handbook of Research on Administration, Policy, and Leadership in Higher Education,* edited by Siran Mukerji and Purnendu Tripathi, 496–517. Hershey, PA: IGI Global.

Policar, Laura, Tracy Crawford, and Vita Alligood. 2017. "Accessibility Benefits of E-Learning for Students with Disabilities." Last modified January 31, 2017. https://www.disabled-world.com/disability/education/postsecondary /e-learning.php.

Porath, Suzanne L. 2018. "A Powerful Influence: An Online Book Club for Educators." *Journal of Digital Learning in Teacher Education* 34 (2):115–28. Doi: 10.1080/21532974.2017.1416711.

Putulowski, Joe R., and Robert G. Crosby. 2019. "Effect of Personalized Instructor-Student E-mail and Text Messages on Online Students' Perceived Course Quality, Social Integration with Faculty, and Institutional Commitment." *Journal of College Student Retention: Research, Theory & Practice* 21 (2):184–201. Doi: 10.1177/1521025117696823.

Qiu, Mingzhu, Jim Hewitt, and Clare Brett. 2012. "Online Class Size, Note Reading, Note Writing and Collaborative Discourse." *International Journal of Computer-Supported Collaborative Learning* 7 (3):423–42.

Quick Facts. 2019. "University of Arkansas at Little Rock." Accessed July 15, 2019. https://ualr.edu/administration/fast-facts/.

Rabourn, Karyn E., Allison BrckaLorenz, and Rick Shoup. 2018. "Reimagining Student Engagement: How Nontraditional Adult Learners Engage in Traditional Postsecondary Environments." *Journal of Continuing Higher Education* 66 (1):22–33. Doi: 10.1080/07377363.2018.1415635.

Ramsdal, Gro Hilde, Svein Bergvik, and Rolf Wynn. 2018. "Long-Term Dropout from School and Work and Mental Health in Young Adults in Norway: A Qualitative Interview-Based Study." *Cogent Psychology* 5 (1):1455365. Doi: 10.1080/23311908.2018.1455365.

Ran, Florence Xiaotao, and Di Xu. 2019. "Does Contractual Form Matter? The Impact of Different Types of Non-Tenure-Track Faculty on College Students' Academic Outcomes." *Journal of Human Resources* 54 (4):1081–1120.

Rapanta, Chrysi, Luca Botturi, Peter Goodyear, Lourdes Guàrdia, and Marguerite Koole. 2020. "Online University Teaching during and After the Covid-19 Crisis: Refocusing Teacher Presence and Learning Activity." *Postdigital Science and Education* 2 (3):923–45. Doi: 10.1007/s42438-020 -00155-y.

Reason, Robert Dean, Patrick T. Terenzini, and Robert J. Domingo. 2007. "Developing Social and Personal Competence in the First Year of College." *Review of Higher Education* 30 (3):271–99.

Richardson, Jennifer C., and Karen Swan. 2003. "Examing Social Presence in Online Courses in Relation to Students' Perceived Learning and Satisfaction." *Journal of Asynchronous Learning Networks* 7 (1):68–88.

Roberts, James C. 2015. "Evaluating the Effectiveness of Lecture Capture: Lessons Learned from an Undergraduate Political Research Class." *Journal of Political Science Education* 11 (1):45–60. Doi: 10.1080/15512169.2014.985104.

Roberts, Joseph W. 2020. "Rapidly Moving Online in a Pandemic: Intentionality, Rapport, and the Synchronous/Asynchronous Delivery Decision." *PS: Political Science & Politics* 54 (1):183–85. Doi: 10.1017/S1049096520001596.

Robles, Marcel M. 2012. "Executive Perceptions of the Top 10 Soft Skills Needed in Today's Workplace." *Business Communication Quarterly* 75 (4):453–65. Doi: 10.1177/1080569912460400.

Roche, Gerard R. 1979. "Much Ado about Mentors." *Harvard Business Review* 57:135–56.

Rodchua, Suhansa, George Yiadom-Boakye, and Ronald Woolsey. 2011. "Student Verification System for Online Assessments: Bolstering Quality and Integrity of Distance Learning." *Journal of Industrial Technology* 27 (3).

Roll, Ido, and Philip H. Winne. 2015. "Understanding, Evaluating, and Supporting Self-Regulated Learning Using Learning Analytics." *Journal of Learning Analytics* 2 (1):7–12.

Romero, Cristóbal, and Sebastián Ventura. 2010. "Educational Data Mining: A Review of the State of the Art." *IEEE Transactions on Systems, Man, and Cybernetics, Part C (Applications and Reviews)* 40 (6):601–18.

Rosenbaum, James E., Regina Deil-Amen, and Ann E. Person. 2007. *After Admission: From College Access to College Success.* New York: Russell Sage Foundation.

Rosenboom, Victoria, and Kristin Blagg. 2018. *Disconnected from Higher Education: How Geography and Internet Speed Limit Access to Higher Education.* Education Policy Program. Washington, DC: Urban Institute. https://vtechworks.lib.vt.edu/bitstream/handle/10919/89125/Disconnectedfrom highereducation.pdf?sequence=1&isAllowed=y.

Rovai, Alfred P. 2003. "In Search of Higher Persistence Rates in Distance Education Online Programs." *The Internet and Higher Education* 6 (1):1–16.

Rovai, Alfred P., and James R. Downey. 2010. "Why Some Distance Education Programs Fail while Others Succeed in a Global Environment." *The Internet and Higher Education* 13 (3):141–47. Doi: https://doi.org/10.1016/j.iheduc.2009.07.001.

Rovai, Alfred P., and Louis B. Gallien Jr. 2005. "Learning and Sense of Community: A Comparative Analysis of African American and Caucasian Online Graduate Students." *Journal of Negro Education* 74 (1):53–62.

Rovai, Alfred P., and Michael K. Ponton. 2005. "An Examination of Sense of Classroom Community and Learning among African American and Caucasian Graduate Students." *Journal of Asynchronous Learning Networks* 9 (3):77–92.

Rovai, Alfred P., and Mervyn J. Wighting. 2005. "Feelings of Alienation and Community among Higher Education Students in a Virtual Classroom." *The Internet and Higher Education* 8 (2):97–110.

Russo, Tracy, and Spencer Benson. 2005. "Learning with Invisible Others: Perceptions of Online Presence and Their Relationship to Cognitive and Affective Learning." *Educational Technology and Society* 8 (1):54–62.

Sax, Linda J., Alyssa N. Bryant, and Casandra E. Harper. 2005. "The Differential Effects of Student-Faculty Interaction on College Outcomes for Women and Men." *Journal of College Student Development* 46 (6):642–57.

Schaarsmith, Amy Mcconnell. 2012. "Growing Number of College Students Choose Online Courses." *Pittsburgh Post-Gazette*, February 16. https://www.post-gazette.com/news/education/2012/02/16/Growing-number-of-college-students-choose-online-courses/stories/201202161337.

Schade, Sarah Ann. 2014. "Reining in the Predatory Nature of For-Profit Colleges." *Arizona Law Review* 56:317.

Schaelen, Tracy. 2020. Distance Education Faculty Coordinator, Southwestern College. Personal communication, June 23, 2020.

Schmidt, Steven W., Christina M. Tschida, and Elizabeth M. Hodge. 2016. "How Faculty Learn to Teach Online: What Administrators Need to Know." *Online Journal of Distance Learning Administration* 19 (1):1–10.

Schrum, Lynne, and Sunjoo Hong. 2002. "Dimensions and Strategies for Online Success: Voices from Experienced Educators." *Journal of Asynchronous Learning Networks* 6 (1):57–67.

Scott-Clayton, Judith. 2011. "The Shapeless River: Does a Lack of Structure Inhibit Students' Progress at Community Colleges?" In *Community College Research Center, Working Paper No. 25, Assessment of Evidence Series*. New York: Columbia University, Teachers College, Community College Research Center.

Scott-Clayton, Judith, and Jing Li. 2016. "Black-White Disparity in Student Loan Debt More than Triples after Graduation." *Economic Studies* 2 (3).

Seaman, Julia E., I. Elaine Allen, and Jeff Seaman. 2018. *Grade Increase: Tracking Distance Education in the United States*. Babson Survey Research Group. https://files.eric.ed.gov/fulltext/ED580852.pdf.

Shattuck, Kay. 2013. "Faculty Participation in Online Distance Education." In *Hand-book of Distance Education*, edited by Michael G. Moore, 390–402. New York: Routledge.

Shea, Peter, and Temi Bidjerano. 2014. "Does Online Learning Impede Degree Completion? A National Study of Community College Students." *Computers & Education* 75:103–11. Doi: http://dx.doi.org/10.1016/j.compedu.2014.02.009.

———. 2018. "Online Course Enrollment in Community College and Degree Completion: The Tipping Point." *International Review of Research in Open and Distributed Learning* 19 (2).

Shea, Peter, Alexandra Pickett, and Chun Sau Li. 2005. "Increasing Access to Higher Education: A Study of the Diffusion of Online Teaching among 913 College Faculty." *International Review of Research in Open and Distributed Learning* 6 (2).

Shevlin, Mark, Philip Banyard, Mark Davies, and Mark Griffiths. 2000. "The Validity of Student Evaluation of Teaching in Higher Education: Love Me, Love My Lectures?" *Assessment & Evaluation in Higher Education* 25 (4):397–405.

Skurat Harris, Heidi. 2020. Graduate Coordinator, Department of Rhetoric and Writing, University of Arkansas at Little Rock. Personal communication, July 30, 2020.

Slagle, Derek, Cassie Gehring, Samantha Wiley, Heidi Skurat Harris, and Reagan Little. 2020. *May 2020 UA Little Rock COVID-19 Assessment of Students, Faculty, & Staff.* Little Rock, AR: University of Arkansas at Little Rock.

Smedshammer, Michael. 2020. Distance Education Coordinator, Modesto Junior College. Personal communication, July 23, 2020.

Smedshammer, Michael, Jenni Abbott, Patrick Bettencourt, Iris Carroll, Amy Duffy, and Steven Miller. 2018. *MJC Online Education Plan 2018–2023.* Modesto, CA: Modesto Junior College. https://www.mjc.edu/governance /distanceedcommittee/documents/mjc_oe_plan_2018_2023_final.pdf.

Smith, Bettye P., and Billy Hawkins. 2011. "Examining Student Evaluations of Black College Faculty: Does Race Matter?" *Journal of Negro Education* 80 (2):149–62.

Smith, Glenn G., Allen J. Heindel, and Ana T. Torres-Ayala. 2008. "E-Learning Commodity or Community: Disciplinary Differences between Online Courses." *The Internet and Higher Education* 11 (3–4):152–59.

Smith, Samuel H., Robert Samors, and A. Frank Mayadas. 2008. "Positioning Online Learning as a Strategic Asset in the Thinking of University Presidents and Chancellors." *Journal of Asynchronous Learning Networks* 12 (2):91–100.

Snyder, Thomas D., Cristobal de Brey, and Sally A. Dillow. 2019. *Digest of Education Statistics 2017 (NCES 2018–070).* Washington, DC: National Center for Education Statistics, Institute of Education Sciences, US Department of Education.

Song, Liyan, Ernise S. Singleton, Janette R. Hill, and Myung Hwa Koh. 2004. "Improving Online Learning: Student Perceptions of Useful and Challenging Characteristics." *The Internet and Higher Education* 7 (1):59–70.

Southwestern College. 2020. "Online Learning." Southwestern College. Accessed July 27, 2020. https://www.swccd.edu/locations/online-learning/index.aspx.

Spector, J. Michael. 2005. "Time Demands in Online Instruction." *Distance Education* 26 (1):5–27. Doi: 10.1080/01587910500081251.

Sridharam, Vasanth. 2012. "The Debt Crisis in For-Profit Education: How the Industry Has Used Federal Dollars to Send Thousands of Students into Default." *Georgetown Journal on Poverty Law & Policy* 19 (2):331.

Stanley, Bolling Craig. 2014. "Online vs. Face-to-Face Instruction: A Comparison of Engagement and Gains for African-American and White Students at Predominantly White Institutions." PhD diss., Department of Educational Leadership and Policy Studies, Florida State University.

Stavredes, Tina M. 2011. *Effective Online Teaching: Foundations and Strategies for Student Success.* San Francisco, CA: Jossey-Bass.

Stavredes, Tina M., and Tiffany M. Herder. 2013. "Student Persistence—And Teaching Strategies to Support It." In *Handbook of Distance Education,* edited by Michael G. Moore, 173–187. New York: Routledge.

Stephens, Nicole M., Stephanie A. Fryberg, Hazel Rose Markus, Camille S.

Johnson, and Rebecca Covarrubias. 2012. "Unseen Disadvantage: How American Universities' Focus on Independence Undermines the Academic Performance of First-Generation College Students." *Journal of Personality and Social Psychology* 102 (6):1178.

Stewart, Carol, Alison Wall, and Sheryl Marciniec. 2016. "Mixed Signals: Do College Graduates Have the Soft Skills that Employers Want?" *Competition Forum* 14 (2):276–83.

Stommel, Jesse. 2020. "Ungrading: An FAQ." Jesse Stommel, February 6, 2020. https://www.jessestommel.com/ungrading-an-faq/.

Stover, Catherine. 2005. "Measuring—and Understanding—Student Retention." *Distance Education Report* 9 (16).1–7.

Strayhorn, Terrell Lamont, and Melvin Cleveland Terrell. 2007. "Mentoring and Satisfaction with College for Black Students." *Negro Educational Review* 58 (1–2):69–83.

Sublett, Cameron. 2020. *Distant Equity: The Promise and Pitfalls of Online Learning for Students of Color in Higher Education.* Washington, DC: American Council on Education.

Sullivan, Patrick. 2002. "'It's Easier to Be Yourself When You Are Invisible': Female College Students Discuss Their Online Classroom Experiences." *Innovative Higher Education* 27 (2):129–44. Doi: 10.1023/A:1021109410893.

Summerlin, James Adrian. 2004. "A Comparison of the Effectiveness of Off-Line Internet and Traditional Classroom Remediation of Mathematical Skills." PhD diss., Department of Education, Baylor University.

Supiano, Beckie. 2020. "Why Is Zoom So Exhausting?" *Chronicle of Higher Education,* April 23. https://o-www-chronicle-com.library.ualr.edu/article/why-is-zoom-so-exhausting/.

Swan, Karen. 2003. "Developing Social Presence in Online Course Discussions." In *Learning and Teaching with Technology: Principles and Practices,* edited by Som Naidu, 147–64. London: Kogan Page.

Swan, Karen, and Li Fang Shih. 2005. "On the Nature and Development of Social Presence in Online Course Discussions." *Journal of Asynchronous Learning Networks* 9 (3):115–36.

Sweeney, Erica. 2015. "Governor, ADHE Announce Draft Plan for Arkansas Higher Education." Arkansas Money and Politics. September 1, 2015. https://armoneyandpolitics.com/governor-adhe-announce-draft-plan-for-arkansas-higher-education/.

Tai, Hung-Cheng, Wen-Chuan Lin, and Shu Ching Yang. 2015. "Exploring the Effects of Peer Review and Teachers' Corrective Feedback on EFL Students' Online Writing Performance." *Journal of Educational Computing Research* 53 (2):284–309. Doi: 10.1177/0735633115597490.

Tajfel, Henri, and John C. Turner. 1979. "An Integrative Theory of Intergroup Conflict." In *Organizational Identity: A Reader,* edited by William G. Austin and Stephen Worchel, 56–65. New York: Oxford University Press.

Tanaka, Greg. 2002. "Higher Education's Self-Reflexive Turn: Toward an Intercultural Theory of Student Development." *Journal of Higher Education* 73 (2):263–96.

Tanis, Cynthia Janet. 2020. "The Seven Principles of Online Learning: Feedback from Faculty and Alumni on Its Importance for Teaching and Learning." *Research in Learning Technology* 28 (0). Doi: 10.25304/rlt.v28.2319.

Tello, Steven F. 2007. "An Analysis of Student Persistence in Online Education." *International Journal of Information and Communication Technology Education* 3 (3):47–62.

Terry, Neil. 2001. "Assessing Enrollment and Attrition Rates for the Online MBA." *The Journal* 28 (7):64–68.

Therrien, William J., and Bryan G. Cook. 2018. "Introduction to Special Issue: Null Effects and Publication Bias in Learning Disabilities Research." *Learning Disabilities Research & Practice* 33 (1):5–10.

Thiry, Heather, Timothy J. Weston, Sandra L. Laursen, and Anne-Barrie Hunter. 2012. "The Benefits of Multi-Year Research Experiences: Differences in Novice and Experienced Students' Reported Gains from Undergraduate Research." *CBE—Life Sciences Education* 11 (3):260–72. Doi: 10.1187 /cbe.11-11-0098.

Thomas, Lisa, James Herbert, and Marko Teras. 2014. "A Sense of Belonging to Enhance Participation, Success and Retention in Online Programs." *International Journal of the First Year in Higher Education* 5 (2):69–80. Doi: 10.5204/intjfyhe.v5i2.233.

Thomas, Rhonda, Karen Kuralt, Heidi Skurat Harris, and George Jensen. 2020. "Create, Support, and Facilitate Personal Online Writing Courses in Online Writing Programs." Working Paper, Little Rock: University of Arkansas at Little Rock.

Thompson, Eileen, ed. 1997. *Distance Education Drop-out: What Can We Do*. Edited by R. Pospisil and L. Willcoxson. Proceedings of the 6th Annual Teaching Learning Forum, Learning through Teaching. Perth, Australia: Murdoch University.

Tickle-Degnen, Linda, and Robert Rosenthal. 1990. "The Nature of Rapport and Its Nonverbal Correlates." *Psychological Inquiry* 1 (4):285–93.

Tinto, Vincent. 2006. "Research and Practice of Student Retention: What Next?" *Journal of College Student Retention: Research, Theory & Practice* 8 (1):1–19.

———. 2007. *Taking Student Retention Seriously*. Syracuse, NY: Syracuse University.

Tomei, Lawrence. 2006. "The Impact of Online Teaching on Faculty Load: Computing the Ideal Class Size for Online Courses." *Journal of Technology and Teacher Education* 14 (3):531–41.

Tu, Chih-Hsiung. 2002. "The Measurement of Social Presence in an Online Learning Environment." *International Journal on E-Learning* 1 (2):34–45.

Tung, Lai Cheng. 2012. "Proactive Intervention Strategies for Improving Online Student Retention in a Malaysian Distance Education Institution." *Journal of Online Learning and Teaching* 8 (4):312.

UCF Facts. 2020. "UCF Facts 2019–2020." University of Central Florida. Accessed July 28, 2020. https://www.ucf.edu/about-ucf/facts/.

UCLA First to Go. 2016. "First-Generation Faculty Initiative." Accessed June 10, 2020. https://firsttogo.ucla.edu/Programs/First-Gen-Faculty-Initiative.

Umbricht, Mark. 2016. "Helping Low-Income and Middle-Income Students:

Pell Grants and the Higher Education Act." *Higher Education in Review* Special Issue (1):24–36.

Urwin, Sharon, Robert Stanley, Malcolm Jones, Ann Gallagher, Paul Wainwright, and Andrew Perkins. 2010. "Understanding Student Nurse Attrition: Learning from the Literature." *Nurse Education Today* 30 (2):202–7.

US Department of Education. 2017. *Education Department Releases Final Debt-to-Earnings Rates for Gainful Employment Programs*. Washington, DC.

Veletsianos, George. 2020. *Learning Online: The Student Experience*. Baltimore, MD: Johns Hopkins University Press.

Villano, Renato, Scott Harrison, Grace Lynch, and George Chen. 2018. "Linking Early Alert Systems and Student Retention: A Survival Analysis Approach." *Higher Education* 76 (5):903–20. Doi: 10.1007/s10734-018-0249-y.

Virginia Community College System. 2001. *Virginia Community College System Organizational Strategy for Distance Learning: Final Report*. Richmond, Virginia.

Vonderwell, Selma. 2003. "An Examination of Asynchronous Communication Experiences and Perspectives of Students in an Online Course: A Case Study." *The Internet and Higher Education* 6 (1):77–90.

Wallace, Tary, Lynn Grinnell, Lou Carey, and James Carey. 2006. "Maximizing Learning from Rehearsal Activity in Web-Based Distance Learning." *Journal of Interactive Learning Research* 17 (3):319–27.

Wallis, Lynn. 2020. *Growth in Distance Learning Outpaces Total Enrollment Growth*. Salem: State of Oregon Employment Department. https://www.qualityinfo.org/-/growth-in-distance-learning-outpaces-total-enrollment-growth.

Wang, Huiming, and Judith Wilson Grimes. 2000. "A Systematic Approach to Assessing Retention Programs: Identifying Critical Points for Meaningful Interventions and Validating Outcomes Assessment." *Journal of College Student Retention: Research, Theory & Practice* 2 (1):59–68. Doi: 10.2190/hyy4-xtbh-rjfd-lu5y.

Ward, Michael E., Gary Peters, and Kyna Shelley. 2010. "Student and Faculty Perceptions of the Quality of Online Learning Experiences." *International Review of Research in Open and Distributed Learning* 11 (3):57–77.

Waschull, Stefanie B. 2005. "Predicting Success in Online Psychology Courses: Self-Discipline and Motivation." *Teaching of Psychology* 32 (3):190–92. Doi: 10.1207/s15328023top3203_11.

Watson, George R., and James Sottile. 2010. "Cheating in the Digital Age: Do Students Cheat More in Online Courses?" *Online Journal of Distance Learning Administration* 13 (1):n.

Wavle, Sharon, and Gamze Ozogul. 2019. "Investigating the Impact of Online Classes on Undergraduate Degree Completion." *Online Learning* 23 (4):281–95.

Wei, Chun-Wang, and Nian-Shing Chen. 2012. "A Model for Social Presence in Online Classrooms." *Educational Technology Research and Development* 60 (3):529–45.

What It Costs. 2020. "Online Finish Strong: What It Costs." University of

Arkansas at Little Rock. Accessed September 1, 2020. https://ualr.edu/online /what-it-costs/.

Whipp, Joan L., and Stephannie Chiarelli. 2004. "Self-Regulation in a Web-Based Course: A Case Study." *Educational Technology Research and Development* 52 (4):5.

Whistle, Wesley. 2020. "College Graduates Are Less Likely to Become Unemployed Due to The Coronavirus." Forbes. Last modified April 17, 2020. https://www.forbes.com/sites/wesleywhistle/2020/04/17/college -graduates-are-less-likely-to-become-unemployed-due-to-the-coronavirus /#1ee1156261e4.

White, Kelley Mayer. 2016. "Professional Development that Promotes Powerful Interactions: Using Teacher Book Clubs to Reflect on Quality in Teacher-Child Relationships." *Dimensions of Early Childhood* 44 (3):28–34.

Willging, Pedro A., and Scott D. Johnson. 2009. "Factors that Influence Students' Decision to Dropout of Online Courses." *Journal of Asynchronous Learning Networks* 13 (3):115–27.

Wilson, Janie H. 2006. "Predicting Student Attitudes and Grades from Perceptions of Instructors' Attitudes." *Teaching of Psychology* 33 (2):91–95. Doi: 10.1207/s15328023top3302_2.

Wilson, Janie H., Rebecca G. Ryan, and James L. Pugh. 2010. "Professor-Student Rapport Scale Predicts Student Outcomes." *Teaching of Psychology* 37 (4):246–51.

Wingo, Nancy Pope, Nataliya V. Ivankova, and Jacqueline A. Moss. 2017. "Faculty Perceptions about Teaching Online: Exploring the Literature Using the Technology Acceptance Model as an Organizing Framework." *Online Learning* 21 (1):15–35.

Wladis, Claire, Katherine M. Conway, and Alyse C. Hachey. 2014. "The Role of Enrollment Choice in Online Education: Course Selection Rationale and Course Difficulty as Factors Affecting Retention." *Online Learning* 18 (3):n3.

———. 2015. "The Online STEM Classroom—Who Succeeds? An Exploration of the Impact of Ethnicity, Gender, and Non-traditional Student Characteristics in the Community College Context." *Community College Review* 43 (2):142–64. Doi: 10.1177/0091552115571729.

———. 2017. "Using Course-Level Factors as Predictors of Online Course Outcomes: A Multi-Level Analysis at a US Urban Community College." *Studies in Higher Education* 42 (1):184–200. Doi: 10.1080/03075079.2015.1045478.

Wood, J. Luke. 2014a. "Examining Academic Variables Affecting the Persistence and Attainment of Black Male Collegians: A Focus on Academic Performance and Integration in the Two-Year College." *Race Ethnicity and Education* 17 (5):601–22. Doi: 10.1080/13613324.2012.733687.

———. 2014b. "Apprehension to Engagement in the Classroom: Perceptions of Black Males in the Community College." *International Journal of Qualitative Studies in Education* 27 (6):785–803. Doi: 10.1080/09518398.2014.901575.

Wood, J. Luke, Frank Harris III, and Khalid White. 2015. *Teaching Men of Color in the Community College: A Guidebook*. San Diego, CA: Montezuma Publishing.

Wood, J. Luke, and Caroline S. Turner. 2010. "Black Males and the Community

College: Student Perspectives on Faculty and Academic Success." *Community College Journal of Research and Practice* 35 (1–2):135–51.

Wood, J. Luke, and Ronald C. Williams. 2013. "Persistence Factors for Black Males in the Community College: An Examination of Background, Academic, Social, and Environmental Variables." *Spectrum: A Journal on Black Men* 1 (2):1–28.

Wood, Kathryn A., Cary Moskovitz, and Theresa M. Valiga. 2011. "Audio Feedback for Student Writing in Online Nursing Courses: Exploring Student and Instructor Reactions." *Journal of Nursing Education* 50 (9):540–43.

Woods, Kathryn, and George Frogge. 2017. "Preferences and Experiences of Traditional and Nontraditional University Students." *Journal of Continuing Higher Education* 65 (2):94–105. Doi: 10.1080/07377363.2017.1318567.

Woods, Robert H., and Jason D. Baker. 2004. "Interaction and Immediacy in Online Learning." *International Review of Research in Open and Distributed Learning* 5 (2).

Woodyard, LeBaron, and Erin Larson. 2018. *California Community Colleges 2017 Distance Education Report.* California Community Colleges Chancellor's Office: Academic Affairs Division.

Woosley, Sherry A., and Dustin K. Shepler. 2011. "Understanding the Early Integration Experiences of First-Generation College Students." *College Student Journal* 45 (4):700–715.

Wray, Michael, Patrick R. Lowenthal, Barbara Bates, and Ellen Stevens. 2008. "Investigating Perceptions of Teaching Online & F2F." *Academic Exchange Quarterly* 12 (4):243–48.

Xenos, Michalis, Christos Pierrakeas, and Panagiotis Pintelas. 2002. "A Survey on Student Dropout Rates and Dropout Causes Concerning the Students in the Course of Informatics of The Hellenic Open University." *Computers & Education* 39 (4):361–77.

Xu, Di, and Shanna Smith Jaggars. 2011a. "The Effectiveness of Distance Education across Virginia's Community Colleges: Evidence from Introductory College-Level Math and English Courses." *Educational Evaluation and Policy Analysis* 33 (3):360–77. Doi: 10.3102/0162373711413814.

———. 2011b. "Online and Hybrid Course Enrollment and Performance in Washington State Community and Technical Colleges." In *Community College Working Paper.* Community College Research Center, Teachers College: Columbia University.

———. 2014. "Performance Gaps between Online and Face-to-Face Courses: Differences across Types of Students and Academic Subject Areas." *Journal of Higher Education* 85 (5):633–59. Doi: 10.1080/00221546.2014.11777343.

Xu, Di, and Ying Xu. 2019. *The Promises and Limits of Online Higher Education: Understanding How Distance Education Affects Access, Cost, and Quality.* Washington, DC: American Enterprise Institute.

Zatynsk, Mandy. 2013. "Calling for Success: Online Retention Rates Get Boost From Personal Outreach." Arlington, VA: American Institutes for Research, Education Sector. January 16, 2013. https://www.air.org/edsector-archives /publications/calling-success-online-retention-rates-get-boost-personal -outreach.

Zavarella, Carol A., and Jan M. Ignash. 2009. "Instructional Delivery in Developmental Mathematics: Impact on Retention." *Journal of Developmental Education* 32 (3):2.

Zembylas, Michalinos. 2008. "Engaging with Issues of Cultural Diversity and Discrimination through Critical Emotional Reflexivity in Online Learning." *Adult Education Quarterly* 59 (1):61–82. Doi: 10.1177/0741713608325171.

Zhang, Ching-Wen, Beth Hurst, and Annice McLean. 2016. "How Fast Is Fast Enough? Education Students' Perceptions of Email Response Time in Online Courses." *Journal of Educational Technology Development and Exchange (JETDE)* 9 (1):1.

Zimmerman, Jonathan. 2020. "Video Kills the Teaching Star: Remote Learning and the Death of Charisma." *Chronicle of Higher Education*, April 24. https://o-www-chronicle-com.library.ualr.edu/article/video-kills-the-teaching-star/.

Index

Grisolia, Alexandra Monteiro, 49
grit, 40–41
group work, 117, 136, 170–71
growth mindset, 40–41

Harmon, Oskar R., 38
Harris, Frank, III, 6, 70
health issues of students, 20
hidden curriculum, 126–27, 135–36
higher education. *See* colleges and universities; community colleges
Higher Education Act (1965), 124
high-income students, 15n
Hispanic students. *See* Latinx students
homelessness, 127
human connection, 42, 50–53, 163–66. *See also* rapport-building strategies; relationship building
humanizing instructors, 84*t*, 85–95, 179; case studies, 189–92; in electronic environments, 43, 68–69; instructor adaptations, 118; purpose of, 83
Hurst, Beth, 102
Hurtado, Sylvia, 63
Huss, John A., 66, 91
hybrid classes, 4, 80–81
hyflex classes, 4

implicit bias, 28
income level and higher education, 22, 125
in-person classes. *See* traditional face-to-face classes
institutional culture change, 194–97
instructors: chance encounters with, 6–7; class size preferences, 97; compassion and empathy of, 43, 137–40, 142–46, 162; contingent versus tenured, 25, 65–66, 151, 182–85; COVID-19 pandemic and, 54, 80; defined, 2n; email examples for, 200–206; engagement of, 65–67; giving up on students, 140–42; growth mindsets, encouraging, 40–41; impact in online classes, 67–75, 75*f*; implicit biases of, 28; meaningful connections with, 74–75, 75*f*, 129–30; modeling behaviors, 68, 104, 106; office hours, 63–64, 88, 126–27, 171–72; presence

and pedagogical warmth of, 42–44, 69, 144, 158, 179; qualifications, 65–66; race and ethnicity of, 128; student evaluations of, 78–79, 89, 152–53, 154*t*, 158–59; student relationships and success rates of, 4–5, 50–53; teaching with rapport, 178–81, 185, 189–91, 193; tradeoffs of building rapport for, 110–11, 151–54, 154*f*; traditional courses, preferences for, 44, 152, 181; transactional distance with, 79–81. *See also* humanizing instructors; rapport-building strategies; relationship building
Integrated Postsecondary Education Data Systema (IPEDS), 16–17
integration into campus community, 42–44
international students, 20
internet access, 128, 138, 174–77
isolation, 43, 62, 66, 129, 181

Jaggers, Shanna Smith, 28, 38, 69, 164, 180
James, Scott, 124
jobs. *See* employment
Johnson, Elaine S., 27, 37
Johnson, Hans P., 35
Johnson, Scott D., 37
Jones, Patrice W. Glenn, 116

Kaupp, Ray, 70
Kennesaw State University orientation, 47
Kentucky Community and Technical College System retention rates, 67
Kezar, Adrianna, 60, 151, 184
Kim, Taehyun, 40
Kuh, George D., 60, 63

Lambert, Leo M., 50, 61
Lang, James M., 48
Latinx students: college enrollment statistics, 122–23, 123*f*, 128; flexibility of online classes for, 19; instructor relationships, 61, 70; online student retention rates, 28
Lawson, Celeste, 37, 53
learning disabilities, 20

Rio Salado College feedback software, 96
Rosenboom, Victoria, 21
rural areas, 21, 176–77

scaffolding, 130
Schaelen, Tracy, 189
scholarships, 187
Scott, Daniel T., 151, 184
self-assessments in orientation, 186–87, 189–90
self-directed learning, 70, 163–64
self-regulation, 40–42
Shea, Peter, 35
skills: assessments and interventions for, 46–48; for online classes, 39–42; soft, 161; for studying, 40; technological, 40, 46, 69, 128; time management, 40–42, 46, 47; working from home and, 22
smartphones, 87, 115–16, 175
Smedshammer, Michael, 87, 91, 192
social and economic mobility, 21–23
socioeconomic status. *See* lower-income students
soft skills, 161
Sottile, James, 138
Southwestern College case study, 189–90
Stanley, Bolling Craig, 19, 129
State University of New York: graduation rates, 52; online classes and retention rates, 35–36
Stommel, Jesse, 43, 139–40, 141, 180
student loan debt, 29, 33–34, 125
students: accessibility of traditional classes, 20; contingent instructors and learning outcomes, 182; demographic changes, 24; engagement of, 62, 74; evaluations of instructors, 78–79, 89, 152–53, 154*t*, 158–59; instructor relationships and, 4–5, 50–53; integration into campus community, 42–44; isolation in online classes, 66, 68; motivation of, 40, 62, 70–71, 74; orientation classes for, 46–48, 51, 185–87; perspectives of, 26–27, 126–29; rapport-building strategies among, 116–18, 136, 170–71; recommendations for, 168–72; sense of self and

self-esteem, 29, 34; skills needed for online class success, 39–42, 46–48; tradeoffs of building rapport for, 160–63; traditional, decreasing number of, 121–22; traditional courses, preferences for, 41. *See also* crises of students; disadvantaged students; peers and peer relationships; relationship building
students of color: accessibility of online classes for, 18–20; asynchronous class outcomes and, 80; college enrollment statistics, 18–20, 122–23, 123*f*, 128; diversity of students and instructors, 128; early alert systems and, 50; instructor relationships, 61, 74; isolation of, 44, 62, 70, 129; rapport and, 6; relationships with instructors, 41–42; social and economic mobility, 22–23. *See also* disadvantaged students
student success teams, 49–50
study skills, 40
support networks, 167–97; administrators and, 177–87; case studies, 188–94; institutional culture change and, 194–97; parents, friends, and mentors, 172–77; students forming, 168–72
surveillance systems, 138–39
Swan, Karen, 124
syllabi, 86–88, 141–42, 170
synchronous classes, 4, 80–81, 165–66
synchronous interaction opportunities, 92–93, 166

Takacs, Christopher G., 61
technology: human connection versus, 163–66; inequalities in, 128, 138, 174–77; Learning Management Systems and, 48–50, 86, 94, 102–3; skills needed for, 40, 46, 69, 128; support staff for management of, 180
Terenzini, Patrick T., 63
texting, 115–16
time management skills, 40–42, 46, 47
Tinto, Vincent, 50, 181
tradeoffs of building rapport, 149–66; for instructors, 110–11, 151–54, 154*f*; Minimum Rapport Experiment and,

tradeoffs of building rapport (*cont.*)
154–60, 157–58*t*, 159*f*; for students,
160–63; technology without humanity, 163–66
traditional face-to-face classes: accessibility of, 20; Best/Worst Study
data on, 64–65, 65*t*; combined with
online classes, 34–36, 35*f*, 170, 174,
187; declining enrollment in, 23–24;
instructor's impact in, 60–64; instructor preferences for, 44, 152, 181;
online classes compared, 32–36, 32–
33*t*, 35*f*, 59–60, 77–78, 151–52, 162;
retention rates and, 26–28; student
preferences for, 41; transferring to
online platform, 92–93, 165
transactional distance, 79–81
Tung, Lai Cheng, 38
tutoring, 73, 164–65

underserved students. *See* disadvantaged
students
unemployment rates, 21–22
ungrading policies, 121, 141
Universal Design for Learning, 20
universities. *See* colleges and universities
University of Arkansas: costs of online
classes, 16; COVID-19 survey, 143–
44; culture of rapport, 184–85; first-
generation students, 132, 174; online
classes and retention rates, 34–36,
35*f*, 174, 176

University of California, Los Angeles
(UCLA) first-generation faculty initiative, 135
University of Central Florida: case study,
192–94; Center for Distributed Learning, 44, 51, 193; online classes and
retention rates, 36
University of Southern Mississippi orientation, 47
University System of Georgia (USG)
eCore, 49–50, 51, 73, 184
Utz, Jenifer C., 47

Veletsianos, George, 79, 104
video and audio messages, 89–92
video feedback, 101
Vincent-Layton, Kim, 87, 91
Virginia Community Colleges, instructor
engagement, 66
Vosicka, Lucie, 47

Watson, George R., 138
welcome emails, 108, 200–201
White, Khalid, 6, 70
Wi-Fi access, 176
Willging, Pedro A., 37
Wood, J. Luke, 6, 41, 70, 80, 191

Xu, Di, 28, 69, 164, 180

Zhang, Ching-Wen, 102
Zoom lectures, 80, 165

Higher Education Books from Hopkins Press

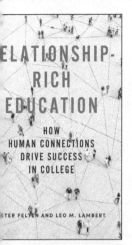